# Movieland

§

**BOOKS BY JEROME CHARYN**

Once Upon a Droshky
On the Darkening Green
The Man Who Grew Younger
Going to Jerusalem
American Scrapbook
Eisenhower, My Eisenhower
The Tar Baby
Blue Eyes
Marilyn the Wild
The Education of Patrick Silver
The Franklin Scare
Secret Isaac
The Seventh Babe
The Catfish Man
Darlin' Bill
Panna Maria
Pinocchio's Nose
War Cries Over Avenue C
Metropolis
Paradise Man
The Magician's Wife (illustrated by François Boucq)
Movieland

§

Jerome Charyn

# MOVIELAND

## Hollywood and the Great American Dream Culture

G. P. PUTNAM'S SONS   New York

§

FOR CUDDLES SAKALL

Published by G. P. Putnam's Sons,
200 Madison Avenue, New York, NY 10016.
Published simultaneously in Canada

*The text of this book is set in Galliard.*

Library of Congress Cataloging-in-Publication Data

Charyn, Jerome.
  Movieland: Hollywood and the great American dream culture.

  Bibliography: p.
  Includes index.
  1. Motion picture industry—California—
Los Angeles—History.  2. Motion pictures—California—
Los Angeles—History.  3. Charyn, Jerome.
4. Hollywood (Los Angeles, Calif.)—History.  I. Title.
PN1993.5.U65C49    1988    384'.8'0979494    88-31806
ISBN 0-399-13423-9

*Designed by MaryJane DiMassi*
*Printed in the United States of America*
1  2  3  4  5  6  7  8  9  10

# Contents

# The Loew's Paradise

1 It wasn't the Capitol, with a bandstand that could collapse and sink right into the cellar or rise up above the stage to reveal Arthur Godfrey and the Andrews Sisters, like warm ghosts out of a Pirandello play. It wasn't the Paramount, where Sinatra sang in 1944, and the lines snaked across Seventh Avenue like a nervous army, looking, looking for "The Voice," who brought pandemonium wherever he went. It wasn't the Roxy, which had a barbershop, 212 toilets, a kindergarten, and closets to house "dragons, drawbridges, and droshkies."

These were *downtown* palaces, with their live attractions to dwarf whatever movie happened to be on the bill. They were the dinosaurs that belonged to cities like New Orleans, Los Angeles, Chicago, Dallas, and New York. And then there was little America, towns like Canton or Biloxi, and boroughs like the Bronx, with their own movie palaces that had nothing but the madness of their furniture and the movies themselves. A town could have two or three palaces, each with a different veneer and a mezzanine that suggested the Yucatán, the gardens of Seville, or a rajah's house, together with statues, stuffed pigeons, and plaster elephants wearing shoes.

I was luckier than some. I had my pick of palaces. The Fairmont sported murals of some medieval land. The Chester, like most movie palaces, had a metal awning called a marquee and balconies so high it was like sitting in a circus, waiting for unicorns to appear on the front wall. But it was nothing like the Loew's Paradise, with its four thousand seats.

The Paradise was a Depression baby. It opened in 1929. Without a marquee. Zoning laws wouldn't permit a metal awning to loom above the sidewalk of the Bronx's biggest boulevard. And so the Paradise reminded you of no other palace. It had a façade that hugged the outer wall and served as a kind of flattened, one-dimensional "marquee," spelling out the particulars of a feature in that familiar white alphabet of moviehouses across America. But it was much more powerful than any old advertising board. The façade was a trompe l'oeil Venetian palace, with stone porches and balconies and recessed windows and its own little roof. But it was a Venetian palace as seen through the eyes of a movie architect, who could plunge in and out of history whenever he wanted to come up with his designs. It had a gigantic clock, over which stood St. George slaughtering a dragon, in his own private niche.

That palazzo look is not surprising. The Paradise was supposed to have been called the Venetian. Loew's had decided not to scrimp on their palazzo in the Bronx. It cost four million and was the most expensive movie palace ever provided for hillbillies from the heartland (Westchester and the Bronx). The Loew's Paradise (né the Venetian) could offer a bit of challenge to those downtown classics, the Roxy and the Paramount, and keep all the hillbillies at home.

The Paradise did have live entertainment, like Dave Schooler & His Serenaders in "CAFÉ DE PAREE," direct from the Capitol Theatre (in 1929). Otherwise, how could it compete? But these minstrel shows that wandered from palace to palace began to disappear as the talkies took hold. Sinatra might play at the Paramount, but he wouldn't have gone up the road to visit with us at the Paradise.

The Boy with the Golden Tonsils took our minds off the war. The frenzy he produced seemed to calm us somehow. But the Paradise survived without him. And it was far grander than the Paramount, which was nothing but a box for Sinatra to sing in.

2 Come to the Paradise, circa 1944. St. George stands at his post, like the guardian of time itself, watching that big clock, guaranteeing the safety of its hours. You enter the lobby and you're in a Spanish patio with mosaics on the floor and a marble water fountain filled with goldfish. The sound of the water is enough to shake your head loose from whatever moorings you have.

The smell of ink has already come off your hands. There are no reminders of public school in this place, not one old witch to badger you about your penmanship. You go deeper into the Paradise and you're in the grand hall, with chandeliers and a barreled ceiling, busts of all kinds of people, gods and wizards and mermaids and someone who looks like Dante's cousin, with a cap made of figs.

And so you proceed from one station to the next. But nothing can prepare you for that crazy garden beyond the mezzanine walls. There's a night sky over your head, a whole orchestrated heaven, with clouds that sail across a swollen field of stars. There are poplar trees, flying pigeons, the complicated walls of a palazzo with an open roof. You have the weird sensation of being outdoors and indoors at the same time, as if the Paradise could produce its own weather.

There was a name for that sort of garden. It was called an "atmospheric," a palace that curled up to nature and wouldn't let you watch a movie without a particular climate. John Eberson discovered the idea. He was the most original of all moviehouse designers and architects. Eberson was born in Austria in 1875, the child of a lumberman. He graduated from the University of Vienna in 1896, served as a horseman in the Emperor's Hussars for a year, and arrived in the United States in 1901. He established his own architectural firm in St. Louis and began to build motion-picture and vaudeville houses in Chicago, Little Rock, Birmingham, Savannah, and other cities with a boldness that hadn't been seen before.

There were no picture palaces in 1906 or 1907, because there was nothing to worship. Actors were still anonymous, and all "picture people" were treated like vagabonds and gypsies—tainted, unholy things. But Eberson's bright colors and sense of interior space helped bring moviehouses beyond their old "peach-box" design. And when the stars emerged after 1910, with names and identities of their own, the first palaces appeared—pleasure domes where movie fans could come to adore their favorite stars. And then a whole new native architecture was born, the picture palace, with an incredibly brief life span: from 1911 or 1912 to the mid-1930s, when the palace had become much too expensive to build. But within those twenty-five years we had an art form that was crazily eclectic, palaces that borrowed and copied and stole from churches, temples, opera houses, pyramids, monasteries, stables, bazaars, and other palaces, and were often as delirious and dreamy as the pictures that played in these baroque and "torridly embellished" gardens. According to Ben Hall, who wrote *The Best Remaining Seats,* such "pleasure domes gave expression to the most secret and polychrome dreams of a whole group of architects who might otherwise have gone through life doomed to turning out churches, hotels, banks and high schools. The architecture of the movie palace was a triumph of suppressed desire."

Ben Hall was much shrewder than he could have imagined. Because that suppressed desire wasn't limited to the architects themselves; it defined the whole damn country. Movie palaces mushroomed all over the place. And the palaces succeeded beyond their owners' expectations, because they met a terrifying need for romance that *was* America. The technology and magic of the twentieth century had projected heroes and heroines on a wall that seemed like ghostly doubles of ourselves, shadows on a "silversheet" that had lives of adventure, love, and risk, while our own Puritan ethos reminded us of Samson's shorn hair, the whores of Babylon, witches and worms. And we began to wake up to the frightening fact that women were sexual creatures; they weren't around simply to serve a man's needs and bear him a trough of children; they had their own ideas of pleasure; their wishes ranged beyond the home and the marriage bed.

We seemed to discover this first at the movies, as if these flickers were a kind of unconscious bridge to our deepest feelings and desires. We fell in love with Gloria Swanson and Garbo and Dietrich, because they had an independence, a distance from us, that we longed for and were frightened of. And then Shirley Temple appeared in 1933 to taunt us with all the pluck of a waxwork woman of five. But something happened to Shirl. She regressed as she got older, going from little mama to an unremarkable girl. Biology got in the way of myth. The Temple craze was over by the time she was twelve.

We forgot about Little Miss Marker and switched our affections to Judy Garland, a chubby child with tits. One of the pleasures of *The Wizard of Oz* is watching Judy grow within the frames of the film from a Kansas girl with baby fat into some kind of woman.

Graham Greene called the film "an American drummer's dream of escape." L. Frank Baum, author of the *Oz* books, was only an "agile salesman." The story of the Munchkins and the Tin Man, Greene says, can't compare with *Alice in Wonderland,* and he's right. It "rattles like dry goods." But it is *our* children's classic. And if the Wizard "turns out to be a Kansas conjurer operating a radio-electric contrivance," isn't that what America is about? He's a lot like "The Wizard of Menlo Park," Thomas Alva Edison, who built the first film studio in the world, a tarpaper shack called the "Black Maria." The fact is, we are a nation of drummers (with desire under the window), and why shouldn't *our* classic be about a huckster behind a curtain, full of "material dreams"?

The palaces themselves were another form of hucksterism. "We sell tickets to theaters, not movies," said Marcus Loew, founder of the Loew's empire. And the art of building movie palaces developed into "one of the richest and most imaginative and transitory schools of architecture since the discovery of the keystone." It was an art and an occupation of excess. If Mies van der Rohe and other fathers of modern architecture felt that less is more, the movie-palace designer believed that more is not enough. He was under constant duress to find another lost culture he could borrow from, mansions he could plunder, styles he could pirate, figures he could stuff. And "as he piled detail on detail, each prism, each gilded cherub, each jewel-eyed dragon became . . . a catapult for the imagination."

Eberson had his own workshop, Michelangelo Studios, which created an entire menagerie of plastic cherubs and mermaids and replicas of all the Renaissance masters. "Donatello's David or the Venus de Milo might have been present in a dozen Eberson theaters, but never in exactly the same place."

There was a sense of play about the palaces, an exuberance that was absent from most other forms of architecture. One of "Michelangelo's" managers might have Eberson's bust appear on a wall, close to Ben Franklin or a couple of Medicis.

Eberson himself was like a minstrel who produced his magic shows in town after town. The very long and narrow path leading to the grand foyer at the Loew's Akron was "actually a bridge that spans the Ohio Canal on stilts of poured concrete. Once across the canal there is a sudden explosion of space" into a Moorish bazaar and banquet hall that "Michelangelo" built.

"Eberson was archeologist, weather man and landscape gardener rolled into one." His idea for the "atmospheric" had come from Florida. That's what he told the Tampa *Tribune*. "I saw the value of putting nature to work and so have borrowed the color and design that are found in the flowers and the trees." Eberson could never have been a disciple of Mies. He had too much love for movie palaces with hidden lanterns that could manufacture a whole fleet of clouds.

**3** But there was something more important than your own shivers inside the Paradise. It was the feeling that this outdoor-indoor garden was Hollywood's own chancellery in the Bronx, a bit of native soil that seemed to connect all of America. That was the power *each* palace had. As the movies defined us, taught hillbillies like myself a little "culture," which meant Groucho Marx or Joan Crawford or Bing Crosby in *Going My Way* (1944), the palaces became our Oz, with Eberson (or some other architect) as the Wizard who provided a network of material dreams.

The Paradise sheltered us in its own fantastic present-past. It opened us up to the childhood fancy of clouds and goldfish and statues in a niche. We found a comfort at the movies in lush palaces where we sought our own lyrical selves, the land between waking and dreaming that's been so hard to define, because it follows the paths of our ordinary lives, the bumpy pull of "consciousness" that's close to a drugged sleep.

The palaces revealed what dreamwalkers we are. They were caverns into our minds, with fixtures and furniture, icons that led us to our seats. We're all Little Nemos in Slumberland, that special "home" Winsor McCay started to sketch in 1905, before we ever heard of movie palaces. Buildings and beds walk around in Slumberland. It's a world on stilts, where a child is always, always looking up. Nemo's dreams *are* his life, and when he wakes up in the final panel of each comic strip, it's a terrible fall into the mundane, as if his childhood were suddenly over. Nemo's bed was a magical place, like the movie palace. And on that bed he dreams with all the "energy, restlessness, and love of motion" that mark us as children of the twentieth century.

# one

# *Faces on the Wall*

**1** I can say without melodrama, or malice, that Hollywood ruined my life. It's left me in a state of constant adolescence, searching for a kind of love that was invented by Louis B. Mayer and his brother moguls at Paramount and Columbia and Twentieth Century–Fox.

I've hungered for dream women, like Rita Hayworth, whose message has always been that love is a deadly thing, a system of divine punishment. Whatever she might say or do, Rita couldn't care less. She was so powerful she could perform the most erotic dance by simply taking off her gloves (in *Gilda*). And just when you thought you had her, fixed forever on the screen, she said good-bye to Hollywood and you and ran off with Aly Khan.

But it wasn't only Rita.

Someone must have sneaked me into a moviehouse while I was still in the cradle, because my earliest imaginings and adventures have come from the screen. While I sucked on a baby bottle I remembered Gene Tierney's oriental eyes. She was in *Belle Starr*, and I was only three. I didn't care about the six-gun strapped to her leg. I didn't care about Dana Andrews or Randolph Scott. They were only flies buzzing around Belle. I cared about her cheekbones, the hollows in her face, the essential beauty she had. It was painful to look at Gene. She stunned you like no other star. Later I would love Dietrich and Garbo and the young Mary Astor (until she cut her hair for Humphrey Bogart in *The Maltese Falcon*). But that was when I had a sense of *history* and could shovel back and forth in movie time and consider myself a fan. But when I discovered Belle Starr's face, it wasn't in some stinking retrospective. I had no idea what films were. I saw her face and suffered.

I've been suffering ever since. At fifty, still a boy somehow, I walk into a moviehouse close to midnight and watch Kevin Costner and Sean Young in *No Way Out,* a rather implausible remake of *The Big Clock,* with the Pentagon and a "masked" Soviet spy in place of a New York publishing empire (what's really missing is Charles Laughton's face). The projector breaks down during a seduction scene in the back seat of a limo. Sean Young disappears from the theater's wall. The audience begins to riot. The images return with no sound track. And we're stuck in spooky silence. It doesn't take a genius to understand how much we depend on the little noises that surround a film—the rustle of a skirt, the opening of a door, the romantic leitmotiv more than the babble, which we can live without. We cannot bear absolute silence in a moviehouse; the shadows on the wall stop reassuring us, even in Technicolor; the faces *feel* sepulchral.

The sound returns, and I can watch Kevin Costner and Sean Young (the beautiful android from *Blade Runner*) in my usual hibernation at the movies. The heartbeat slows. I'm like a bat with folded wings. Costner's conventional handsomeness soothes the blood. He's easy to look at. A star. But Sean Young dies a third of the way through the film. And we move from romance to a convoluted manhunt. I carry around all the illogic of a disappointed child. I want her to rise from the dead and return to Kevin Costner. Of course she doesn't. It's Hollywood in its seventh generation, not Dalí or Buñuel.

Still, I get up from my seat with the same exhilaration I often feel at the end of a movie, as if I've been through a period of profound rest, no matter what maneuvers and machinations are on the screen. Those thirty-foot faces always hold my eye.

2  Movie time has its own logic and laws, related to little else in our lives. I don't mean by this that watching a movie is more "authentic" than reading a book or attending the theater or making love. We dream our way through all these events, involved with the crazy continuum of present, future, and past, which never really figured in the safe mechanics of Sir Isaac Newton, the greatest scientist who ever lived. Sir Isaac believed that the universe was a magnificent but tight machine where "the whole future depends strictly upon the whole past."

Our own century, the century of Hollywood and Hitler, has pushed us further and further away from Newton's corner. The wildness and randomness we've discovered in the universe, we've also discovered in ourselves. And not even Louis B. Mayer and his mother's famous chicken soup (dispensed at the MGM commissary for thirty-five cents a bowl) could keep this randomness out of films. He could nourish his stars on the MGM lots, groom them, reinvent their lives and their looks, but he couldn't control their faces on the moviehouse wall. Those faces had a darker message than any one L.B. subscribed to. They had their own wild resonance. They scared as much as they delighted. The simplest screen was much bigger (and darker) than any of the movie moguls. The studios could tyrannize the content of a film, declare a land of happy endings, but they weren't sitting with you in the dark. They could control Joan Crawford, but not the hysteria hidden behind those big eyes, or the ruby mouth that could almost suck you into the screen. The stars were very strange creatures. They had the power to hypnotize whole generations in ways that Sir Isaac couldn't have guessed. The stars were like the doubles of our own irrational, perverse selves. In matters of Hollywood, our feelings were often mixed: we were tender and murderous toward the stars. They were like a demonic parent-child, lover and stranger, and we were *always* involved in some sort of incestuous relationship with them, with those faces (and bodies) on the wall.

If I read *The Sound and the Fury* or *Middlemarch,* I'm filled with the aromas of either book, with past readings and relationships to the characters, with a whole continent of language and scenes, but the books don't frighten me. I can enter into their dream songs, and leave at my own will. But if I'm watching *Casablanca* on the wall, I'll let my eye slip past the phony details, the studio-bound streets, the laughable sense of a fabricated city, and drift into that dream of Humphrey Bogart and Rick's Café Américain, which exists outside any laws of physics, like the eternal dream of Hollywood itself, a little dopey, but with a power we can't resist. I don't crave popcorn while Bogart lisps. I'm a ghost "on the wrong side of the celluloid," almost as immaterial as those figures I'm watching, involved in their ghostly dance. I'm Bogart and Ingrid and the pianoplayer Sam and Paul Henreid's perennial wooden face. We lend ourselves,

give up boundaries in the dark that we'd never dare give to a
lover. We are ghosts absorbing other ghosts, cannibals sitting in
a chair. . . .

I can remember the moviehouse where I saw *They Died with
Their Boots On*. The RKO Chester. It was part of a special treat.
I'd gone with my uncle and my older brother. It was at night.
And I was barely five. It was the first time I could link a partic-
ular movie to a particular palace, and therefore it's my first
memory as a moviegoer, sadder than seeing Gene Tierney as
Belle Starr, because I can't recollect the circumstances surround-
ing her face. *Boots* starred Errol Flynn. It was about Custer's
Last Stand. I couldn't have known who Custer was. I hadn't
even graduated from kindergarten. But I remember horses'
hoofs, Custer's mustache, his coat of animal hair, and Chief
Crazy Horse (Anthony Quinn).

I've never seen the film again. But I haven't forgotten that
call to death as Custer rides to meet the Sioux. It didn't matter
that I was in short pants. I understood the vocabulary of this
film. It was as if I'd been a moviegoer all my life. My uncle and
brother were held in the suspense of the story, even though
they must have heard of Little Bighorn. They were older, wiser,
more schooled in the American way. But I could read faces on
a wall. And I saw something amiss in Errol Flynn's eyebrows,
in that dark knit of his face. I shivered in my seat and pondered
the enigma of those side balconies with boxed-off chairs that
never made sense in a moviehouse, because you had to observe
a film at such a deep angle all the action seemed to curve away
from you, to fall right out of your grasp. I counted my fingers.
I combed my hair with a pencil. Anything, anything rather than
watch the massacre I felt was coming. I didn't want Errol to
die. He had long hair, like a girl. He was much prettier than
his screen wife, Olivia de Havilland. This was her last film with
Errol. She was always a nub of virtue around his neck, whether
the film was about Robin Hood, Custer, or Captain Blood. But
I wasn't a film historian at five. I was crapping in my pants at
the RKO Chester, and I couldn't keep my eyes off Errol Flynn.

Custer dying with all his men depressed me for months. It
wasn't that I had discovered death at the movies. There was
polio and other diseases. A neighbor falling off the fire escape.
Bombings in Europe that my brother had talked about. But

screen dying is like no other dying in the world. I'd gotten used to Custer's long hair. I belonged with the Seventh Cavalry. There was almost a religious conversion in the dark. I'd become whatever Custer was. And when he died, the loss was just too great.

**3** There was an actress I noticed in 1944. She played Velvet Brown, an English girl who wins a horse. Into her life comes a former jockey who was the star of the film. Mickey Rooney himself, twenty-four years old, but looking fifteen. He was one of the biggest box-office draws in the world, "burying" Shirley Temple in 1939. I liked his dash. But it was the girl who drove the eyes out of your head. I'd seen her before in *Lassie Come Home*. But I was crazy about Lassie and not the girl. And suddenly there she was, the child-woman, Elizabeth Taylor, in *National Velvet*. The most beautiful actress in Hollywood at eleven. Liz had a kind of angelic look, but the face was so stunning that the voluptuous woman was already there in her eyes, like some dark lady in waiting. She was the one girl I ever really wanted to marry. I got her photograph at the Loew's Paradise, and it hung over my bed like a love charm. She was five years older than the little moviegoer, but I swore to catch up. I'd kick Rooney in the pants. I'd become a mogul.

I was loyal to Liz for about a year. Then I took her photo down from the wall. I graduated to Gilda. Half the Western World fell for Rita Hayworth, the love goddess who was so shy she couldn't bear to be in a crowd. She'd been married to Orson Welles, but the goddess was jealous of his every move. She grew estranged from Orson, and hired his former secretary, Shifra Haran, to accompany her on a voyage to the French Riviera. Shifra Haran had to carry ten thousand dollars in cash to take care of the goddess, who was "prey to persistent depression." Aboard the ocean liner to Cap d'Antibes Rita lived like a ghost. She "couldn't stand being looked at." She ate in her cabin with her companion-nurse and "would go walking when it was darkest, when there weren't too many people around. She was virtually a prisoner in her room."

But this seclusion never hurt her on the screen. Rita erupted in 1946. It was as if the world had woken from the war and exploded into sex. Rita sat on her own atomic atoll, with energy at the root of her red, red hair. It didn't matter that her hair was dyed, or that her forehead had been plucked, or that the song she sang in *Gilda,* "Put the Blame on Mame," was "ghosted" by Anita Ellis. Ellis would become her ghost again. She sounded like Rita Hayworth. And Glenn Ford was her perfect foil. Handsome and passive, without a touch of humor, he couldn't really contain Rita's storm. The camera didn't seem to know what to do with her face, other than record its carnivorous beauty. Gilda could have eaten you alive.

Her beauty, says critic Michael Wood, was not "an exceptional gift but an accentuation of normal good features into an ideal form, the sort of poisoned inheritance that could fall to anyone." *Poisoned inheritance.* "Here was a sex object disassociating herself from all the excitement . . . simultaneously too ordinary and too beautiful."

But there was a deeper ambivalence. She was the shyest of girls and the most brazen. The camera did for Rita what it did for other goddesses, gave her a kind of release. She had the haunted look of all film beauties, women *and* men. She rushed into our lives through her image on the wall and wouldn't let go. She tried to repeat her success with Glenn Ford in *The Loves of Carmen.* But she was only Gilda in a Spanish veil. And as she lamented to Shifra Haran: "Every man I've known has fallen in love with Gilda and wakened with me."

She'd fallen captive to her own image on the screen, Rita Hayworth, the prisoner of sex. Husbands, lovers, alcohol. And romance floated past her like some pirate ship. She couldn't recapture her audience after her flight with Aly Khan. She was constantly making a comeback. She tried the theater and couldn't remember her lines. People blamed it on the alcohol, but she'd developed Alzheimer's, that disease of forgetfulness. And she died in the care of her daughter, Princess Yasmin.

But it was more than the pirate ship of romance that ruined Rita Hayworth. More than her marriages. More than her fights with Harry Cohn (king of Columbia Pictures), or that poisoned inheritance of her face. America has always been very skittish about its love goddesses, as if an audience could only get so near, and then had to retreat from the fire. Look at Kim Basinger, a woman as carnivorous as Rita and even more beautiful. The *new* Hollywood casts her as one "strawhead" after the other, a playmate to Bruce Willis, or Mickey Rourke and Robert Redford. Redford sleeps with Kim in *The Natural* and hits home runs to the image of Glenn Close in centerfield.

Even without a Hollywood Production Code that wouldn't permit marriage beds or a woman's navel to be shown on the screen, we haven't rid ourselves of the Puritan ethic. Louis B. Mayer was speaking for most of America when he said that he didn't want "whores" at MGM. Leo the Lion could only tolerate so much of sex. Kathleen Turner can take off her clothes in *Body Heat* and *Prizzi's Honor,* but she doesn't have that hungry look. She makes love like a beautiful technician. She's not lost in the musk of her own body, like Marilyn . . . or Kim Basinger.

We've adored our love goddesses and been frightened of them. Brando also had that dangerous look. He was some kind of "goddess." His sexuality disturbed a whole generation. He fell to earth in 1950 like a furry being from another planet. He was dark, had terrific biceps and a sensuous mouth. He was a paraplegic in *The Men,* his first film, and Teresa Wright didn't know what to do with Brando. The reality of the film was that Marlon was much more sexy than Teresa Wright. She was like a walking package around the whirlwind of his desires. And the country, which had fallen asleep again and was scared to death of Communism, longed for Eisenhower and tolerated the bulbous, blinking face of Richard Nixon. It wanted mom and pop, vanilla ice cream, and searched for its heartland and the lost frontier. And into that timid, sleeping country came Brando, and Elvis, and Marilyn Monroe, with a kind of magnificent stink. They were un-American. They didn't wash the way we did. Norman Mailer remembers Marilyn Monroe from her days at the Actors Studio. Marilyn had a red nose. "She smelled dank—an odor came off her." But that odor has obsessed Mailer for life. Marilyn inhabits his head like some moonwalker, overripe, as all sexual creatures are.

And while Senator Joe McCarthy took on the State Department, the U.S. Army, Congress, Hollywood, the Soviet Union, and whatever other red and pink devils were lying around, Brando "feminized" the American screen. In *Viva Zapata!, The*

*Wild One, Julius Caesar, A Streetcar Named Desire, On the Waterfront,* and *The Men,* he was the real love interest, and whatever women were around lived in his shadow, even Vivien Leigh. And then it all stopped. Brando became more and more mannered and baroque. He would mugger in most of his films, do a series of impersonations, like a thickening ape, until he ended up as Superman's dad, earning millions for a moment that seemed to punctuate his own invisibility. *Our* Brando had fallen off the edge of the screen. He'd retired to Tahiti, like Gauguin. But he wasn't discovering modern, magical art in those island faces. He was in retirement from himself, exiled, like the Napoleon he once played, searching for his own Désirée. Yet he wasn't that different from Greta Garbo. "I had made enough faces," she announced after completing *Two-Faced Woman* in 1941.

*Making faces.* Isn't that what films are all about? Brando had tired of his screen face, and so had Garbo. And for almost fifty years now she's become the phantom of New York, appearing at lunch counters, disappearing into Central Park, her romantic presence as strong as ever. Time has frozen around her. Dietrich ages. Rita dies. But Garbo's absence-presence is like a song to Hollywood itself. Does it matter very much that TV and tennis, rock stars and nighttime soap operas have grabbed hold of America? We still have Greta Garbo, and that long, long romance of her face on the wall.

**4** Hollywood was the first global village. Long before jumbo jets and Telstar communications, the world swam with Esther Williams, skated with Sonja Henie, danced with Ginger and Fred. Gary Cooper was more recognizable, more beloved, than any king or president. Clark Gable wouldn't wear an undershirt in *It Happened One Night,* and haberdashery stores shuddered at their loss of revenue. American movie stars didn't have to bother creating fashions, their very looks made a whole planet shiver with delight. We forget how beautiful almost all of them were. Barbara Stanwyck may have been the ice mama of the Fifties, the Western Witch (*Cattle Queen of Montana, The Maverick Queen,* etc.), but she was gorgeous and fragile as Stella Dallas. William Holden grew surly and tough in *Stalag 17*, but he was once the golden boy of Hollywood. Gene Tierney waltzed through World War II in film after film that made me sick with desire. It hurt your eyeballs to watch Tyrone Power (one of the first "female" men) in *Alexander's Ragtime Band*. Even at five I wanted to kiss Alice Faye. If Louis B. Mayer outlawed toilet seats, if he forbade all the "natural functions" on screen, if he got us to believe that movie stars never had to piss like you or me, he was able to manufacture an idealized atmosphere, a universe where the stars lived for romance. This was the mark of Hollywood, its greatness, and its absurd quest. I grew up believing that Yvonne De Carlo was just around the corner. All you had to do was blink and find Ali Baba and the Forty Thieves. Even Paul Henreid, with his wooden mouth, could become a pirate on the Spanish Main.

I still dream of Henreid dueling with Walter Slezak, who was as familiar to me as my own face. I saw myself as fat Walter. He was my favorite villain. The world divided itself into a long, bitter, and passionate duel between Henreid or Tyrone Power *and* Basil Rathbone, George Sanders, Henry Daniell, or Walter Slezak, over the body of Maureen O'Hara. It didn't matter how often the duel was played out. Maureen O'Hara must have exhausted herself, racing from set to set, living in one of the artificial oceans on the back lots of Warner Brothers and Twentieth Century–Fox.

All that swagger, that preposterous choreography of pistols and swords, was only the lines and ligaments of romance. Whoever won got Maureen O'Hara, or some other wench, who would drive Tyrone Power bananas for the rest of his life. Poor Walter Slezak didn't really count. The most important duel was between the lovers themselves, like Gregory Peck and Jennifer Jones in *Duel in the Sun* (1946). It was a film that destroyed me and every single equation I had about the prospects of a normal, happy life removed from the screen. Jennifer was some kind of half-breed. And Peck was the rancher's son. Both of them had the highest cheekbones in Hollywood. They couldn't bear to be with or without each other. That, I understood, very early on, was tantamount to love. If it couldn't suck at your blood, it was worth nothing at all.

*Duel in the Sun* is probably one of the longest, emptiest epics of all time. But I adored the sheer meanness of the film, its caterwauling, its hymn to greed, and its monomania: lovers had to crawl across the desert and kill each other, or it wasn't romance. David O. Selznick hoped *Duel* would be another *Gone With the Wind;* it wasn't. But I can still hear the ominous jingle of Peck's spurs, feel those dark caverns in his face, the lithe movements of a merciless man. Lewt, Lionel Barrymore's boy, who wears his lean saddle pants, murders Charles Bickford, and seduces Jennifer Jones. It was here that my erotic cradle began to rock and rock and rock. I didn't like *The Best Years of Our Lives* (the critics' choice of 1946), with all its little problems about soldiers and sailors returning from the war. I wanted high opera, not Fredric March as a banker with a sergeant's stripes.

And I've been lost ever since in the caverns of Lewt McCanles' face, waiting for my own love-death. Tristan and Isolde go West. But it wasn't funny, because to discover *Duel in the Sun* at nine or ten was to be caught in a state of erotic arrest. I saw Lewt and Pearl (Jennifer Jones) as a particular conundrum, paradigms of American culture and all its plangent songs.

I wasn't the only one who suffered. Hollywood fashioned a poetics of love that was found nowhere else on the planet. It was a democracy of beautiful faces, an homogenized landscape of sex. In movieland, the Hollywood of Mayer and the other moguls, there was no *auteur*'s theory about directors sculpting all those shadows on the wall. Directors and writers and cinematographers were vague articles that were listed in the credits, and then disappeared. "When I was twelve or thirteen," Federico Fellini recalls, "I went to movies all the time—American movies. But I did not know there were directors of movies. I always thought the actors did everything."

And that's how it seemed to most of us. *They* were the magic quotients, the presences that held us in our seats. In "Autobiography of a Spectator," the late Italian novelist Italo Calvino says: "For me movies meant . . . the current Hollywood production." Calvino became a "serious" moviegoer around 1937 (the year I was born). "American movies of that time could boast an array of actors' faces unequaled before or since. . . . What we know as the 'Hollywood firmament' constituted a system to itself, with its constants and its variables, a human topology . . . from the broad and languid mouth of Joan Crawford to the thin and pensive one of Barbara Stanwyck." Calvino understood the legacy of Louis B. Mayer's (and Jack Warner's) exquisite circus of women and men. American films favored a kind of alabaster look, a flawless photogenic dream that "did not teach us to see real women with an eye prepared to discover unfamiliar beauty." Screen women became "phantoms of carnal aggressiveness," like Harlow and Crawford, and such powerful creatures "prevented you from being satisfied with what little (or much) you might encounter and it drove you to project your desires farther, into the future, the elsewhere, the difficult."

And I've never seemed to crawl out of that situation Calvino describes. The faces and bodies I adore have always led me back to shadows on a wall. Calvino realized the dilemma of the moviegoer. That descent into the cave isn't all out of fun. We're driven to it, because "the film of which we self-deceptively thought we were only spectators is the story of our life." And that's why we're mesmerized from the moment we enter the cave. The screen caresses our history, shapes us as we shape those phantoms on the wall; and as we watch, we discover our own design. We become Cassandras, predicting pasts and futures, futures and pasts.

5 Cassandra sits in her palace. She's a little boy of seven. She's watching a guy with a cleft in his chin. Call him Cary Grant. He plays Ernie Mott, a wandering tinker and penny hoodlum in Hollywood's idea of London's East End (*None But the Lonely Heart*). London was very exotic to a boy of seven. But I was sick to death, same as Ernie Mott. Both of us were in love with June Duprez. She had that dark, dreamy air of a Brooklyn-Bagdad princess.

June seemed out of place as a cashier at a London carnival, all blonded up, and married to George Coulouris, who wasn't much of a movie star, looking like a snake. She couldn't have belonged to George. She wasn't his type at all. I considered her a more beautiful cousin of Maria Montez. I could understand why thieves and buskers would fight over her, a dreamy girl like that. Cary Grant is subdued. His mom, Ethel Barrymore, is dying, and she ends up in jail. The London bobbies have caught her with stolen goods.

Ernie Mott lives across the street from Jane Wyatt. Even at seven I understood that a girl who sat night and day with a cello couldn't have much sense. She was like some phantom idea of the good. But Cary Grant fell for it. June Duprez disappears from the film. Ernie Mott has his dying mom (Ethel Barrymore won an Oscar for her role) and the cello girl. But I've been pondering the metaphysics of that film for forty-three years. Because this was a different Cary Grant, not that guy of all graces who "seemed a born aristocrat." He's lower class in *None But the Lonely Heart,* a Cockney brat without his usual flair (when we meet him he's dressed like Chaplin's tramp). A street kid who's close to Archibald Alexander Leach, the poor boy from Bristol who copied Noël Coward. "I pretended to be somebody I wanted to be and I finally became that person. . . . Or he became me. Or we met at some point. It's a relationship."

*None But the Lonely Heart* stutters along for two hours, but it haunts us in a way that much better films haven't. It's filled with a kind of patriotic bathos, a call for democracy and good-will out of all that London fog manufactured at RKO in the middle of World War II. But we don't believe in any future for Ernie Mott. He'll always be a penny bandit. And he's lost June Duprez.

Barbara Deming, in her marvelous book, *Running Away From Myself,* feels that Ernie Mott is a mama's boy, "struck helpless before the fact that he is to be left motherless." Like other heroes of the Forties, he's lost in a kind of masculine maze. Deming suggests an American landscape that is like a ticket to hell. She finished her book in 1950, but it wasn't published until 1969, when America, awakened by the mess of Vietnam, had begun to grow up about the content of its movies. No one wanted to look into that crazy mirror in 1950. Movies were movies, after all. Mayer and MGM. But Deming understood that a kind of group portrait had emerged from Hollywood films of the Forties, "a dream portrait" that was filled with ghosts.

Ernie Mott acts out some secret dream of the 1940s, that male fear of the female who had suddenly become both consumer and breadwinner during World War II. But Cary Grant's performance echoes more than that. He'd come out of the Bristol slums, belonging to Elias and Elsie Kingdon Leach. His dad was a garment worker who died an alcoholic. His mom went mad. The boy ran away from home to join a group of acrobats. He walked on stilts for a while. He worked in musical comedies, developed a new persona with the help of Noël Coward. He was an established star by the time he played Ernie Mott, forty years old, married to Barbara Hutton, the Woolworth heiress.

He had an incredible comic touch, a manic energy that created "windows" for the actors and actresses around him, opened them up because his timing was perfect. But he's lethargic as Ernie Mott. He emerges from the fog with his bull terrier, comes home to ma. "Black as the ace, I am," Ernie says, but we don't believe him. There's a kind of scratchy love play between Ernie and Ethel Barrymore. She's fond of her tinker son, but she can't tell him. He's a sucker for women, Ernie is. Black as the ace, with a heart of gold.

But he seems to be walking on stilts. The truth is, Ernie can't take care of himself. He can fix a watch, shoot a rifle, but he's like that acrobat Archie Leach, a boy who's run away from home and can't stop running.

I felt stuck to Ernie, back in 1944. I'm stuck to him now. Ethel Barrymore could have been my own mom. Jane Wyatt is only one of the women I ought to have married. And June Duprez is that love doll I've followed across a thousand movie walls and can't seem to catch. Calvino was right. Each time we descend into the cave we encounter the story of our life.

# two

# Portrait of the Artist as Buffalo Bill

1 Suddenly it's 1972.
Most of the palaces were gone. The Roxy had been razed years ago. I'd haunt the revival houses, looking for Groucho and W. C. Fields. Their misanthropy soothed me, made me feel part of mankind. I'd bark at the moon from my window over Riverside Drive. Visit my girlfriend. But something wasn't right. Movies shouldn't have had such awesome power in the middle of my life. Friends of mine were getting remarried, having sons and daughters, honing themselves for something big. And all I could consider was *Duck Soup*.

And that's when I met him in my elevator. Didn't say a word. I was mummified. His eyes were as blue as some ocean fever. He was with his actress wife. She smiled, understanding the state I was in. But he was as cold as Billy the Kid. And I felt the fool. Couldn't keep myself from goggling at him. As if he'd come down off the screen like an adventurous god to have a rendezvous in an elevator with the ultimate movie addict. It was my building, after all. I lived here. What the hell was Paul Newman (and Joanne Woodward) doing in my house?

Ah, it was no big deal. He was visiting my neighbor, Frank Corsaro, a friend from the Actors Studio. But how could Corsaro know that Newman was the first star of my adult life? Unlike Marlon Brando. Brando belonged to that boyhood I'd always be in. He was frozen into the very blood of my adolescence, with his biceps and his sex appeal, like a secret feminine side, some dark sister of the soul. Just watching Brando was almost an act of incest. I loved him with that crazy love of a fourteen-year-old kid. I wore muscle teeshirts. I learned to mumble like him.

A whole generation had fallen for that son of a bitch. We were marooned in the dull, dead Fifties of Dwight David Eisenhower, and Brando's was the only face that seemed to count. Before Presley. Before Dean. And before Marilyn starred in *Niagara* and *Gentlemen Prefer Blondes*. Of course Brando betrayed us. How could he not? He belonged to movieland.

"It was like I'd been asleep, and I woke up here sitting on a pile of candy," Brando said about his own success. "You're just sitting on a pile of candy gathering thick layers of—of *crust*."

My dark sister was dead. And by this time I was at college, fighting Communism as a member of the Naval ROTC. I didn't last long as a cadet. A couple of months, that's it.

Friends of mine went on to graduate school. I worked in the Parks Department as a playground director. It was a form of exile. I was nothing but a moviegoer. And that's when I started to notice Paul Newman. I saw his first film, *The Silver Chalice*. He mumbled like Marlon's kid brother. He was very, very bad. But the blueness of his eyes froze the frame. His body was lean as a knife. Yet the "actor" in him was lethargic, unformed, and he flooded the screen with his own hysteria, like a frightened ghost. I saw him in *Somebody Up There Likes Me*. I saw him in *The Left-Handed Gun*. The hysteria was under control, but there was still something schizoid about him, as if he couldn't shed Marlon Brando and find a persona that was properly his. I saw him in *Exodus*. He was a star. He occupied his own blue-eyed country on the screen.

"The expression of beauty tends to eliminate expression itself," says sociologist Edgar Morin. And that's how I felt about Paul Newman, the handsomest movie star on earth. There had never been that kind of fierce male beauty. Eyes staring out of a skull that always seemed to engage you, Newman's skin a powerful, pulsing mask. But something was missing for me. The beauty seemed purposeless, as random as an uncalled-for act of grace. He was the "blueeyed boy" e. e. cummings talked about in "Buffalo Bill's," a sharpshooter with a trigger finger controlled by Mister Death. He didn't have the touch of mercy about him, that human hand. I admired him, but he couldn't make me suffer, as Brando had done.

And then I saw Newman in another film, *The Hustler* (1961), directed by Robert Rossen (né Rosen), a kid from the Lower East Side who'd become involved in the Hollywood witch hunts. Tagged as a Communist, he was called upon by the House Committee on Un-American Activities to identify the names of other Communists in movieland. Rossen said no. He wouldn't finger his own friends. The studios blacklisted him, and he fell into that hole Hollywood created for people like him. He was a walking invisible man. Rossen brooded for a while and started "naming names." His testimony tore at him and he never returned to Hollywood. He shot *The Hustler* in the East. It was almost a companion film to *Body and Soul* (1947), starring John Garfield, another haunted man who fell afoul of the Committee and dropped dead the night before he was scheduled to "talk."

A tough street kid, Garfield spent the last years of his life like Kafka's K., feeling guilty and floating in all the ambiguities of the "Law." But he hadn't been ambiguous in *Body and Soul*, playing a boxer who becomes champ by courting the bad guys. The film had a marvelous feel of the street. And the dancing Garfield does in the ring could have been the very dance of his life: the delinquent who found a career by miming movement and mumbling words in some little corner as tight as any ring. Discovering how to act had saved Garfield, but becoming a movie star had brought him to the attention of the Committee. Who would have cared what friends he had if he'd been another journeyman actor, and not a star?

And in *The Hustler* Rossen tried to grapple with some of Garfield's story, the texture of failure and success, all the peculiar twists of talent, and the kind of vulturous deadness that attaches itself to talent, eats it alive. Newman is "Fast Eddie" Felson, a pool hustler from Oakland who's come to the Big Town to beat Minnesota Fats (Jackie Gleason), the best money player in the world. This is a different Newman, not an acting mask. He's lithe. All the laziness is gone. He isn't a beautiful sleepwalker. We can feel the swagger in his body. He's full of danger now. The match begins. "You shoot a good stick," Fats says to Eddie.

And Eddie says to his partner (Myron McCormick) about Minnesota Fats, "That fat man. Look at the way he moves. Like a dancer."

Fats wins, and then Eddie wins, sixteen thousand dollars, but he won't quit, because the match isn't about money, it's about some crazy code of honor. Eddie wants the fat man to admit his defeat. The fat man goes to his "banker," Bert Gordon (George C. Scott), whom we first see wearing dark glasses and drinking a glass of milk. Bert looks Eddie up and down and says to Fats, "Stick with this kid. He's a loser."

Eddie gets drunk. The match goes on and on. The fat man washes his hands and face. "You look beautiful, Fats. Just like a baby," Eddie says, with a drunken, exhausted smile. Rossen has shot the film in black-and-white, and Newman can't show off his blue eyes and Technicolor face. He has to depend on his wits. There's a vulnerability in that smile, a feeling of pain that binds Newman to Eddie Felson and destroys that distance between the actor acting and ourselves. We've entered into the drama and the dream of the film, given ourselves over to Eddie and the fat man. We watch with our own sense of fear.

Eddie loses, of course. And later he asks Bert, "What beat me?"

"Character," says Bert.

There's a double pull to that remark, because "character" is what Newman has acquired in this film. He isn't Mister Death's own "blueeyed boy," or that beautiful mask beyond the land of expression. He's a guy who's discovered his craft and found himself in Fast Eddie Felson. Perhaps it's Eddie's own deep flaw, his need to wound himself, that touched Newman, opened up *his* wounds. Because it's the first time that prettiness itself isn't the central part of a Paul Newman picture. The face on the wall has begun to grow lines and has learned to growl.

Fast Eddie deserts his partner and begins to drift. He meets Sarah Packard (Piper Laurie) at the bus station. She's a drifter like him, but she's also lame. "You're too hungry," she says after they kiss. Eddie leaves Sarah outside her door. At a poker game he meets Bert Gordon, who offers to back Eddie in big-time hustling. But Bert wants seventy-five percent of the take. Eddie refuses Bert's offer. He feels humiliated. He finds Sarah again. He moves in with her and they have a kind of drifter's romance. He starts to hustle, but he's doomed, because he can't show how good he is, or he'll give himself away. He prowls the pool halls like an isolated animal. The fact is, Minnesota Fats is the only man he can really play. He grows careless at a waterfront bar, reveals the depths of his game to a small-time hustler, and the hoods at the bar grab Eddie, shove him into the toilet, and break his thumbs. We see his face pressed against the glass, hear him scream, and we've gone outside movieland and gotten caught in the grit.

Eddie recovers and looks for Bert. Twenty-five percent of something, he says, is better than a hundred percent of nothing. Bert decides to take Eddie on the road and test him against a Kentucky blueblood named Ralph (Murray Hamilton) who gets a kick out of playing hustlers. Eddie brings Sarah along. It's Derby week in Louisville. Bert taunts Sarah, but he's also attracted to her. He wants everything Eddie has. He sleeps with Sarah, and she kills herself in Bert's bathroom, knowing she's lost Fast Eddie to Bert and the art of big-time hustling. Eddie comes home to his Louisville hotel and finds Sarah dead. He tries to kill Bert, but the cops hold him down.

Of course Fast Eddie plays Fats again. "All of a sudden I've got oil in my arm." He beats the fat man, and Bert insists on his rightful share. He'll be satisfied with twenty-five percent. Eddie won't give him a dime. Bert warns Eddie not to walk into a big-time pool hall again. But Eddie doesn't suffer over that. We see the sadness in the fat man's eyes. He belongs to Mister Death.

*The Hustler* takes us into the shadows, insists on black-and-white in a Technicolor world. It has the courage to investigate cowardliness and those dark corners of the psyche where few American directors had gone before. It's a film about human dirt. And Robert Rossen got extraordinary performances out of Newman, Scott, Gleason, and Piper Laurie. She was a girl from Detroit, Rosetta Jacobs, and Hollywood had turned her into a starlet who kept appearing in "Arabian" romances, like *Son of Ali Baba* and *The Prince Who Was a Thief,* until she was little more than a sexy, sanitized infant. But Rossen had revealed her "face" to us, and it looked like Rosetta Jacobs rather than Piper Laurie.

But we shouldn't forget Paul.

I clung to him after *The Hustler,* as if Brando had come back in a cooler form, some blueeyed Bill running from Mister Death . . . and *The Silver Chalice.* He was sensitive on the subject of being like Brando's kid brother. "I wonder if anyone ever mistakes him for Paul Newman. I'd like that." But he didn't have to worry. He'd buried the Brando image by now. His persona was rooted in rough, gravel tones. He was the rebellious, lonely bandit of *Hombre* and *Hud,* and the warmer, lonely bandit who played Butch Cassidy, Judge Roy Bean, and Henry Gondorff in *The Sting.* The face had grown even more beautiful, and at the beginning of *Butch Cassidy and the Sundance Kid,* there's a close-up of Butch, shot in sepia, where he looks like some stranded angel of the West, as forlorn as America, that lost country of a brand-new continent. But after *The Sting* (1973), Newman was quiet for years, more of an icon than an actor, winging his way through whatever role he had, as if it didn't seem to matter so much. He'd joined the company of Gable and Gary Cooper, those "rough trappers of movie space," whose presence in a film was enough to guarantee an audience. But his face was no longer pressed against the glass, as it had been in *The Hustler.* He couldn't "break onetwothreefourfive pigeonsjustlikethat," as Buffalo Bill had done.

And then he fooled me. He played a Boston Irish lawyer, Frankie Galvin, in *The Verdict* (1982), and it was the performance of his life. Newman himself was in that no-man's-land between fifty-five and sixty. And Galvin must have touched a nerve in him. Frankie was a lawyer at the end of the line, an ambulance chaser who wanders into funeral parlors looking for work. The landscape he inhabits could have belonged to Leopold and Molly Bloom. The Boston that director Sidney Lumet shows us had the feel of Dublin; the river Charles was almost as black and bleak as the Liffey. The film was shot in muted reds and browns. But the most powerful landscape was Newman himself, with his wondrous white hair, his hawklike profile, a gorgeous bird of prey. No longer a boy, Newman had the beginnings of a chicken neck. Yet the marvelous decay of him, the mighty face broken a bit, the eyes staring out of a slightly worn map, pulls us closer and closer to Paul, and he reveals a side of him he'd never risked before: a kind of cold fear, the stink of failure, the sense of an approaching doom.

Galvin goes up against "the prince of fuckin' darkness," Ed Concannon (James Mason), Boston's most successful trial lawyer, in a case involving the negligence of two doctors. Frankie has to fight Concannon, the courts, the Catholic church, witnesses who vanish on him, and a girlfriend who's really Concannon's spy. And whether he wins or loses, Galvin realizes, "there is no other case. This is the case."

Newman got his sixth Academy Award nomination, but not even Frankie Galvin could bring him that little gold statue. The gods were against him. He had to go up against the great Mahatma Gandhi, and Gandhi won. The Mahatma took the form of Ben Kingsley, an Anglo-Indian actor in his first film. It was a spooky performance, as if Harold Pinter were standing behind Ben, giving the Mahatma a touch of menace. *Gandhi* was a much more ambitious film than *The Verdict,* full of historical furies and the bones of war. And Kingsley's performance took it beyond the sentimental reaches of a religious epic. But there was nothing in the film that could touch Paul Newman eating a raw egg in a glass of beer, playing pinball, soaking his face in a sinkful of ice. Newman had gone outside impersonation, had pulled Frankie Galvin into himself, danced around in the void. He should have won that Oscar.

The Academy recognized Paul Newman as the Mahatma of American films and awarded him a special Oscar in 1985. Perhaps the sachems of Hollywood felt guilty that they'd shut out Paul. Newman might have denied it, but that special Oscar did seem like "a gift certificate to Forest Lawn." That's not something that should have happened to Henry Gondorff or Butch Cassidy. His screen personas kept boiling in my head. "The star," says Edgar Morin, "is more than an actor incarnating characters, he incarnates *himself* in them, and they become incarnate in him. . . . Gary Cooper ennobles and enlarges all the heroes he plays: he *garycooperizes* them."

Newman doesn't ennoble or enlarge. He limits his characters, narrows them down to jumping, comic skeletons. But the effect is almost the same. He *newmanizes* Henry Gondorff, Butch, Frankie Galvin, and Roy Bean, gives them *his* flesh on the wall, and also assimilates Gondorff and Bean "into his own personality."

It's a sort of ghostly cannibalism. Pirandello, perhaps our greatest inventor of ghosts, believed that the film actor "feels as if in exile—exiled not only from the stage but also from himself." But it's this very exile, that schizoid sense of self, that provides movies with their ultimate power. The camera, wrote Walter Benjamin, "introduces us to unconscious optics as does psychoanalysis to unconscious impulses." And it's the unconscious optics of the face that often give film its "shock effect." Because nothing, nothing haunts us as much as the human face. And that first close-up of Butch, staring out at us like an old photograph suddenly come alive, fills us with sadness *and* adventure. The sadness of a lost world and the euphoria of having that world reinvented for us in front of our eyes, with that beauty of the face.

The life and times of the Mahatma, no matter how well they're presented on the screen, can only come to us *through* Ben Kingsley's face. The enigmatic smile, the Pinteresque pause of the voice reveal Gandhi to us, evoke a landscape, just as Butch Cassidy *becomes* the West. If faces are only one more article for the camera to dwell upon, they are exquisite articles, without which all the props we can conjure up—pieces of furniture, burnt skies, a particular motorcar, a mirror from some golden age—would only be marvels in the land of the dead.

Still, the marriage of performer and performance is never complete. The movie actor does exist in a kind of exile. Butch Cassidy is and isn't Paul Newman, as Edgar Morin might say, and Paul is and isn't Butch. "Once the film is over, the actor becomes an actor again, the character remains a character, *but from their union is born a composite creature who participates in both, envelops them both: the star.*"

2   Met Paul Newman again a couple of years after he lost that Oscar to Ben Kingsley. It must have been 1985. I'd become a member of a unit at the Actors Studio reserved for playwrights and directors. I loved Pirandello and Pinter, Brecht and Jean Genet, some of Joe Orton, but most of the theater pieces I saw seemed like endless gardens of talk. What can you expect from a moviegoer? I had all the prejudices of a rotten child. But the Studio had an aura of its own for movie addicts. It had been the home of Brando and Marilyn, Jimmy Dean, Dustin Hoffman, Joanne Woodward, Jane Fonda, Robert De Niro, Geraldine Page, Sidney Poitier, Anne Bancroft, Sally Field, Rod Steiger, Eva Marie Saint, Ellen

Burstyn, Eli Wallach, Ben Gazzara, Steve McQueen, Shelley Winters, Al Pacino, Patricia Neal, Mickey Rourke . . . and Paul Newman. Four generations of movie stars had come riding out from under Lee Strasberg's overcoat. He was the magic rabbi, the wizard of the East, who had more to do with Hollywood's "merchandise" than any mogul. The rabbi had been dead three years when I started attending classes at the Studio, but he inhabited the place, haunted it, as if nothing could get done *without* his approval. I could feel that stern little man sitting behind me . . . next to Norman Mailer.

It was Mailer who'd brought me into the house. He'd become involved with the Studio in 1958, while he was working on a dramatization of *The Deer Park*. Lee Strasberg was a "heavy, powerful, central influence" at the time. Elia Kazan, one of the Studio's founders, was "enormously successful," but the Studio was still "Strasberg's bailiwick." He appeared at all the acting sessions. "He had an unpleasant voice," Mailer recalls. "He was not a warm man. There was a chill in the air when he spoke . . . and a sense of oppression." Strasberg seemed to belong to some "high priesthood."

Mailer has his own rabbinical side. And two high priests don't usually get along together. Strasberg didn't like to shake hands. He was a purist who never had the time to finish high school. He could walk past you without saying hello. But the actors he's worked with *and* criticized, like Marilyn and Al Pacino, had adored him and his gruff, "gangsterish" ways. Strasberg was a lot like Hyman Roth, the gangster he'd played in *The Godfather, Part II*. Hyman Roth had started him on a career as a character actor in the movies at the age of seventy-three. But no career could cripple his teaching or deplete his energies. He danced with the Rockettes in a gala at Radio City Music Hall three days before he died.

Critic Harold Clurman had said of Strasberg as a teacher-director that the "effect he produces is a classic hush, tense and tragic, a constant conflict so held in check that a kind of beautiful spareness results." It came out of "an acute awareness of human contradiction and suffering."

Strasberg was the "father of Method acting in America," but it was Marlon Brando who brought The Method into the heart of our own movie culture with his electric, mumbling style that played upon a perverse sexual danger. Brando was that outlaw in all of us, male and female. And The Method was a means of rooting his entire persona into a part, of discovering a character's "prehistory" along with his own, so that a performance, moment by moment, was filled with psychic energy and a raw, radical truth, as if an actor's insides were being ripped away to reveal that poetic skeleton under the skin.

I believed in such a skeleton until Brando gave it up. But The Method remained a secret religion for me, tied to that wish I'd always had (shared with most of my generation), of becoming a movie actor, another Marlon Brando. And now I sat in the holy temple, the house of Brando and Kazan and Strasberg, together with Shelley Winters, Eli Wallach, Mailer, Arthur Penn . . .

I'd written a play for the unit, a two-acter about King George III in his eightieth year, when he was deaf and blind, and his wastrel son, also George, was prince regent. I'd always loved that old man, Father George, who was mocked by half the world as the king who lost the American Revolution. I didn't care. I was still loyal to George. After all, he was the last king the thirteen colonies had, the monarch who was hiding in our historical closet, because the land of democratic principles didn't like to consider that it had some "despot" in its own family tree.

My play was a farce, of course, with the king sitting on a throne that was a huge chamberpot. And the actors at the Studio had a difficult time puzzling what the play was all about. It was hard to bring The Method into madcap comedy. But I was willing to act out all the roles myself. And then one day, as I was coming down from the bleachers in the Studio's main classroom, I saw the blueeyed boy. His hair was much sparser than it had been in my elevator. But the eyes had the same oceanic fever. He could have pulled the moon down with those eyes. And I was still the fool. Couldn't stop staring at Paul, actor, husband, father, racing-car driver, popcorn maker, and president of the Actors Studio.

3     It was like chasing Melville's white whale. The guy didn't like to give interviews, sign autographs, or appear in public. He'd rather eat popcorn. But as private as he was, he probably had the most recognizable face

on earth. He'd become an icon, like Brando and Marilyn and Bogart and Clint Eastwood, an image that was fixed in our psychic landscape, with a climate all its own. A poster of him appears on Jon Voight's wall in *Midnight Cowboy*. You can also find his face in bars and bowling alleys in any city, town, or country village, real or imagined.

I'd seen him only once at the Studio, but I wouldn't have badgered him there. I wrote to Paul. The movie addict was preparing a book, blah, blah, blah. . . . A month went by. Nothing happened. Then a letter arrived with Newman's name on the back of the envelope.

The blueeyed boy was in Florida. But his assistant wrote that Paul would be happy to give me half an hour when he returned from the land of Ponce de León. And so I went to see Paul Newman. He was closeted on Madison Avenue, in a back office of the Disney empire. It was Paul's hideaway, like those bandit rocks of Butch Cassidy's Hole-in-the-Wall Gang. But these rocks were in the heart of Manhattan.

The sign on the wall said "The Disney Channel," with a gold sillhouette of Mickey Mouse. Mick wore the mask of America, innocent, dopey, efficient, sweet. He'd been the number-one star in the world, beating out Gable and Cooper and Shirley Temple in all the popularity polls.

He had more names than a mouse ought to have. He was Michel Souris in France, Topolino in Italy, Miki Kuchi in Japan, Muse Pigg in Sweden, Mikki Maus in Russia, Miguelito in most of Latin America. The Mouse even took part in World War II. During D-Day "Mickey Mouse" was the code name of the Allied Supreme Command. And the Mouse was just as popular in less momentous ways. King George VI wouldn't step into a London movie palace unless he could watch Mickey Mouse.

And there I was in one of Mickey's cribs, waiting for Paul Newman. Paul's assistant, Marcia Franklin, led me through labyrinthian corridors to a wooden door with a sign that said

ATTENTION
CHIEN BIZARRE

She sensed how nervous I was, and she smiled. But she'd locked herself out, and just as she started searching for the key, the door opened. We went inside. There was no one to greet us. I put my winter coat on a couch, thinking Paul Newman was around the bend somewhere, in another part of the forest. Marcia disappeared, and I could feel the prickles at the back of my neck. Newman was a couple of feet away, sitting behind a desk. He wore a green sweater and was nibbling on something out of a silver bowl.

I sat down and couldn't help noticing the noose that hung over his desk. I figured it was a souvenir from the Hole-in-the-Wall Gang. I didn't try to play on him like a harp, warm him up with some brilliant question. Told him how much I'd liked Frankie Galvin. "You should have won an Oscar," I said. And I asked him how close he felt to the character of Frank.

He swiveled in his chair. His face had the rough look and temperature of a drill sergeant. "I know what it means to feel uncomfortable with yourself," he said, talking of Frankie Galvin. "It doesn't take much to resurrect that emotional state. . . . Oh, shit, I don't want to sound pretentious."

"But Frankie's at the edge," I insisted. "He's on a tightrope he can't get off. His only future is to fall."

Paul looked at me out of those luminous eyes. He was as lean as Fast Eddie or Butch. "I've not been there," he said, "but I've been pretty close. . . . I don't care that much about results. My instrument [as an actor] at that particular time and place was tuned for that character. I had a lot of fun, really, literally, I had a lot of fun getting lost in that character."

"It worked," I said, "because it's not your usual happy ending. Frankie doesn't go off with the girl [Charlotte Rampling as Laura Fischer]." Laura keeps ringing and ringing Frank, but he never picks up the phone.

The studio had wanted a "reconciliation" between Frank and Laura Fischer.

"Sidney [Lumet] was asked to capitulate," but he didn't, and Frankie is left on his tightrope, perilously alone.

My curiosity about the noose was getting in the way of my questions. I couldn't think. "Is the noose from one of your films?"

"No," he said. "Just for visitors."

The blueeyed boy had caught me. He *was* Henry Gondorff, the great sting artist.

I asked him about the half-breed he'd played in *Hombre,* the stillness of the character. The half-breed hardly ever moves, hardly ever talks. But when he does move, it's with a graceful, electric violence, a dancer distilling death.

"I stole that from an Indian in an Indian reservation in New Mexico. Stillness was exactly the key."

"But it couldn't have only been a steal," I said. "I don't care how much you copied from that Indian, or how much you stalked him. The half-breed has blood in his eyes. The white men hate him. The Indians hate him. And you walked that wonderful line of a man who lives in both worlds and belongs to none."

Newman dug into the silver bowl again. "I'm going to eat and drink comfortably tonight. This is doing terrific things to my ego."

Ah, how the hell do you talk to an icon? He didn't have to follow Indians around any more. He could feel his way into a role. "I don't have to wrestle so much. I get it quieter."

"What about Henry Gondorff?" I asked. "Redford is nominated for an Academy Award, but the whole picture hinges on you. You had Gondorff in your pocket. You were the magic source. Gondorff was always under control. The film would have evaporated without you."

But he wouldn't share my enthusiasm for Gondorff. "I didn't feel it demanded very much." He'd been thinking of Gable while he inhabited Gondorff's skin. "Gable was my external picture."

"External picture? How come?"

"He was a man of extreme relish. If you got into trouble, you could always fall back on that."

Since Paul had mentioned an actor out of his own past, I started to dredge up his childhood. I knew he was a kid from Cleveland. His father had owned a sporting-goods store. I wondered about the movie palaces he'd visited, and I asked him how important movies had been to him as a boy.

"Not inordinately important. I didn't think very much about films. It was very long ago. *The Perils of Pauline* . . . double features."

"Did you have a favorite actor?"

He said no. Nor did he have a favorite actor now. He was

like Buffalo Bill, riding the "watersmooth" stallion of his craft, an actor all alone.

I asked him about *The Hustler*.

"I'm very dissatisfied with [my] films of that period. I was working too hard."

"But it's a film about hunger," I said. "All that exuberance was necessary."

"I watched twenty minutes of it and felt embarrassed. . . . It's only taken me thirty years to become confident. That's not to be confused with arrogance. The less you care about the result of it, the less you think of result when you're playing the character. But my confidence will probably go down a lot. There's not enough work out there to keep your instrument oiled. Since you work less frequently, there's so big a stake, so much riding on every film. I'm only working every two, three years."

That's because each picture was like its own corporation, with millions spent on an actor's smile. But in the old Hollywood, the town of Mr. Mayer, when the big studios had to bring out a picture every six or seven days to meet the demand of moviehouses coast to coast, and the stars themselves were hired hands, Gable might be in three, four, five pictures a year. During the Thirties Gable himself could fill the house. You didn't need movie titles or the mention of other stars. Just Clark Gable.

"I spoke to a tennis player of real consequence [Newman wouldn't name him], and he thought of himself as being ungifted. . . . I'm not a natural talent. I'm a learned talent."

He must have had Brando on the brain. Or Jack Nicholson.

"But you're such an intelligent actor," I said. "And I think that's more important."

But Newman said he'd "sacrifice intelligence for talent, for the natural gift." And he was sorry he'd made so many rotten films. "I'm always much more aware of my failures than my successes."

And like some phantom of the moviehouse I rattled off all the good films he'd made in the last thirty years, including Robert Altman's *Buffalo Bill and the Indians,* the only film in Newman's "fallow period" (during the mid and late Seventies) that I really admired. It was a left-handed look at American history; like a cousin of Melville's *The Confidence Man,* it examined showmanship and chicanery, and revealed Bill as a likable fraud and narrow man who walked about in his own hallucinated presence. There's so little substance to Bill, he didn't even possess a shadow. And Newman played that neurotic showman and captain of the Wild West with a mischievous charm.

But he didn't agree. "I couldn't get rid of Roy Bean in Altman's film. Roy Bean. That's what I think was a good performance. It was really a wonderful film [John Huston's *The Life and Times of Judge Roy Bean*]. A great character."

Huston's film had a funny, mythic side. It was about some badlands of the imagination, west of the Pecos, where Judge Roy Bean, a reformed desperado, determined the law. He drapes himself in the Texas flag and presides over the town of Vinegarroon. The film was like a picaresque novel set in one place. Every sort of adventure arrives in Vinegarroon. Bean, with his blue eyes sticking out of a bearded face, was like some Don Quixote of the Panhandle, a visionary without his wits. But I preferred Walter Brennan's Roy Bean in *The Westerner* (1940). Brennan played Bean with much more menace. Newman seemed outside his own myth. There was no surprise in his performance. It was a masquerade, with Newman in a dime-store mask.

The film had wonderful comic moments. John Huston plays Grizzly Adams, a mountain man who comes to Vinegarroon to die, but first he has to find a home for his bear. "Zachary Taylor, my oldest boy, named after the twelfth president of the United States . . . I prefer his company to that of men."

The big black bear kisses Bean, and it's like high romance in Vinegarroon.

When I asked Paul about the other actors he'd played with, whether he'd learned from them, he said, "I got an awful lot from that bear in *Roy Bean*."

"What about working with someone like John Huston? Did you feel—"

"Privileged."

Huston "had a great deal of respect for actors, and you had no alternative but to return that favor. It was a nice situation, just for starters."

We talked about his own life as a director.

*Rachel, Rachel* captured the terrific loneliness of people Newman himself had played. Joanne Woodward, the spinster schoolmarm, had a touch of Butch, Frankie Galvin, Roy Bean, and that lonely, hallucinating Buffalo Bill—hunters and seekers of families who hug the moviehouse wall with their blueeyed isolation. "I probably enjoy the demands of work as a director more . . . but it's hard to release yourself from the applause of being an actor."

And that got us onto the subject of fame. Paul Newman, the star, who couldn't eat a lamb chop in a public place without being pestered. Did he hate the intrusion of it?

"Yes, I hate it. Yes, it's a terrible intrusion, most of it is graceless. But when you start losing it [fame], you're acutely aware of it, not because you're mad at losing it, but it's a signal that your power is diminishing, and your choice as an actor is also diminishing . . . your choices are diminishing in a diminishing market. I don't like the publicness of it all. I don't like the intrusion of it. [But without it] you have lost your bargaining power. I ain't working. I've lost something."

Must have been deaf. He was Henry Gondorff, for God's sake. He was Butch. He could have made another half-dozen films about the Hole-in-the-Wall Gang. And he'd just come off winning an Academy Award as Fast Eddie in Martin Scorsese's sequel to *The Hustler,* called *The Color of Money.* Newman had grabbed the gold statue on his seventh nomination.

"What have you lost?"

"I ain't working. There aren't that many good choices to be made."

He continued to munch out of his silver bowl.

I got a little nosy. "What are you eating?" I asked.

"Popcorn kernels. I'd offer you some, but it's nearly finished."

I couldn't get that image of Henry Gondorff out of my head, Henry in his undershirt, fixing an old merry-go-round that was the "front" for a whorehouse in Chicago, where Henry was lying low. He looked like my father with his mustache and his undershirt and his black hair. I loved Gondorff. He was as near to Bogart as anyone could get, the little guy as mythic man, with that quiet, calming sadness. Gondorff. The name alone was worth a million. Silly and magical at the same time.

"That mustache you wore in *The Sting,*" I said. "You don't usually wear a mustache."

"I had a mustache in *Color of Money*."

Ah, but what a difference that mustache had made. In Scorsese's film it serves to hide Eddie Felson's face. It has no mythic overtones. Eddie is now a liquor salesman. He's also a "stake horse" who backs other pool sharps. "I'm too old," he says. "My wheels are shot."

He backs Vincent Lauria (Tom Cruise), who's a "natural," like Eddie had once been. He goes on the road with Vince and Vince's girlfriend Carmen (Mary Elizabeth Mastrantonio), who was Al Pacino's sister in *Scarface* (1983). She's the daughter of incest—there's a funky quality about her—and she should have been some princess of the night who unsettles Eddie and Vince, but the film is static. It has a curious lethargy, because there's no magic between the two men. They inhabit different timescapes. Tom Cruise looks like Clark Kent. He has none of the pain and hunger Eddie had in *The Hustler*. He's a smiling, dancing cartoon. *The Color of Money* is about the pretended hunger of the Eighties. It has no central core. It doesn't ride into the far country of Scorsese's other films, *Mean Streets* (1973), *Taxi Driver* (1976), and *Raging Bull* (1979), with that urban nightmare he's mapped so well. The paranoia is gone. And in its place is a ritualistic concern for money. In scene after scene, money moves from fist to fist. Eddie himself mouths wisdoms about the "color" of money. He says to Vince: "You remind me that money won is twice as sweet as money earned." That's meant to be a hustler's credo. But it has a hollowness without the old Fast Eddie Felson.

Newman is still lean as a knife in *The Color of Money*. But his face is a broken mask. He's hiding from us. "Hey, I'm back," he says. But we don't believe it.

And so he won his Oscar from an Academy with a guilty conscience. The sachems must have been dreaming of those other fiercely comic lonely guys when they watched *The Color of Money*. They'd celebrated an icon who'd endured over thirty years. And I asked Paul how it felt to be a walking idol.

"You can't help but think of yourself as a fraud," he said. "You can't live up to the size of the people [Gondorff, Butch, etc.] who have been written for you."

But the blueeyed boy was being unfair to himself. No one but Paul could have played Henry Gondorff, invested that character with so much fun. He *was* Butch Cassidy, he *was* Frankie Galvin, and that "hombre" with the still eyes, murderous and gentle, like some angel of a man who'd plugged himself into the modern psyche.

He'd finished the popcorn and it was time for me to go.

There was one scene in *The Color of Money* where Tom Cruise embraces Paul, and Paul starts to stiffen. I don't think that stiffening was rehearsed; it wasn't a gambit; it hadn't come out of some actor's bag of tricks. I had the feeling that Paul didn't like to be touched. He wasn't a hermit, as Howard Hughes had been near the end of his life. But he was a very private man, at a distance from the world, and that pulling back lent his performances the sadness of a lost photograph. He didn't threaten us the way Brando did. He didn't explode. But he calmed us inside the cave.

I saw Mickey's silhouette on my way out, gilded emblems of the Mouse's ears and nose. Paul Newman and Mickey Mouse. The two caballeros. They'd come riding into our century, one with his enormous yellow shoes, his button nose, and white gloves, the other with his blueeyed handsomeness, and both of them had given us more pleasure than any man or woman from an earlier time could ever have dreamed. They were the movies. Mickey and Paul.

# three

# *Gilda's Glove*

**1** I remember something Charles Laughton told Tyrone Power once upon a time. Be careful. If Power, the movie star, wanted to act on stage, he would have to shed a particular demon. He might be an actor reading his lines, but he would "also be the monster, made up of all the characters [Power had] played on the screen." And Power would have to dispose of that monster by breathing and looking like a man. Perhaps. But the monster would still be behind every move. That mingling of time, roles half-remembered, words uttered from an echoing wall.

Consider Orson Welles. He was a mythic creature from the moment he was born. A family friend, Maurice Bernstein, who happened to be an orthopedist, examines Orson at eighteen months and declares him a genius. With the help of Dadda Bernstein, Orson paints, performs his own magic act, writes poetry at six. But he's too ill to go to school. Dadda keeps him at home because of his asthma and rheumatism. But it's no crime. The boy is deep into Shakespeare long before puberty. He travels around the world with his dad and doesn't start school until he's ten. He edits a book, *Everybody's Shakespeare,* with his headmaster, Roger Hill. Both his mother and father are now dead. Dadda becomes his guardian. He does more magic tricks and decides to become an actor. At sixteen he appears with the Abbey Theatre in Dublin (he's already six feet two). At nineteen he's on Broadway. At twenty-three his head appears on the cover of *Time*. He'd scared the pants off America with his radio adaptation of H. G. Wells' "The War of the Worlds," which told of Martians landing in New Jersey the night before Halloween.

Welles already had his own company, the Mercury Theater, with three productions on Broadway, but a lot of his fame had come in a more peculiar manner. He was the radio voice of Lamont Cranston, "The Shadow," who could vaporize himself at will. Cranston was almost as industrious as Orson Welles. Both were magicians. But Cranston had devoted his life to the theater of crime. He was his own walking laboratory. An amateur, like Sherlock Holmes, he could read minds and frighten murderers and thieves to death with the booming registers of his voice. His very laughter could knock a man down. But how could Welles have known that he was acting out his own autobiography on the radio? He would also become an invisible man, with a habit of disappearing from wives, creditors, hotels, countries, film projects, and his own fame. Even while he was in his twenties, critics called him the world's youngest has-been. Welles went to Hollywood at the invitation of RKO. He described that studio as "the biggest electric-train set any boy ever had." The Shadow knows.

"He has the manner of a giant and the look of a child," said Jean Cocteau. And both the giant *and* the child set to work on *Citizen Kane*. It was a movie that Mayer of MGM tried to kill, because Welles had parodied newspaper tycoon William Randolph Hearst and his mistress, Marion Davies; and Hearst, who had "little odd eyes, like a whale's," might have taken vengeance on all of Hollywood, a company town with as much individual heroism as a mouse. But in spite of Louis B. Mayer, *Kane* was released. It was kept out of most major moviehouses. It was ignored in the Hearst press. RKO could barely advertise it. But the movie was seen and marveled at. "Overnight," said Kenneth Tynan, "the American cinema had acquired an adult vocabulary, a dictionary instead of a phrase book for illiterates."

Perhaps this was what the moguls were really afraid of; a film like Welles' might awaken that sleeping child, the American audience. Andy Hardy couldn't exist in the same crib with Charles Foster Kane. And Mayer had bet his life on Andy Hardy. He'd made Mickey Rooney one of the most popular stars in the world, the rival of Mickey Mouse. Both of them were all-American boys. They celebrated the ordinary, the universal openness of the American dream. But war had come to Europe. And Shirley Temple could no longer fill the moviehouses; she was a doll with growing pains: a tired old lady of twelve. And who could have known that *Gone With the Wind*, the most popular film in

our solar system until *E.T.*, had signaled the end of something?
That special kind of infantilism Hollywood created out of America's own need for romance had helped keep us in a cocoon.
But even though the cocoon would last well into the war, a
dark sensibility grew up around it. Suspicion. Worry. Fear. The
world of *Citizen Kane*.

Welles had brought all the bravura of a twenty-four-year-old
boy to the making of the movie, all the weird sound effects he'd
picked up from The Shadow, his own booming voice, his sense
of grouping figures on a stage, as if he were encamping his own
little army, his belief in an ensemble, which allowed RKO to
"lend" him his Mercury players. Thus he invented *Kane* out of
Herman Mankiewicz's script and a boy's bearish energy. Welles
was everywhere in *Kane*. It was his first film. He had nothing
to measure himself against except his own burly self. In "Raising
Kane," Pauline Kael notes that "the dark, Gothic horror style,
with looming figures, and with vast interiors that suggested castles rather than houses . . . suited Welles; it was the visual
equivalent of The Shadow's voice—a gigantic echo chamber."

And it's the echo chamber that defines so much of *Citizen
Kane,* as if The Shadow had come out of hiding, and Lamont
Cranston had moved from the radio to films. There's no deny-
ing the genius of his cameraman, Greg Toland, who created an
overpowering mood for *Kane,* a sense of figures stranded in a
fishbowl, a kind of sculpting of the human form, as if we were
watching an enormous, floating bier, a death ship with its own
willful design; or the genius of Mankiewicz's script, with its
geometric pinpointings of Kane's life; or the genius of Welles'
troupe, with Joseph Cotten, Everett Sloane, Agnes Moorehead,
Ray Collins, Paul Stewart, and others like Dorothy Comingore,
whom Welles himself had molded for the film, and my old
friend George Coulouris, that snakelike man from *None But the
Lonely Heart*.

Whatever genius surrounded him, Welles was still the magician at the center of the storm. It's no accident that Everett
Sloane is named "Bernstein" in the film, like that Dadda of a
doctor who'd helped to raise him. And Kane's autobiography
belongs as much to Welles as it does to William Randolph Hearst.
Like Kane, Welles is "taken" from his parents and sent out into
a mysterious world. But more than that, it's not the tale itself

that deepens into art. It's the sheer buoyancy of Welles. From the moment we see him, we cannot take our eyes off Charles Foster Kane. He's the ultimate monster: Welles, Kane, William Randolph Hearst, and Lamont Cranston. The Shadow wearing flesh. And Kael reminds us that "film is so vivid and the actor so large and so close that it is a common primitive response to assume that the actor invented his lines. . . . Welles carries on in a baronial style that always reminds us of Kane. Kane seems an emanation of Welles."

But it really doesn't matter how the monster was formed. Welles blunders through *Kane* like a pitiful giant. We observe him young and old. And our eyes never stray from the wall. It's not the convoluted structure that holds us, the tale within the tale, the cheap little mystery that links a dying old man to his childhood sled. It's The Shadow coming out to play with us.

2   Welles isn't the only monster on the wall. Humphrey Bogart had been a movie actor for thirteen years when we discover him in *Casablanca*. He'd been a thug with "nigger lips" throughout the Thirties, the bad guy who was always the second fiddle to James Cagney or Edward G. Robinson or Pat O'Brien or Leslie Howard or Joel McCrea or Sylvia Sidney or some Dead End kid, like Leo Gorcey and Billy Halop. He had a few good roles. *Dead End. The Petrified Forest.* But he was constantly dying. He died in more films than any other actor in the world, except perhaps Jean Gabin, who had romantic notions about dying in every film. But Bogart wasn't Gabin. He was a kind of walking, twitching corpse. Yet he hadn't been a gigolo like George Raft.

He was the son of a surgeon. He liked to suck on a silver spoon. His mother, a commercial artist, had used him as a model for the Mellins baby. Mellins had once been "standard for babies. On the product was a picture of a beautiful baby, a dream baby." Humphrey Bogart. The ex–Mellins boy was thrown out of the Phillips Academy in Andover. He joined the navy during World War I. It was aboard the *Leviathan* that he supposedly acquired his famous lisp. Bogart suffered a shrapnel wound while the *Leviathan* was being shelled. It left him with a "partly paralyzed lip." The *Leviathan* sounds like a phantom tub, dreamt up by Jack Warner's publicity department. No matter. Bogart had the lisp.

He sneered. He died. He went on dying in other films. "He was the loneliest guy in town." But the climate changed around 1941. Bogart's face belonged to the Forties. That monkey's grin suddenly turned handsome. The tight, corkscrew body took on a sexual tone. It was an America of shadows, about to enter a war. And Bogart's unconventional looks, his nervous ways, felt right. He appears in *High Sierra,* a killer again, Mad Dog Earle, but now we pause to look at his face. His tight skull interests us. There's no James Cagney to get in his way. He befriends a crippled girl. And the Bogart who will enchant us is about to be born.

He graduates from Mad Dog Earle to Sam Spade, Dashiell Hammett's nervous detective in *The Maltese Falcon.* He's in love with Brigid O'Shaughnessy (Mary Astor), but he lets her go to jail. He grins like a jackal. He's tough, tight, and unromantic, and we're beginning to fall in love with Humphrey Bogart.

1943. *Casablanca.* It feels like one more fake exotic film. The old Warner Brothers cast is assembled: Peter Lorre, Sidney Greenstreet, Claude Rains. We're expecting fog and foreign intrigue in the back lots at Burbank. But we couldn't have anticipated Rick's Café Américain. Casablanca itself disappears from the frame, and the whole planet moves into Rick's Café.

We catch a glimpse of Rick playing chess. His hand. His white dinner coat. And then that brooding face, and it's as if we'd never seen Humphrey Bogart before. He's like a figure out of Goethe stuck in a comic-book world. Romantic. Hopeless. Lost.

Yet Bogart arrives almost by accident. George Raft had been offered the role of Mad Dog Earle. "Raft wouldn't die in the picture," remembers Raoul Walsh, who directed *High Sierra.* Walsh would have accommodated George Raft, but the Hollywood censors insisted that Mad Dog Earle had to die. So that "dier," Humphrey Bogart, was brought in. "You couldn't kill Jimmy Stewart," said Walsh. "But you could kill off Bogart. The audience did not resent it."

Raft is the bigger star. He's seen all the time with Betty Grable. He'd been in *Scarface, Madame Racketeer, Rumba, Each Dawn I Die.* He gets top billing over Bogart in *They Drive by Night.* The fan magazines are in love with his dark suspenders, his dark shirts. Everybody wants him to marry Grable. He's offered the role of Rick in *Casablanca*. Raft turns it down. He becomes the ghost of Humphrey Bogart's rising career (he'd turned down *Dead End* and *The Maltese Falcon*). And we wonder, Would he have remained a star if he'd been the love of Ingrid Bergman's life in *Casablanca*? He'd have romanced her in his elevator shoes, sat with Dooley Wilson, gone off into the fog with Claude Rains, and *Casablanca,* with all its noble sentiments, would have been forgotten in six months.

Raft was a figure out of the Thirties, at ease in a world of gold diggers. But the gold digger was gone. The poor little shopgirl was now working in factories and defense plants. Rosie the Riveter didn't need a millionaire. And with one little turn, in a backdoor Casablanca, with a dreamlike mythic café, Rick's, with Nazis and Frenchmen, all the lost and damned of the world, waiting, waiting to get on that clipper plane to Lisbon . . . and America, we meet Humphrey Bogart, part Caliban, part Prospero and God knows what, the mysterious, lonely, isolated man with his own black angel, Dooley Wilson, otherwise known as Sam. Bogart's lisp is perfect in the film. It removes him from every other man. Into the movie walks Ingrid Bergman, twenty-four, as Ilse, his lost love from Paris. She gets the black angel to play "As Time Goes By." And Bogart begins to brood with Sam. "Of all the gin joints in all the towns in all the world, she walks into mine."

We have a flashback of Ilse, Rick, and Sam in Paris (1940). The Germans are coming. Bogart wears a dark suit. Sam has his piano. And Ilse is Ilse. We watch her with Rick's eyes. She's supposed to run away with him and Sam. But she never shows up. It's raining. Bogart wears the trenchcoat that all moviegoers will learn to adore. He's bitter, vulnerable, and from that moment on, Paris is the city of lost love.

And Hollywood has never been the same. A sort of B film, derived from an unproduced play, *Everybody Comes to Rick's,* becomes an image of America itself. It's hard to think of anyone, male or female, growing up in the Thirties, Forties, Fifties, or Sixties, who hasn't been touched by Rick's Café. It's the touch of Hollywood itself.

The French, the Germans, the Italians, the Japanese could create masterpieces like *Grand Illusion, M, Open City,* or *Ikiru,* films that the moguls would have considered much too pessimistic. Where's the love interest? Louis B. Mayer would have asked. What about the happy ending? Hollywood would hire Fritz Lang and Peter Lorre, the director and the star of *M,* a movie about a child murderer that turns in upon itself, like an amazing corkscrew, as Lorre, with an "M" marked on his back, tries to explain his own demons to the underworld of Berlin, who've captured Lorre and sentenced him to death, because his very existence has threatened their own profitable relationship with the police. *M* is a kind of Brechtian opera without song. But Lorre's cry to the underworld screams in our ear, forces us to examine who the hell we are. It's not designed to comfort us in the dark. Lorre's chubby, childlike face seems to make monsters of us all. *We* partake of his death. *We* convict him, as we convict ourselves.

Mayer never read scripts. But the idea of such a movie would have enraged him. He'd have demanded that a pair of lovers be thrown into the pot. Some police inspector, played by Richard Dix (borrowed from RKO for such a minor vehicle), and a queen of the underworld who reforms herself and marries Dix, while the murderer is shoved into the background. But whatever the limits of MGM, all its sugared life on screen, only Mayer's Hollywood could have conceived *Casablanca* and *Gone With the Wind.*

Its message was that no one in America need be exempt from love. The newsboy could marry the millionairess if only he was industrious enough, and looked a little like Gable. Nothing got in the way of romance. In *The Last Tycoon,* F. Scott Fitzgerald has his film producer Monroe Stahr explain the basic melody of any motion picture. "We've got an hour and twenty-five minutes on the screen—you show a woman being unfaithful to a man for one-third of that time and you've given the impression that she's one-third whore."

But this "future wife and mother" is in love with a guy named Ken Willard. She thinks of him all the time. "Whatever she does, it is in place of sleeping with Ken Willard. If she walks down the street she is walking to sleep with Ken Willard, if she eats her food it is to give her strength to sleep with Ken Willard. *But* at no time do you give the impression that she would ever consider sleeping with Ken Willard unless they were properly sanctified."

Thus Fitzgerald's fictional producer, Monroe Stahr, had captured the *miracle* of MGM and the other majors: a kind of mad eroticism that not even the Hays Office (Hollywood's own league of censors) could have destroyed. Love finds its way, from Shirley Temple to Andy Hardy. Temple could flirt with horses, dogs, Alice Faye, Randolph Scott, or Abraham Lincoln, in *The Littlest Rebel*. And Andy Hardy had so many girls around him—Lana Turner, Judy Garland, Esther Williams, Kathryn Grayson, Donna Reed—he might as well have lived in a harem.

Desire bubbled inside Hollywood's Production Code. No marriage beds. No bellybuttons. But gliding erotic ghosts. Harlow's bust, sheathed in silk, almost spilled onto the screen. And the incredible movie marriage of Ginger Rogers and Fred Astaire was like constant foreplay between an awkward-looking crane and a raucous blond duck. Astaire seemed to have no gender without Ginger Rogers. He was lost on the screen until she danced with him, and then there was a kind of hypnotic pull without a single kiss. No other country in the world could have produced an "innocent" gold digger like Rogers and an ugly, long-chinned character like Astaire who developed a phantom grace as he moved around the floor. Together they acted out the wonderful warfare of sex that was almost an American invention, an American toy. Fred and Ginger couldn't really get along until they started to "dance." Fred was the fragile one. He seemed about to fall. And Ginger was always in the middle of some storm. And yet they found a delicious peace. Like Mickey and Minnie Mouse.

Their kingdom was Hollywood. Tinseltown. La-la-land. Nathanael West saw it as a great burning jungle, a village of masks that had no interior, no particular heart. It was filled with players and freaks. Hollywood was where sluggish armies of extras crawled from lot to lot and lived among castles with tar-paper turrets; sleepwalkers, grotesques caught in a landscape of palm trees and dying people. "Few things are sadder than the truly monstrous."

West is one of the heroic ghosts conjured up in Otto Friedrich's picture of Hollywood in the Forties, *City of Nets*. Friedrich provides a remarkable portrait of various exiles in Hollywood, from Brecht to Thomas Mann and Theodore Dreiser, who lived among the stars like an invisible man.

Brecht was more complex than "Cary Grant or Betty Grable," I agree. The very idea of Bert Brecht *and* Hollywood is almost the plot of a surreal novel. Brecht couldn't have discovered a better asylum. But why does it trouble me that Brecht plays so significant a part in Friedrich's Hollywood, "while Grant and Miss Grable play almost none"? I couldn't imagine Hollywood without Cary Grant. And I'd love to know why Grable dropped George Raft and married bandleader Harry James in '43. Actors, Friedrich says, are "less interesting than writers, gangsters, musicians, tycoons, and sex goddesses." Wasn't Grable some kind of goddess? With her shiny teeth and perfect smile?

She was the pinup queen of World War II. In *Guadalcanal Diary* (1943), William Bendix shaves while looking at a photo of Betty in a white bathing suit, "she who unofficially won the war." That same photograph "was marked off in sections to teach fliers how to read aerial maps."

Rita Hayworth would dethrone her after World War II. But Betty Grable had that dream look America desired. You could almost believe that she'd go out with Raft for a year and never spend the night. Her films seldom play in the revival houses. But she was the first Technicolor star. Color "becomes" Betty Grable. There was something luscious about her that would have been damaged by too much complication. She had the face of a wartime bachelorette, the girl who would always be true to her soldier. You could go and fight a war and not have to worry about Betty Grable.

3   The worldwide appeal Hollywood has always had, even now, when the mythic town of Louis B. Mayer no longer exists, is that it was a machine created for children. *The Godfather* is *Gone With the Wind* in modern baggage. Less romantic perhaps, but still a saga for twelve-year-olds. And Steven Spielberg is the ultimate children's puppeteer. His films carry all the freight of a masterful cartoon. Hollywood has entered so deep into the collective will of the

century that it's almost impossible to be alive and not to have felt its influence. We're all "moviegoers," living in an extraordinary web, dream works that sustained us and turned me into a curious kind of dwarf, waiting for my own Gilda.

But Gilda wouldn't come again. She'd been there once for Rita Hayworth. It was the ideal moment, September 1945. The war had ended. Rita was estranged from The Shadow, Orson Welles. Harry Cohn was chasing her around his office. She had a nine-month-old baby, Rebecca Welles, and a little of her own "baby fat." She was shy, nervous, depressed, when *Gilda* began. The film's producer, Virginia Van Upp, acted as a liaison between Rita and Harry Cohn. She refashioned the dialogue for Rita. The shooting started without a leading man. Glenn Ford was thrown into the fray. He had a kind of passive beauty, with jug ears and a weak jaw.

*Gilda*. It was almost *Casablanca* again, with a gambling casino and a foreign locale: Buenos Aires. But this casino had none of the mythic properties of Rick's Café. It was filled with glass and plaster vines, like an indoor jungle. Glenn Ford even had Bogart's white gambler's coat. But he didn't lisp or resemble a romantic monkey. You couldn't dwell too long on his face. It was boyish and frozen, with bits of animation in his eyes. He worked for Ballin Mundson (George Macready), who had a long scar on his cheek that was like a crooked slice of the moon.

"Hate is the only thing that has ever warmed me," Ballin says. He puts the casino in Glenn Ford's hands, disappears, and returns with a wife. Rita Hayworth. So far it's a rather conventional story. We hear Rita sing (it's the voice of Anita Ellis). And then we meet her. Her head jumps into the frame like a jack-in-the-box. And from that moment we're caught in the web of the film. The imbecilic plot about a tungsten cartel doesn't bother us. It's Gilda we look at, Gilda all the time, even though Glenn Ford narrates the film. There'd been no one like her until now. Not Mae West with her husky look. Not Harlow.

It's as if all the erotic energy that was held in during the war fell to Rita Hayworth. She'd come out of some dark bottle. She banters with Johnny Farrell (Glenn Ford). And soon we realize they'd been lovers before. "Johnny is such a hard name to remember and easy to forget."

Ballin knows his wife (and Rita Hayworth). "You're a child," he says, "a beautiful, greedy child." He puts Farrell in charge of her. And Farrell-Ford promises he'll take care of Ballin's wife, "exactly the way I'd take and pick up his laundry."

And now we're in a landscape that has little to do with Argentina. "I hate you so much I think I'm going to die from it," Gilda says to Johnny. And we've entered the country of poisoned love. The lines matter less than Rita's own planetary moves. A strange hum surrounds her. She's uninhibited on the screen, her body involved in a constant swaying line. Gilda's the girl with musical hips. And the first time we see her dance, it's like she's making love with every manchild in the audience. Now we understand why Ford is up there on the screen. He's a stand-in for all of us.

During carnival she says to Johnny, "You're out of practice, aren't you? Dancing, I mean . . . I could help you get back in practice. Dancing, I mean."

*Dancing.*

It seemed much less daring than a kiss. But it was how the stars "practiced" making love on screen during the years of Hollywood's self-imposed blue laws. The Hays Office wouldn't have tolerated a five-minute kiss. But Gilda could dance her head off, with or without Glenn Ford. Her two solos are much more sexy than her carnival dance with Ford. Anyone over the age of five in 1946 ought to remember her phantom striptease, "Put the Blame on Mame," but the dance she does in Montevideo, when she disappears from Johnny, is wilder and not so full of burlesque. For Gilda, caught between Ballin and Johnny, Buenos Aires had become her jail. But she turns lithe, like a jungle cat, as she sings "Amado Mío," with all the revelation of her red hair. It's not the frenzied dancing of Carmen Miranda, with fish eyes and an hysterical rubber smile.

We grow attached to Gilda's naked midriff. Her legs fall away from her skirt like beautiful prancing knives. Her hair is in her eyes. It cuts her head like the sharpest silk in the world. Gilda devours the frame. She leaves us sitting there like little boys.

Then Johnny Farrell tricks her into returning to Buenos Aires. And she punishes him with "Put the Blame on Mame," the strip dance that would become an icon around the world. But Gilda's only having fun. We marvel at the smoothness of her

back. I could have sworn that Gilda removes *both* her black
gloves, but the left glove stays on for the duration of the dance.
How could I have swallowed up a detail like that? I have the
image in my head of Gilda in black, bumping to the music and
peeling off those long black gloves, as if her white arms were all
the nakedness I'd ever need. I was wrong. Gilda removes the
other glove when the dancing is done, hurls it at the audience
like a declaration of war.

"We were both such stinkers, weren't we?" Gilda says to
Glenn Ford after the melodrama is over. She'll return to the
States with Johnny Farrell. The film ends here and we see the
Columbia monogram and "mascot," not Leo the Lion, but a
woman holding a torch in her right hand. And it feels like magic,
because we've become so involved with Gilda, we're convinced
that the woman with the torch is Rita Hayworth, the new Columbia mascot.

*Gilda* reaches everywhere, but what about Rita, the theater
urchin and professional waif, dancing since she was twelve. Just
another love goddess.

In a Hollywood ruled by men, women had to wear protective
coloring, like salamanders in the sun. The studios exploited
women, used them sexually—Darryl Zanuck of Twentieth
Century–Fox always had his four-o'clock siesta, when a starlet
would visit his office, and all studio business would stop. But
in some curious manner, the women stars triumphed more than
the men, as if they had to develop a secret language, almost
speak in code, whether it was Dietrich, Garbo, or Joan Crawford. Three chubby girls. The studios reinvented their faces,
Hollywoodized them, but they had a dream language, a movement, a smile, a touch, that was much more powerful than the
best of Spencer Tracy or Robert Taylor.

Then Gilda came along. And the reality was that men were
tricksters, little boys, whether they ran a studio like Zanuck and
Cohn, had a swordcane like George Macready and could say to
Glenn Ford that it was "a faithful, obedient friend. It is silent
when I wish to be silent. It talks when I wish to talk." Was
that scarface discussing his own sexuality? Who cares? He's
stabbed in the back with his own sword. And Gilda goes home
with Johnny, who's a bit of a fool, but it's the guy she's crazy
about. "Nobody could ever dance like you, Johnny."

Most of Europe had to suffer through a war without Hollywood films. Gilda arrived in 1946. She was much better than the Truman Doctrine or the Marshall Plan. All the brashness of America, its energy, its innocent belief in romance, the childish eroticism underlying all its Puritan songs, seemed to be gathered in Gilda. The sweep of her hair. The pull of her torso that was like an act of spontaneous copulation with some imaginary man. Where did her sensuality come from? The Shadow? Harry Cohn? The studio lights? All that magic-making of movieland seemed to tumble right out of Gilda's glove.

She tossed it at us and it was almost like a reenactment of *The Great Train Robbery* (1903), the first "story picture." Its actors were anonymous, since the old studios, like Edison and Biograph, didn't want "stars" who would demand high salaries and make their pictures much more expensive. *The Great Train Robbery* was twelve minutes long, which must have seemed like a saga to the audiences of the time, fed on a diet of six-minute films about firemen and horses eating hay. Bandits hold up a train, flee, and "fight to the death behind their fallen horses." This should have signaled the end of the film. But a resurrection occurs. One of the bandits rises from the dead "and shoots five bullets straight into the audience." That's how narrative art began in American film. The audience went insane with fear and delight. Some people screamed. Some closed their eyes. Some ran from their seats.

Nobody ran from Gilda's glove. But it had a bit of the same hysteria. That trancelike involvement of an audience with a face and a body on the wall. The bandit's five bullets destroyed the "distance" of the screen (probably a bed sheet or a curtain in 1903), just as Gilda's glove obliged us to complete her dance.

We grabbed at Gilda, ignored that shy person who liked to dance in front of a movie camera. She stumbled in and out of love, became an alcoholic, lost her memory until she had to be cared for like a child. But that's not what we want to remember. We were cruel in our devotions to Rita Hayworth, as we were cruel with almost every other star. We idolized her lost power, her sense of play. The rumba she did. All the enchantment of Gilda's glove.

# four

# *Angel on My Shoulder*

1937.

Mussolini opens Cinecittà (City of Film) on a gigantic plain outside Rome. Cinecittà has enough territory to house a dozen Colosseums. It's like a tremendous corral, another one of Mussolini's empires, with an artificial ocean and sound stages that look like temples of doom. Il Duce is ambitious. His engineers and masons and architects have fashioned for him the most glorious studio complex in Europe. He hopes to rival MGM and Hollywood itself. He wants to conquer the world by becoming Benito the Starbuilder, Louis B. Mayer. But he can't find another Garbo or Gable. His most glamorous star is Myria (née Myriam) di San Servolo, the sister of Mussolini's own mistress. Cinecittà has no Italian Gary Coopers. It makes little romantic comedies in Mussolini's enormous tombs. Heroines are always yapping into a white telephone. Not even the Italians themselves want to see such "white telephone" romances. They prefer American films, which are all dubbed, because Mussolini doesn't want any foreign ideas arriving in Rome and corrupting the Fascist state. But the more he censors Hollywood, the more eager Italians are to watch Gable, Cooper, Dietrich. American movies "were the world," remembered Italo Calvino of those Cinecittà years. "For me only what I saw on the screen had the properties of a world—fullness, necessity, coherence—while off the screen heterogeneous elements accumulated, apparently assembled at random, the materials of my life which seemed to me completely lacking in form."

Calvino worshipped that high Hollywood style, with its "transfiguration of female faces, legs, shoulders, and cleavages; it made Marlene Dietrich not the immediate object of desire but desire itself, like an extraterrestrial essence." Yet "for all Italian moviegoers, only half of each actor and actress existed: the figure, but not the voice, which was replaced by the abstraction of dubbing, by a conventional speech, alien and insipid, as anonymous" as a printed title on the screen. Such stilted talk was outside any universe Calvino could recollect. It had "no relation to any spoken language of past or future." But those voices were still "like the sirens' song," because every time Calvino passed a moviehouse he "felt the call of that other world which was the world." *Hollywood*.

And when Italy started banning American films, Calvino became one more casualty. "This was the first time I was deprived of a right that I enjoyed; more than a right, it was a dimension, a world, a space of the mind; and I felt this loss as a cruel oppression. . . . I still speak of this today as a lost happiness, because something thus disappeared from my life and was never to reappear."

It was a fall from paradise. And nothing out of Benito's City of Film could replace that paradise for Calvino. Cinecittà "counted for so little. . . . Italian films also seemed dubbed in those days, even if they weren't."

1937.

Louis B. Mayer sits in his white office, with his white carpets, his white leather walls, his white desk, his white piano, and his four white telephones, in the movie capital of the world. Cinecittà wouldn't have entered his dreams. He might have worried about MGM's loss of revenue in Fascist Italy, but not a Roman MGM. The Duce can make all the comedies he wants in that tomb near the Tiber. He can invite all the little kings of Europe to Rome. Hollywood has its own mark of royalty. Dukes and kings come from everywhere to meet the stars. Cooper and Crawford and Dietrich and Garbo and Gable are phantom faces that can float across any ocean, cover continents, and rest on the wall of caves in the simplest, darkest town. They're among the first international ghosts we've ever had, their silvered heads more famous, more adored, than figures out of any bible or historical past. And recently (since 1928) they've learned to talk. So we can listen to Cooper's drawl, hear Garbo's anguish as she loses yet another lover, watch Dietrich sing while she's wearing men's pants.

Thirty-seven wasn't such a fabulous year for films. A few children's classics, like *Lost Horizon* and *The Prisoner of Zenda,* which offered us a new country, Ruritania; a new prince, Black Michael; a wonderful, smiling villain, Rupert of Hentzau; a beautiful villainess, Madame de Mauban (Mary Astor); and Ronald Colman, who enjoyed a double life as the king and his own distant cousin.

But the year's biggest hit was *Snow White and the Seven Dwarfs,* Walt Disney's first feature-length cartoon. It was released in December, and most of the profits spilled into 1938. Frank S. Nugent of *The New York Times* called *Snow White* a classic, as important to films as *The Birth of a Nation* "or the birth of Mickey Mouse." Snow White appeared in forty-one countries. She was Schneewittchen in Berlin, Biancaneve in Mussolini's Rome. The girl grossed eight million, more than any other film of its time. But Schneewittchen didn't get twenty thousand letters a week, like Shirley Temple. Shirley didn't need the Seven Dwarfs. She was nine years old and the queen of movieland. Children's salons opened all over the country to copy her curls. She played Wee Willie Winkie, the little sweetheart of a whole British regiment, in 1937.

Eighty million Cassandras went to the movies every week. Over five hundred features were produced, sixty at MGM alone. Shirley Temple's salary for 1937 was $300,000. Mayer's was $1,296,503. He earned more than any other man in the United States.

*Life* magazine was already a year old. It camped out in Hollywood, together with five hundred other correspondents, who worried more about David O. Selznick's search to find Scarlett O'Hara than about Mussolini or Hitler—fictional characters far from the rumblings of movieland. Hollywood had become *Life*'s adopted country. The magazine guarded movieland with a ferocious concern (Garbo was featured in the very first issue). Jean Harlow appeared on the cover of *Life* in May 1937, a month before she died of uremic poisoning at the age of twenty-six. And Dietrich was shown in her bathtub the same year, with one beautiful knee rising out of the bubbles.

Hollywood had cornered the whole damn movie market. Jean Gabin was okay for Italy and France. But he didn't look like Gary Cooper. Gabin was warm, human, alive. Cooper was a long-legged ghost who never got excited on the screen. Parisians flocked to see him as Wild Bill Hickock in *The Plainsman*. He had that dream image of America, the land of inarticulate cowboys, calm, yet close to violence. You could discover Gabin's feelings in his eyes. His whole face was like a weather map, while Coop was a magnificent sleepwalker, a silent knight. He wouldn't even kiss Calamity Jane.

The top ten stars at the box office (according to the Quigley Poll of motion picture exhibitors) were:

1. Miss Shirley Temple
2. Clark Gable, king of the lot at MGM
3. Robert Taylor (Garbo had made him a star in *Camille*)
4. Bing Crosby
5. The Thin Man, William Powell
6. Jane Withers, a little monster of eleven (Shirley's only rival)
7. Ginger and Fred
8. Sonja Henie
9. Wild Bill Hickock, often known as Gary Cooper
10. Myrna Loy, the Thin Man's wife

But 1939 was a much grander year. We had *Gone With the Wind, Gunga Din, Stagecoach, Wuthering Heights, The Wizard of Oz. Ninotchka* alone could have wiped out most of 1937. But that was the year I was born, and it's as if every film *until* 1937 belongs to some ancient, yet recognizable, past. I don't mean that squabble about silents and talkies, and which was the greater art. Most of us have developed amnesia about silent films, except for Charlie Chaplin and a few of the myths, like Fatty Arbuckle's Coke bottle and Garbo's love affair with John Gilbert. Hollywood planned it that way. It declared that everything, except this week's bill, was obsolete. It couldn't afford a history. It had too much invested in its current stars. If John Gilbert failed in his first talkies, forget about him (he died in 1936). Robert Taylor was the *new* John Gilbert, and Taylor was enough.

Hollywood didn't conspire in my devotion to 1937. It's when my imagined memory begins as a moviegoer. It's the epic I was born into, the beginning of that endless reel. In talking about the great screwball comedies, philosopher Stanley Cavell insists that these films "declare that our lives are poems, their actions

and words the content of a dream, working on webs of significance we cannot or will not survey but merely spin further. In
everyday life the poems often seem composed by demons who
curse us, wish us ill; in art by an angel who wishes us well, and
blesses us."

And in my own head, I've been riding that angel since 1937.
*Anything* filmed that year titillates me, suggests a kind of wak-
ening, a sudden, thrilling love of the world that I couldn't get
from books. *The Sound and the Fury* is my favorite American
novel: its music deepens into pain, its different voices have the
texture and feel of a movie, but it doesn't matter to me that
the book was published in 1929. It doesn't really belong to any
year. It has a total, willed life that *The Prisoner of Zenda* could
never have. The affairs of Ruritania are delightful mush. I adore
Rupert of Hentzau and the pleasure he takes from his own vil-
lainy (it's the closest Douglas Fairbanks Jr. ever came to his dad,
the original Black Pirate), but I could fold all of Ruritania into
my pocket. It doesn't reverberate beyond the moviehouse wall.

Ruritania is magnificent mind candy, no more palpable than
Rick's Café. Yet I respond to it like a birth certificate. I watch
the images on the wall, those silly gatherings of the plot, and I
suffer vertigo, have a terrific sense of loss, a sudden appetite for
1937. I don't run to the history books. I don't think of FDR
and his dog Fala, or the Duce and his sound caves at Cinecittà.
Instead I think, Mary Astor, Madeleine Carroll, they were *alive*
in 1937, and it's like a magical quotient. My history becomes
their existence on the screen. And then I travel further into
movieland. *The Adventures of Robin Hood* (1938). I'm one year
old while Errol Flynn is toying with the Sheriff of Nottingham,
and I wrap myself into the consciousness of that film. The bandits of Sherwood Forest are the only 1938 I'll ever need.

Of course it's crazy. Richard the Lionheart didn't follow
Neville Chamberlain to meet with the German Chancellor in
Munich. Friar Tuck never sat in Hitler's lap. But I dream of
those faces and the lives they had. And why should I worry if
my education as a moviegoer exists somewhere between Popeye
and Proust?

Movies evoked a "climate" that nothing else ever will, that
attending angel Stanley Cavell talks about. Movies, and their
precursor, the comic book. I sat like a dummy at school from

the age of five. I learned all the tortured tricks: multiplication tables and vocabulary lists. But I owe more to Donald Duck (the comic-book character) and Captain Marvel than to the teachers I had. Comic books gave me more insights into time and space than all those lessons and lists. I couldn't have realized then that they were movies in slow motion. But they were more imaginative, funnier, and more poignant than the children's books we were told to read (little lessons in morality about the good cow). Because they introduced the idea of the irrational, took leaps into the unknown. They were contraband, those comic books. They encouraged idleness and had a meanness of heart that was familiar to most kids. And they intertwined with the movies themselves. It's hard to recall finally which came first. Did Errol Flynn's swordplay prepare me for Marvel and Donald Duck and their powerful language of panels and balloons? But one thing is certain. I was raised by Donald Duck and Louis B. Mayer. If Donald disappeared from my life, the land of Louis B. Mayer didn't.

I've been a moviegoer from *Belle Starr* and *They Died with Their Boots On* to Steven Spielberg's *Empire of the Sun* (the very last film I saw as I write this page). That's forty-seven years. And those years contain a melody I've found nowhere else, a constant song that's endured the collapse of movie empires, the fall of Louis B. Mayer, the end of my own marriage, the absence of Marlon Brando, the death of Jimmy Dean.

I was moonstruck like an imbecile when I saw *Prizzi's Honor* (1985). It felt like a film out of my childhood, as if John Huston had completed some loop and returned to that energetic landscape of *The Maltese Falcon:* both films were full of grotesques with an operatic pull. They were playful as only a child knows how to play. Jack Nicholson was like the Wolf Man without whiskers. And Anjelica Huston was his personal witch, Maria Ouspenskaya with a longer nose and a prettier mouth.

But the point is that movies were our childhood, and that childhood has persisted, at least for some of us. And why? Is it the fabric of America itself that has kept us in a moving cradle? We're a country of wishes and expectations, frozen into some idyll where all things are possible, where each of us can become a movie star, like Norma Jean Baker, who was born in the City of Angels and traveled sideways in time to become *Marilyn*.

We're the country of movie stars, because the stars, like ourselves, represent a kind of extended infantilism, beauties waiting for the big chance.

2 Movies developed earlier in Italy and France. Our first classic was *Fred Ott's Sneeze* (189?), which took one of Thomas Edison's mechanics through all the convolutions of a sneeze in front of Edison's own movie camera. But the French and the Italians were creating little epics about the moon and Pompeii while America had Fred Ott. World War I destroyed whatever dominance the French and Italians had over us. And movies became America. The first American movie capitals were Fort Lee, Manhattan, and the Bronx. Films were shot on rooftops, around the schedule of the sun. But Thomas Edison had a stranglehold on most movie patents. And he hired detectives to chase maverick movie producers around the country and destroy whatever equipment they had. The mavericks ran to Southern California, where they had unlimited sunshine (like a miraculous lamp) and could dash across the Mexican border if Thomas' detectives arrived. Some of them parked in a lemon grove called Hollywood. One of the first studios in the area was actually part of a zoo. Zebras settled in with cameramen, and soon Hollywood became an enchanted village. The locals disliked these "movies," or wandering picture people, and wouldn't rent houses to them, so the picture people stayed at the Hollywood Hotel. And movieland was born out of a dusty little oasis next to a tar pit. Real estate values boomed. Oil was discovered around the tar pits. Hollywood had water problems and annexed itself to L.A. It was one more village in a landscape of villages, connected by high-speed trolleys. The City of Angels was a trolley town. And Hollywood was the end of the line.

But it was no Cinecittà with phantom caves. It had what the Duce could never buy or bring to his City of Film. Faces that the world wanted to see. They were anonymous at first, shadows with fictional names. And fan mail began to arrive for these fictional characters. Broncho Billy, the hero of primitive Westerns, was idolized throughout the world. One of the characters Mary Pickford played was so popular that Pickford was soon called "Little Mary" no matter what role she was in. And Roscoe Arbuckle, who played "Fatty" in a series of shorts, was universally known by that name. It was Fatty who was accused of raping Virginia Rappe (or Rappé), not Roscoe Arbuckle. It was Fatty whom Will Hays (Hollywood's self-appointed censor and czar) banished from films. And Fatty, who once upon a time was as beloved as Chaplin's tramp, trundled across movieland like a 320-pound ghost.

But audiences wouldn't allow the early film companies to keep their actors and actresses as anonymous as performing seals. And thus that strange phenomenon, the movie star, arose out of a worldwide curiosity, with Hollywood as the phantasmagoric place where the stars lived and worked. *Movieland*. And because it had no past, Hollywood didn't have to compete with itself. All it had was a lost tribe of Indians (the Gabrielinos) and a tar pit, where the skeletons of saber-toothed tigers were found. It was like a prehistoric menagerie. And Hollywood grew up into the twentieth century, like the stars themselves.

Soon its very streets were recognizable all over the world. The town was turned into a set. "Private homes were used for domestic dramas. Banks were used on holidays, Saturday afternoons, and Sundays for hold-up scenes. Stores were robbed regularly before the cameras." And that's how a dream city began, with melodramas and comedies manufactured out of dust and wind and the grinding of a camera. Cowboys came down from the hills to act as extras and join the colony of picture people. The population swelled. Hollywood was a sleepy village of five thousand souls in 1910, without the studios and the stars. By 1920, "Hollywood's population jumped 720 percent." Bathing beauties arrived from everywhere with the hope of becoming the new Gloria Swanson or Lillian Gish. The town fathers tried to discourage this stampede. But Hollywood kept growing and growing. People wanted to eat where the stars ate, follow them around like the stars' own phantom selves.

The heart of this dream city was the Hollywood Hotel, with its Dining Room of the Stars and its dances and teas. Pola Negri, Douglas Fairbanks, Lon Chaney, Norma Shearer, Valentino, and Louis B. Mayer all lived there for a while. That sleepy town which had started by shunning picture people disappeared with its lemon groves and its country stores and its ban on alcoholic beverages.

The Babylonian set that D. W. Griffith had built for *Intolerance* (1916), stood on Sunset Boulevard for several years, with pillars and stairways and elephant gods that watched over movieland. Charlie Chaplin moved indoors to his own studio on La Brea Avenue, but Mack Sennett's Keystone Kops traveled through Hollywood, stopping trolleys and motorcars, and menacing people with cotton billy clubs.

All the great comedians were like anarchic kids. Fatty, Harry Langdon, Buster Keaton, Harold Lloyd, Mabel Normand, Laurel and Hardy, and Chaplin himself. Keaton was so childlike he could barely tie his own shoes or understand the hieroglyphics of a checkbook, yet he could choreograph the most intricate machinelike maneuvers for a moviehouse wall. And dancing with Fatty Arbuckle, remembered Louise Brooks, "was like floating in the arms of a huge doughnut." He loved to bounce people off his belly, splash the ceiling of the Hollywood Hotel with pats of butter that he would shoot off his napkin. And when Fatty died, it was discovered that his sexual parts had never matured: he had the genitals of a child. Chaplin was far more serious, and frugal with his money (Fatty loved to give parties), but the persona he developed on screen caused much more mischief than Arbuckle could ever have dreamed.

*All* the stars were children. They inhabited a universe that was totally self-absorbed. Mary Pickford was almost as perverse as Chaplin. She played Little Mary, the girl with the golden curls, a self-sufficient dream child, who was as funny, sweet, and delirious as America itself. The country wouldn't allow her to grow up. She endured her first screen kiss in 1927, when Little Mary was thirty-four. She retired soon after that. "I left the screen because I didn't want what happened to Chaplin to happen to me. When he discarded the Little Tramp, the Little Tramp turned around and killed him. . . . I wasn't waiting for the little girl to kill me."

And Little Mary, who was the first millionairess in films, was chaperoned by her mother, Charlotte Smith, even after she married Douglas Fairbanks (Mary's second husband) in 1920. "To the very last day she [Charlotte] lived, her word was law." And what about Fairbanks himself? He remained a smiling Peter Pan most of his life, jumping through windows and sliding down banisters in one children's paradise after the other. The Twenties belonged to Doug; it was his very own decade. Children and adults mobbed him wherever he went, and demanded some spectacular leap from Doug, as if there were no distance at all between Doug and the Black Pirate he played, or D'Artagnan and the Thief of Bagdad. He was "the screen's most adored superman."

His romantic involvement with Mary Pickford seemed much more vital than any affair of state. Kings could drown, currencies could fall, but *theirs* was the first cinematic marriage. Little Mary and the Black Pirate. America's royalty began with them. They went to Europe on a six-week honeymoon, and it was the most publicized wedding trip the world had ever seen. Roses dropped from the sky (with the help of an airplane) when they landed in Britain. And Doug had to climb a balcony at the Ritz Hotel while thousands of Londoners cheered him from the street. They wouldn't let the Black Pirate go without some kind of cakewalk. Cameramen followed Mr. and Mrs. Fairbanks everywhere: the couple couldn't escape to Venice for a gondola ride without "an accompanying barge of cameramen," and Doug had to dance up "the side of an American warship in the harbor."

Then they retreated to Pickfair, their mansion in Beverly Hills, and reigned as king and queen of movieland. Pickfair could have been one more movie castle. Robin Hood's house on a hill. Guests "ate from a solid-gold dinner service, with a footman behind every chair." A single dinner might include several stars from Hollywood's British colony (Ronald Colman and C. Aubrey Smith), Albert Einstein, Lord and Lady Mountbatten, and Babe Ruth. But it wasn't a happy marriage.

The king and queen separated in 1933 and were divorced in 1935. Both of their film careers were finished by then. Mary took a third husband in 1937, Charles "Buddy" Rogers, who'd given Mary her first screen kiss. But Pickfair had little magic without a king. Doug died in December 1939. And the announcement of his death carried much more hysteria in London than the latest war news. "Doug's dead, Doug's dead," the newsboys cried all afternoon. He'd been America for two generations of Brits. He embodied the notion of unashamed romance. Doug's adventures out of the past—Robin Hood, D'Artagnan, Robinson Crusoe—had really been dreams of the New World and all its optimism, a land of pirate princes. Hollywood had convinced the entire world that D'Artagnan was a good American boy.

Little Mary drew deeper and deeper into Pickfair. She talked about that character she'd played. "It was easy for me to act the part of a child because I adored children. I forgot I was grown up. I would transform myself into a child." And somehow the transformation held. Little Mary took to her bed in 1965, and lived "on light food" and a quart of whiskey a day.

**3** Doug and Mary didn't knock around in my skull like Gilda or Gary Cooper. I came to them as a boy of fifty. They were both extraordinary mimes, and the personal Bagdad they created wasn't so removed from my life as a moviegoer, that prolonged childhood in the cave. After all, I had Douglas Fairbanks Jr. as Rupert of Hentzau and both Corsican Brothers. He might have been a dancing shadow of his dad, but when I saw him in *The Prisoner of Zenda,* he was the only Douglas Fairbanks I'd ever heard about.

If movies retarded us, kept us small, hypnotized us as we sat in that cave, they also introduced us to the fury of adults, faces that could kiss and cry and worry themselves to death about all sorts of foolish notions. At nine or ten we had to ponder the growing pains of matrimony and divorce. We watched Joan Crawford compete with men in business and the arts. She adopts a violinist (John Garfield) in *Humoresque* and then kills herself by waltzing into the sea.

Crawford looked a lot like my mother; they both had big eyes and hollow cheeks. My mother was also a "pony" ( the shortest girl in a chorus line). Or at least I thought of her in some imaginary chorus, a jazz baby, like Joan. And my father had Gable's mustache and Bogart's "nigger lips." I was movie mad, and that cave, which took me out of my home and the life I had as a delinquent (real or not) and turned me into Ali Baba, with genies that could soothe my boiling brain, carpets that could fly me into the middle of any romance, happened to mock me in the end, because Ali Baba was that same delinquent in the dark: Jerome Charyn. And I was only one more actor in that endless reel, a small-time Gregory Peck. And the angel who blessed us inside the moviehouse, who wished us well, was also the angel of death. He'd come to us mercifully, with pictures and song, but the message he had to deliver was that we'd live and die, like those other shadows on the silversheet.

4 Philosophers and film critics and even harebrained boys and girls have all noticed the resemblance between movies and Plato's myth of the cave, as if Hollywood itself had bridged those twenty-five hundred years between Socrates and Louis B. Mayer. In Book VII of Plato's *Republic,* Socrates, our first film critic, is talking to Glaucon, one of Plato's elder brothers. He's trying to convince Glaucon that the ideal ruler of his Republic would be a philosopher king, who isn't in love with sensation but with that order of reality which is not subject to opinions or shifting moods. But the problem arises as to what reality is. Does it fall somewhere along that curious line between shadow and substance? And is the substance we dream of only one more mask? Plato's image of the cave has tantalized the West like a singular butterfly that moves from dark to light, dark to light, with a will of its own. That butterfly is perhaps another angel of death, teasing the very life out of us.

Imagine, says Socrates, an underground vault or a cave which has an entrance open to sunlight as wide as the cave itself. In this cave are lost souls who have sat there as prisoners ever since "they were children, their legs and necks being so fastened that they . . . cannot turn their heads. Some way off . . . a fire is burning," and between the fire and the prisoners is a road, in front of which we have a wall, "like the screen at puppet shows" that separates the puppeteers and the audience.

And there's all sorts of activity behind the curtain wall, "including figures of men and animals" that resemble "wood and stone and . . . other materials." And Socrates asks Glaucon if the prisoners could recognize "anything of themselves or their fellows except the shadows thrown by the fire on the wall of the cave opposite them.''

Of course not, answers Glaucon, since these prisoners can't move their necks.

And, says Socrates, ''would they not assume that the shadows they saw were the real things? . . . And if the wall of their prison opposite them reflected sound, don't you think that they would suppose, whenever one of the passers-by on the road spoke, that the voice belonged to the shadow passing before them?''

Socrates wonders what would happen if a single prisoner were set free and cured of his ''delusions.'' Wouldn't it drive him mad if he could look directly into the fire? And suppose he were dragged out into the sun and could comprehend the new order of things? Wouldn't he feel a kind of pity for the prisoners in the dark? And suppose he returned to his old seat in the cave? Wouldn't he feel blinded in the dark? And his fellow prisoners ''would say that his visit to the upper world had ruined his sight. . . . And if anyone tried to release them and lead them up, they would kill him if they could lay their hands on him.''

And so we have the riddle, the very riddle of our lives. The cave isn't about truth or wisdom. Plato's Republic is as fanciful as Ruritania, or a kingdom of Groucho Marx. Our own century has reminded us that philosophers know how to murder even more precisely than brutes. Stalin was a talmudist of sorts. And Goebbels had a Ph.D. There isn't much divinity in learning any more. The philosopher kings who invented Auschwitz adored all the plumes of art. They listened to Beethoven in the middle of all the burning they did. And movies stare out at us because they're the child of unreason. Plato's cave is both the sun and the dark, and we're its prisoners, enlightened or not. That angel of art is the puppeteer who lures us in the moviehouse. And we're all children in his wake, fascinated by those shadows on the wall.

When the Austrian-born philosopher Ludwig Wittgenstein wanted to relax, he'd go into a moviehouse near Cambridge University, sit in the front row, and watch a Western (or films with Carmen Miranda and Betty Hutton, his favorite stars). The screen pulled him away from language and all the conundrums he wrote about. But movies were congenial to Wittgenstein for many reasons. He believed that sentences themselves could be cast into "pictures," and that existence was also a kind of picture, a revelation of the real. But at the movies Wittgenstein was like a child, a prisoner of Plato's cave. His neck never moved from the screen. He also approached philosophy with a child's wonder, all the clarity of a six-year-old. In some profound way Wittgenstein never grew up. He had no wife, no children, and almost no attachments. For years he lived in a hut. But he was a moviegoer, like the rest of us. And one can imagine what a treatise on Westerns by Wittgenstein would have been like. A sentence-song, a piece of delightful grammar.

Like the movies themselves, which have a grammar and a special kind of interior monologue. The other day I saw *Dark Eyes,* an Italian film made by a Russian director. But it was pure Hollywood, a film assembled with silky glue. Marcello Mastroianni follows his married "mistress" back to a small provincial town in Russia, declares his love, and says he can't live without her. Mastroianni plays a fool. He dances through the picture. He never walks. The Russian lady has a little dog, Sabatchka. She's silly, beautiful, forlorn. And we expect her to be enigmatic. But no. She answers Mastroianni—that is, the character he plays. She cannot live without him either. Of course, he dances away from her and never returns. But I cried at her remark. The Russian lady was marvelous and mad. She marked me with the sad designs of her life. Film critic David Denby describes the characters in *Dark Eyes* as "grown-up children floating in a state of delicious or painful torpor."

It sounds like a complaint. Yet those two particular *children* share a kind of torpor I'm familiar with. The lassitudes of love. That very business we dread and cannot live without. And the dream Hollywood of Nikita Mikhalkov's *Dark Eyes* (he also directed *Oblomov,* about a "lover" who cannot get out of bed) performs one of movieland's essential tasks. We fall in love with those faces on the screen as children fall in love, with heartbreak and deep fissures in our blood.

Louise Brooks, one of the great cryptic beauties of the silversheet, abandoned her autobiography, "Naked on My Goat," because she understood that no person's life would make much sense without revealing his or her sexual phantoms, all those powerful loves and hates, and Louise wasn't willing to do that.

But the films we adore become *our* autobiography in Brooks' special sense. We attach ourselves to faces that hurt us and delight us and become our erotic measures. Garbo and Gable. Dietrich. Brando and Marilyn. . . .

"I didn't know Marilyn Monroe," said Louise Brooks to critic Kenneth Tynan, "but I'm sure that her agonizing awareness of her own stupidity was one of the things that killed her." And eroticized her too. That "retarded" girl wounded whole generations of us. She was constantly naked, even with all her clothes on. Didn't we feel our own death in that funny, sad face? The ripeness of Marilyn came at us like a scream. And we loved Joe DiMaggio twice as much after he married the girl. They didn't have Pickfair. They weren't king and queen, like Doug and Mary. He was a bit old-fashioned, a guy who'd spent half his adult life in a pair of blue-and-white pajamas. And she was the dimpled goddess who didn't believe in underpants. They were married nine months. And DiMaggio was the husband who mourned her most. One more prisoner with his neck to the wall.

5 We go to the movies to get out of our skin, to seek Gullivers with gorgeous heads, and we discover a coherence in all their silly moves, a line that connects them to our own erotic life; they fall in love like crazy people, selfish, without consideration, until we realize that they're acting out our deepest wish: to find that perfect mate, our heart's desire, whoever it is.

As a boy, in a Catskill bungalow colony, I remembered those colony wives coming home from a Gable movie with the dark blood of romance in their eyes, a hunger I'd never seen before. I could hear them making love with their husbands that night. The whole bungalow colony quaked. Those wives had tasted *their* angel of art. They'd gone into the cave and returned like miraculous, buttery cows. They smiled for most of the week, with a delicious heaviness about them. And I couldn't have realized then that Louis B. Mayer had been responsible for that. Born somewhere between Vilna and Minsk on a summer night in 1882 or 3 or 5, he worked like a dray horse from the time he was six, went to Canada and learned a rough, brutal English, became a junkman and then a movie distributor in the United States, because it was a business that wasn't established enough to keep out Jewish furriers and peddlers, like Mayer and Zucker and Goldfish (alias Samuel Goldwyn). He dodged Thomas Edison's detectives, ran out to Hollywood to help create MGM, and had a profounder dream of America than most of the natives. L.B. lived in a Technicolor world. He discovered Garbo and Gable. He took a chubby Swedish girl with a flat chest and big feet, starved her a little, and turned her into the most exquisite face ever photographed on the silversheet.

Mayer built an empire that no other studio ever matched, and he built it around his stars. He was a temperamental son of a bitch. He had fistfights with Charlie Chaplin, John Gilbert, Sam Goldwyn, and Erich von Stroheim. He blacklisted anyone who got in his way (you couldn't work in movieland if Mayer didn't want you around). He started the Academy Awards and helped establish Will Hays as Hollywood's censor. He would have fainting fits whenever it was convenient for him. He'd cry shamelessly in front of his stars. He nourished them with his mama's chicken soup. He destroyed more careers than any other mogul. He was the capricious father of a tribe, playing Moses long before Charlton Heston ever got the part. He'd sit for hours with his female stars, solve their marriages and their divorces.

"At Columbia they had Harry Cohn, who thought every actress on the lot owed him sex, ditto Zanuck at Twentieth, ditto Joe Kennedy and then Howard Hughes at RKO. At MGM we had a certain dignity; we didn't feel like whores," Joan Crawford recalled. If one of Mayer's female stars had ever dared live with a man without marrying him first, "Louis B. would have had a stroke. . . . I don't think he liked the fact that we were sexually operational." But on the screen Mayer's stars were sexual wraiths who entered our blood, so that we could barely separate ourselves from them. That's what the cave was about. We went from the muddle of our lives into the dark, in search of those planetary beings. "Men didn't line up for Valentino," Crawford said. "But they sure as hell put the big okay on Clark [Gable]."

That's what the stars were. *The big okay.* We flourished so long as we had them. We borrowed their rhythm, found that necessary peace.

# five

# Mogul

**1** Louis B. Mayer was involved in a wondrous marriage. I'm not talking about his two wives, Margaret (the daughter of a kosher butcher) and Lorena, whom he liked to rumba with. They might have been the objects of his desire, but for the twelve years between 1924 and 1936 he had an additional "bride," a boy genius who'd been running film studios since he was nineteen, who fired Erich von Stroheim when he was twenty-two, married Norma Shearer, the princess of MGM, had several heart attacks before he was thirty, served as the inspiration for *The Last Tycoon,* and was probably the one authentic prince Hollywood ever had.

His name was Irving Thalberg. He had big brown eyes. He was five feet six and never weighed more than a hundred and twenty pounds. He was Louis B. Mayer's chief of production at MGM. "This frail half-sick person holding up the whole thing," as F. Scott Fitzgerald said of his Last Tycoon. He worked nineteen hours a day. He could juggle the content and the shooting schedules of half a dozen films in his head. He wouldn't greet dignitaries, like a normal prince, or give interviews. Irving didn't have the time. He was too busy killing himself for some infernal ideal that few people could ever understand. The clock he ran to was a movie clock. He was like an incarnation of the movies themselves. A silver shadow that couldn't stop. He held story conferences in limousines and funeral parlors. And when he took visiting executives around to a bordello, "he would sit in the hallway, in a rocking chair, reading *Variety.*"

Together with Louis B. Mayer he ran Hollywood's biggest principality, MGM, a walled empire in Culver City that ruled Hollywood in those years when Hollywood ruled the world.

Paramount made better films. Nothing in the Mayer-Thalberg inventory could compare with Ernst Lubitsch's *Trouble in Paradise,* or the early Marx Brothers, or Mae West. But Lubitsch and the Marx Brothers helped bankrupt Paramount. And Mayer thrived with his stars. He had two hundred and fifty contract players in 1935, and the other studios had to make deals with L.B. if they wanted to borrow Gable or Harlow. He had an actual army of four thousand souls—carpenters, musicians, schoolteachers (MGM had a schoolhouse for its child stars), ambulance drivers, wigmakers, writers, chefs . . . at least a hundred and fifty professions were practiced on the MGM lots. A world within a world that manufactured still other worlds for an entire planet of moviegoers. And holding that construction together was Irving and L.B., who were involved in a kind of constant rumba, a ritual of love and hate. Irving was the only man in Hollywood whom Mayer seemed to fear. And Irving's "love" for Mayer was mingled with contempt. Mayer took three-month vacations. He preferred to dine with bankers and politicians rather than picture people. He never read scripts. And the immense burden of production fell on that "frail half-sick" boy. But it was a marriage, nonetheless. Tweedledum and Tweedledee, Mutt and Jeff, Shem and Shaun, Irving and Louis B. Mayer. "He needed me," Mayer lamented, long after Irving's death. "I was his sounding board and wailing wall."

Writer and film director Kevin Brownlow says that "history has shown him [Mayer] to be a childish, melodramatic paranoiac," but he was a paranoiac who "made more stars than all . . . the producers in Hollywood put together." But it wasn't only stars he made. He built MGM around the idea of chicken soup. He wanted to feed all his workers like his own family. His studio had greatness, he said, "because our people are bound together by love. We have no hate here, we have love. I love Irving. I love everybody . . . except John Gilbert, Sam Goldwyn, and Charlie Chaplin."

Of course it's crazy. There was much more bile in and around L.B. than he would have liked to admit. Maureen O'Sullivan, Tarzan's wife, who wore the sexiest outfits of any jungle goddess until the Hollywood Production Code obliged Maureen to cover her loins, thought Mayer was "terrifying." His little family at MGM would shiver at the sight of Louis. No one could ever be sure of his moods, or of his next fainting spell. "He could help you or hurt you badly," recalled Danny Kaye. He'd court you, cry in your face, and then kick you off his lot. Nothing was ever final with Mayer except the sanctity of motherhood. He'd fall in love like a little boy. Jean Howard, a starlet he happened to adore, said Mayer reminded her of "a mental adolescent in perpetuity." He'd chase her with flowers, do the rumba, but never ask her to bed. Dancing, it seemed, was his only cure for insomnia.

But he was still Mayer of the chicken soup. When his son-in-law, David O. Selznick, ran up a big gambling debt and needed an instant supply of cash one night, L.B. called the managers of friendly moviehouses in L.A. and had them bring him all their cash receipts. And there was often confusion on the lot because of his dad, Jacob, who lived with L.B. out in Santa Monica. That old man would arrive in a chauffeured car and behave like the boss of MGM. It could have been a Marx Brothers movie. The emperor of Hollywood, Louis B. Mayer, with his four white telephones, didn't have the heart to contradict his dad. He allowed the old man to rule for the day.

The writers in movieland, who were mostly invisible men and women tucked away in little rabbit holes somewhere, mocked L.B. and the other moguls. Dream peddlers with their imperfect English and crude, sentimental ways. They'd come off a cattle boat, sold junk or jewels and furs, and emerged as film pirates who broke Thomas Edison's Trust, and seized Hollywood for themselves. And Mayer was the most powerful, and therefore the worst, of the moguls. He never forgave King Vidor for showing the top half of a toilet tank in *The Crowd*. Men and women didn't go to the toilet in the land of Leo the Lion. They kissed and held hands. "We'll have sex in motion pictures," Mayer told a reporter in 1926. "But it will be normal, real, beautiful sex."

There might be vamps in Mayer's America, bad girls, but no whores. A bad girl could mend her ways, turn into Cinderella in the second reel, or go and drown herself. Such were the laws at MGM. Mayer refused to back Walt Disney and help finance Mickey Mouse, because he was convinced that women would never go see Mickey. They were much too scared of mice.

Who the hell was Louis B. Mayer? His own father couldn't

be sure where the family name had come from. The Jews of the Russian Pale learned to be wizards in order to survive, altering their names *and* personalities after each pogrom. And because of those pogroms, no one can really pinpoint where Louis was born, except for some crooked line between Vilna and Minsk. Or when: 1882? 1885? It was summertime, and Louis picked the Fourth of July as his birthday. He'd celebrate it with a picnic at MGM, like the American boy he'd become. And because he seems foolish now, terribly old-fashioned, we forget the sway he once had over movieland. He'd come out of nowhere, created himself, a junkman who wore a pince-nez. Louis B. Mayer. He added that "B." at the time of his first marriage. Said it stood for Burton. But he had no middle name. He was as amorphous as the stars he made. But he'd been the master of the whole works. Whoever visited Hollywood visited him.

And behind L.B., in constant motion, was Irving Thalberg. He died at thirty-seven, without seeing movieland escape him, as Mayer did. Irving didn't become a dinosaur, like D. W. Griffith. But film historians are skeptical about him. He's a villain in college surveys, the man who took *Greed* away from Erich von Stroheim and had it cut to pieces. His vision of what was allowable on screen was no broader than L.B.'s. He had a curious mixture of concentration, ruthlessness, and naiveté. "Irving was a sweet guy but he could piss ice water," according to one of his associate producers.

When MGM art director Cedric Gibbons insisted that a "moonlit ocean" be dropped from a film about Paris, since Paris didn't have any ocean that Gibbons could remember, Thalberg told him not to bother about that. "We can't cater to a handful of people who know Paris."

He was, after all, the prince of movieland. He could risk any illusion. Oceans in Paris. Eiffel Towers in Prague. The Chrysler Building in downtown L.A. Audiences would buy *all* of Gibbons' backgrounds. "Whatever you put there, they'll believe that's how it is."

2 Thalberg didn't have any of Mayer's mysterious roots. There were no pogroms in the family album. He was a child of the middle class, born in Brooklyn (19 Woodbine Street) on May 30, 1899. His father, William, was a German-Jewish immigrant with a lace shop on lower Fifth Avenue. Henrietta, his mom, was practically an heiress. Her side of the family had a big department store, Heyman and Sons. Irving was a "blue baby," cursed with cyanosis, the sign of an imperfect heart.

He didn't develop like a normal child. His arms and legs stayed thin. He was in and out of bed so often he had little else to do but read. The doctors predicted a short life. But Henrietta wasn't offering that "blue baby" to any angel of death. She became his private nurse. She'd give him enemas and rub his body, and he was reading Kant by the time he was twelve.

Soon he was well enough to attend Boys High, but he had a bout of rheumatic fever at sixteen and had to return to bed. And there, like Jay Gatsby himself, Irving wrote out a list of maxims for the rest of his life.

He would trust no one but himself.

He would live each day as if that day were the only day he had.

He wouldn't lie. He wouldn't steal.

He wouldn't listen to foolish people. . . .

Sounds like Horatio Alger, D'Artagnan, and the ghost of Kant. It was nonsense and the curious wisdom of a boy who'd lived half his life in bed. Henrietta wanted him to go to law school, but Irving didn't have the time or the patience.

He taught himself to type, studied Spanish and shorthand at a commercial college, and became the secretary to Carl Laemmle, who founded Universal in 1912 and was one of the first film pirates and pioneers. Like Louis B. Mayer, Laemmle was fond of having his family around. An eccentric little man, five feet tall, he was born in Laupheim, Germany. Uncle Carl is the culprit who helped introduce the whole business of stars. He stole "The Biograph Girl" from Biograph when actors and actresses were still anonymous on screen and advertised her as Florence

Lawrence, the first star with a name (she got out of pictures and swallowed rat poison in 1936).

Irving reorganized Uncle Carl's entire office, like some magnificent floor manager, corrected Laemmle's English (the boy was a first-class scribe), and was sent to Universal City, Laemmle's four-hundred-acre "ranch" in the San Fernando Valley. It was the first California movie kingdom; the kingdom was in a mess. "Trying to control Universal was like trying to control a game reserve; the studios had been operating for only four years, and jack rabbits and mountain lions still treated it as their rightful domain. Tracking down a company and rounding up lost extras was like going on safari."

Irving had never traveled before; the only wildlands he knew were the marshes of Queens. He climbed aboard the Twentieth Century Limited with his hot-water bottle, a boy of nineteen. The journey took four days and nights. He arrived in California, got a room at the Hollywood Hotel, and went around in long woolen underwear.

He tamed the mountain lions. But somebody had to look after the ranch. And that's how Irving became head of production at Universal. He wasn't even old enough to sign the company's checks. The Boy Wonder took a struggling actor, Lon Chaney, and turned him into the Hunchback of Notre Dame. *Hunchback* was the biggest hit of the season.

And then there was the Stroheim affair. D. W. Griffith had established the reputation of the director as a kind of demigod. Producers were little bald men who walked around with money in their pockets while their directors wore puttees and campaign hats and shouted orders into megaphones that might be ten feet long. When Irving came onto the set of *Foolish Wives,* Stroheim asked, "Since when does a child supervise a genius?"

Stroheim was extravagant with Uncle Carl's cash. He built a full-scale model of Monte Carlo on the back lots of Universal City. But since he was the star as well as director of the film, Irving could do little about Stroheim's Monte Carlo. The first cut of *Foolish Wives* was six hours. Stroheim got it down to four. Then Irving and Uncle Carl took the film away from Stroheim and lopped off another two hours. *Foolish Wives* was an enormous success.

And Stroheim went back to work for Uncle Carl on *Merry-*

*Go-Round*. This time he outfitted his extras with silk underpants carrying the insignia of the Imperial Austrian Guard. The silk was never seen, but Stroheim insisted that those underpants helped create a mood for the film. When Irving interfered with him again, Stroheim went into a rage. "I am an artist. . . . I don't go by schedules prepared by lunatics with stopwatches, dummkopfs counting words on a page. I embroider, I paint, red here, blue here. . . . What do you know? Where do you come from? An asylum, maybe?"

Irving fired him, and it was the talk of Hollywood. Nothing like this had ever been done before. Erich Oswald Hans Carl Marie Stroheim von Nordenwall, whose father had been a colonel in the royal dragoons, his mother a lady-in-waiting to Empress Elizabeth of Austria, . . . and a kid from Brooklyn who'd barely graduated from Boys High. Later, of course, it would be discovered that Irving's lineage was no less than Erich's. Stroheim wasn't the son of a cavalryman. His father was a Jewish hatmaker. Erich had been in the Austrian army (an auxiliaryman stationed on a horse), but he was also a deserter who arrived penniless in the United States. He would become a man of many careers, according to his own account: prison guard, fly-paper salesman, singer, soldier, stable hand, lifeguard at Lake Tahoe. He apprenticed himself to D. W. Griffith and was soon acting and directing on his own. He played Prussian officers during World War I and was billed as "The Man You Love to Hate." He couldn't walk into a Hollywood restaurant without being hissed at. He wore a monocle like the Prussian officer he'd become, and he'd give advice to other directors on military matters.

Then Irving got in his way, and "Von" went to another studio (Samuel Goldwyn) to film Frank Norris' novel *McTeague*. But Irving himself got into trouble. Uncle Carl's plain-looking daughter, Rosabelle, grew infatuated with Irving and started to fall in love. The romance between Irving and Rosabelle is a rather clouded affair. Either Irving loved Rosabelle too little or too much. He broke with Uncle Carl and went to work for that other mogul, Louis B. Mayer, who had his own small production company on Mission Road, next to a zoo. It must have seemed like a demotion for Thalberg, moving from Uncle Carl's principality to a kind of rag-and-bone shop run by Mayer. But

Marcus Loew, the moviehouse magnate, bought L.B.'s little outfit and merged it with two other companies to form Metro-Goldwyn-Mayer. L.B. was general manager and Irving was his production chief. They inherited Sam Goldwyn's studio in Culver City . . . and Erich von Stroheim.

Von had taken Frank Norris' novel, shot it scene by scene, and turned it into a forty-two-reel film he now called *Greed*. The film ran seven hours. Von cut it to five. He wanted it shown in two parts, with a light supper in the middle, as a divertissement. It was a delicious idea, and might have made perfect sense in 1989. But neither Mayer nor Thalberg had Stroheim's vision. The film was released in ten reels (without a divertissement) and was a total flop. Still, even in its butchered state, *Greed* has a relentless, ghostlike quality and a driving sense of doom, despite all the incomprehensible breaks; like a wondrous mouth with missing teeth.

**3** MGM was only a little giant, not to be compared with Paramount, which had De Mille and Gloria Swanson and Clara Bow, or United Artists, formed in 1919 by Chaplin, Mary and Doug, and D. W. Griffith, or that enormous acreage Irving left behind with Uncle Carl at Universal City. It was Hollywood, after all, and film companies could come and go, like those pirates who'd arrived in California, running from Edison's people. Mayer wasn't as even-tempered as Uncle Carl, and no one thought the Boy Wonder would survive very long with the junkman. But Irving had matured in movieland. He was twenty-four. He'd given up woolen underwear and become a fixer. He could patch up any film. He was the producer-magician who could sense a structural flaw and locate the melody of a given scene. The Thalberg legend began to grow. "Of this slim, slight, nervous man it was said he lived in a motion picture theater all his waking hours and knew instinctively whether the shadows on screen would please the public."

Irving wasn't as marvelous (or mystical) as all that. He was a prince of the commonplace. He knew how to deliver "rainbows in the dark." He didn't have Stroheim's black dreams. He was Horatio Alger with a technical gift, a genius of sorts, whose imagination never really developed much beyond high school.

That made him a perfect "reader" of films. The audience that he was pleasing was only himself. And if he had a literary bent, a love of fireside classics, it's exactly how a bedridden boy would react to the world. If he did Shakespeare, it was Shakespeare for children. There were no undersongs in a Thalberg film, no darker meanings, like the best of Walt Disney, all the witches and crows and perverse, funny creatures that surround Snow White and Bambi and Pinocchio.

Irving picked up the Marx Brothers when they no longer had a career in Hollywood. He told them that *Duck Soup* "had more laughs than a picture needed." The Brothers did *A Night at the Opera* for MGM, their first success. Groucho idolized Irving. So did Buster Keaton. But he thinned their talents, led them to the ordinary.

He had his first heart attack when he was twenty-five, while *Ben-Hur* was being made. Irving wasn't supposed to recover. The whole studio was paralyzed; it was like a haunted village without Thalberg; MGM fell into a deep gloom. But within a week, Irving was lying in bed in his hospital room with the rushes of *Ben-Hur* projected on the wall.

He was responsible for bringing a cross-eyed actress named Norma Shearer to MGM. It's difficult to define her charm on screen. She wasn't beautiful. She wasn't tall. She didn't have Garbo's bones, Dietrich's smile, or Crawford's mouth. But watch her in *The Barretts of Wimpole Street*. She's almost silly as the suffering Elizabeth Barrett, but she steals the screen from Charles Laughton and Fredric March. She's like a magnificent, wounded statue with an otherworldly look. You might titter, but you can't take your eyes off "Elizabeth." She was the daughter of a Canadian businessman who fell on hard times. When she first met Thalberg in Hollywood, she mistook him for an office boy at MGM, according to one of movieland's classic myths. But somehow I don't believe it. Irving didn't dress like an office boy. He had the quiet feel of power that not even a cross-eyed princess could have failed to notice.

They were married in 1927 and lived in a mansion on Sunset Boulevard with Irving's mom and dad. Henrietta was the real chatelaine. She'd rub his back the way she always did, and "administered enemas when necessary." The biggest brain in movieland still belonged to mama.

4 "Everybody has two businesses," Irving liked to say. "Their own and the movies." Hollywood had become a boom town. There were world premieres of motion pictures almost every week. Searchlights would cross the sky like incredible blue and white fingers until all of Hollywood was a burning lamp. The "birth" of the stars had brought about the phenomenon of the picture palace. In Akron, in San Antone, on Peachtree Street in Atlanta, Canal Street in New Orleans, Fordham Road in the Bronx, theaters bloomed, like the blood and bone of some new American dreamland.

But the picture palace in Hollywood was a dreamland unto itself. The Pantages, Grauman's Egyptian . . . I'm not talking about the nuttiness of the landscape. The hieroglyphics on the walls, the ushers in Egyptian hats, the deep, deep court like the well of some demented god who happened to be a moviegoer. Where else could you stand in line and catch a glimpse of Garbo and Gilbert, Norma and Irving (who looked like a star, even with his long nose), Doug and Mary, Mae West . . .

The stars had come down from their mansions in the hills to be stared at and mingle with one another. And it didn't matter how pretentious or narrow their lives really were, with all those butlers and cars like battleships. It was movieland, after all, where everything was outsized. The butterflies in Bevery Hills "had the proportions of bombers." The most revered shadow on the silversheet might be a dipsomaniac, or collect pieces of string, or do nothing, nothing at all.

Mayer's publicity department and the fan magazines may have fabulated the most imbecilic fairy tales, but they couldn't have gotten very far without us. We were Mayer's little accomplices. We demanded romance. We didn't want any distance between the shadows and the shadow plays. We were all Plato's children, trapped in the cave, seeking our heart's desire in the dark. Because the stars gave each of us a secret life. And we wouldn't permit them to drop away from their exquisite selves on the wall. How could they have families of their own if they belonged to us? They had to dress and walk and eat their dinner just as they did on screen. If Jack Gilbert appeared at the Pantages, he couldn't afford to be anything other than the ghost he'd become, or we might grow suspicious and turn from those shadows on the wall, feeling betrayed.

L.B. understood this better than anyone in Hollywood, and that's why MGM succeeded beyond a junkman's dreams. He gathered stars. He let Irving knit and weave. Mayer couldn't alter a shadow play, but he knew how to arrange an abortion, cover up any scandal that might surround his stars. The junkman had his own police department, bigger and much more complicated than the police of Culver City, the town MGM was in. "I am like a fireman with my shoes always on," said Whitey Hendry, MGM's police chief. He saw how pampered and spoiled the stars could be. "They've become Frankensteins to us." But he always protected them for Mr. Mayer. MGM made whatever laws it needed to survive in Culver City.

And the junkman found the stars and nurtured them. It was a simple formula, followed by all the big studios. "It takes ten years to make a star overnight." But the junkman had the patience. If he was going to manufacture Cinderellas, he wouldn't let them march without glass shoes. He maintained "his rule of illusion . . . which decreed that great players must present themselves to the public as glamorous figures, wear beautiful clothes . . . drink champagne." Mayer determined the lives of all his Cinderellas and Frankensteins. Nothing was left to chance. The junkman's own scribes answered the stars' mail. His publicity people "became expert at imitating all signatures. When Garbo refused to supply hers for this purpose, it was copied from her contract."

Stealing signatures was the start. "Phone calls to the players were screened, invitations accepted or declined . . . romances promoted or destroyed, elopements and marriages arranged or rent asunder." It was a kind of choreography lesson: the big dance. And for the newcomers, those whose images weren't established on the wall, the junkman constantly sought their screen face. Lana Turner, who was probably the most luscious sixteen-year-old on the lot, with soft features and big startled eyes, began as a brunette. Her hair grew lighter and lighter, her features coarsened, until she was that hungry blonde in *The Postman Always Rings Twice*. It was a face you couldn't forget, touched with that disease of transformation, the signature of MGM. But it was a critical moment for Lana, caught somewhere in time between a blond harpy and a girl of sixteen. She would go on to be a goddess, but she'd never have that power again. . . .

*Postman* was long after Irving's time. Lana wasn't a face he'd ever work with. He'd been feuding with the junkman over money. He wanted a bigger piece of the profits. He threatened to leave the land of Leo the Lion. He'd start his own company, Thalberg Productions. The junkman was mortified. He offered some of his own profit shares to Irving. And the Thalberg people, the five or six producers who were part of his coterie, who ate with him in the executive cottage, felt a touch of relief. "As long as Irving lives, we're all great men."

5 He took ill after the MGM Christmas party in 1932. Had another heart attack. He'd never command MGM's entire production force again. The junkman called in his son-in-law, David O. Selznick, and others loyal to him. Now, instead of the Boy Wonder, he'd have his own "peerage of producers." When Thalberg returned from a holiday in Europe, he was just one more potentate on the lot. He had to scramble around to get stars for his own productions. He wanted Gable to appear in *Romeo and Juliet*. Gable balked. "I don't look Shakespeare, I don't talk Shakespeare, I don't like Shakespeare, and I won't do Shakespeare."

And Irving had to settle for Leslie Howard as Romeo. The picture failed, even though it starred his wife. Lost a million for MGM. It was one of Irving's last productions. He died of pneumonia on September 14, 1936 (he'd caught a head cold on Labor Day and never recovered).

Gable was one of the ushers at his funeral. A message from Franklin Roosevelt arrived, sharing America's grief with the widow. According to Samuel Marx, MGM's story editor, Louis B. elbowed one of his underlings after the funeral and said with a smile, "Isn't God good to me?"

I wonder if it was really an apocryphal remark, something half-overheard that could heighten the rift between him and Thalberg and prove that the junkman was some kind of devil. Still, it was a remark that L.B. could have made. He'd watched the Boy Wonder turn from him and gather a power base. Irving alive was always a threat. But the junkman didn't have to worry about a dead producer.

Some movie addicts see a sad decline in the MGM "product" after Irving was gone. I don't. The gloss was still there. And so was Gable and the rest of MGM. The studio talked about finding another Thalberg. But that talk has been going on for fifty years. We've had new Boy Wonders, but none of them with Irving's shyness *and* flair. "He was like no other character in the entire film capital," said writer Anita Loos. Loos' collaborations with him were "almost like love affairs."

The junkman was never able to inspire such affection. He'd loved Irving like some lost son (Mayer himself had a pair of daughters). But he couldn't control Irving, and there were always those squabbles about money which grew worse and worse until L.B. and the Boy Wonder hardly talked in the end. He didn't want another Thalberg around.

It wasn't the absence of Irving that undermined Louis B. Mayer (he had ten good years on his own). It was the very star system that he'd promoted and helped to perfect. After a while, those talking shadows didn't want to be dressed by L.B. He couldn't keep Hollywood a kiddie town. He gathered Rooney and Garland and Elizabeth Taylor around him. But Rooney rebelled and joined the army. Garland grew anorexic. And Taylor grew tits. "I have a woman's body and a child's emotions," she said, and there was nothing the junkman could do about that. The stars had become too capricious for publicity departments. They were ghosts in Technicolor now and they demanded Technicolor lives.

Mayer absorbed himself in the Hollywood witch hunts. "The more McCarthy yells, the better I like him."

He lost MGM. He did the rumba a lot with his second wife. He was often gloomy. Dying of leukemia, he mumbled, "Nothing matters. Nothing matters." He was inside his own heart of darkness, and he no longer had all the puffed candy of MGM. One more ex-mogul, without his own "firmament" of stars.

6 The junkman is a creature out of the past, but Irving sticks to the blood. He won't lie still. There was a melody about him, a song that seems utterly modern, despite his naiveté and all the enemas administered by his mom. In *Prater Violet,* Christopher Isherwood calls Hollywood a half-world, a town that had lost its third dimension. Thalberg was part of that town. Indeed, the half-world was his. He could be very cruel, stranding people outside his office for days at a time on his "Million-Dollar Couch." He kept everybody waiting. Louis B. The Marx Brothers. Scott Fitzgerald. It was Thalberg who hired and fired Fitzgerald more than once, who stuck a "shadow" behind his back (teams of other writers) to work on the same script, until Fitzgerald became the court jester of Hollywood, the formerly great writer as drunken fool. Fitzgerald of the glazed eyes who went everywhere with a Coca-Cola bottle because his system could no longer tolerate the least bit of wine. But Scott saw a good deal through his glazed eyes during all the years of his "crack-up." He felt that third dimension, the heartbreak behind Thalberg's cool mask. "Thalberg has always fascinated me," he wrote the editor of *Collier's* about the Hollywood book he was working on, the story of Monroe Stahr. "His peculiar charm, his extraordinary good looks, his bountiful success, the tragic end of his great adventure . . . he is one of the half-dozen men I have known who were built on a grand scale."

The court jester couldn't even sell his stories any more. His lyricism meant nothing to the Thirties, that time of the proletarian novel. He'd ceased to function as a writer (his royalties in 1936 were under a hundred dollars). He'd have turned into another Melville, a lost soul of the imagination, if it hadn't been for the movies. At least he had the Garden of Allah, that bungalow colony on Sunset Boulevard, with its swimming pool built like the Black Sea. He could drink his Coca-Cola with other people who had "disappeared." The Garden of Allah was stuffed with writers who were never heard from again. It was a meeting place and a mausoleum. But Scott moved out of the Garden of Allah and created Monroe Stahr.

Stahr is the most perceptive portrait of Thalberg we have,

much more striking than any biography that's been done, because Fitzgerald wasn't obliged to dance around with the linear
facts of Thalberg's life. These facts can't provide us with a motor. Thalberg was much too elusive. But Fitzgerald's fiction has
a lyric pull. It lends Monroe Stahr a poetic skin that allows us
to deal with Thalberg's contradictions. *The Last Tycoon* couldn't
have happened if Fitzgerald hadn't seen the fictional man in the
mogul who kept him waiting outside his door. Fitzgerald died
of a heart attack before he could finish the novel. It's a
"wounded" book, as incomplete as Thalberg himself. As such,
there's a kind of perfection to the state it's in. Brilliant and
broken, like Irving, it leaves us with all his mystery and the
mystery of what the completed book might have been. And so,
without intending it, Fitzgerald has written about the puzzle of
*all* personality, the poetics that cannot end, like the dreamland
of the movies.

The narrator of *The Last Tycoon* is Cecilia Brady, a college girl
who's obsessed with Stahr. Her dad is Monroe's partner, Bill
Brady, one of the original movie pioneers. Cecilia was seven and
Stahr twenty-two when he began to work with Brady, and she's
had a crush on him ever since. She's an authentic daughter of
the Golden West. "Rudolph Valentino came to my fifth birthday party," she tells us. And Cecilia accepts Hollywood "with
the resignation of a ghost assigned to a haunted house."

She's a moviegoer, like the rest of us, but she's caught in a
double web. She grew up on movies *in* movieland itself. A ghost
among ghosts.

And Stahr? "He was born sleepless, without a talent for rest
or the desire for it." He'd come out of the Bronx rather than
Brooklyn, but Fitzgerald had the right to move a couple of
boroughs around. Like Thalberg, Monroe had gone to stenog-
raphy school and had married a movie star. But Monroe's wife,
Minna Davis, was dead, and he had no children, no home other
than the studio itself. And of course he had a bad heart. It's
1935 when the novel begins. And like all the moguls, he'd been
through "the great upset, when sound came" and careers were
lost. And movies themselves had lost their language of pantomime. The first sound films were deadly affairs, static movements around a stationary microphone. Spoken dialogue had all
the resonance of a foghorn. Then Hollywood discovered the

boom mike, and actors could dance around again, in a wind of words. But Cecilia's dad couldn't have made his pictures without Monroe Stahr. "Of course, he talked that double talk to Wall Street about how mysterious it was to make a picture, but Father didn't know the ABC's of dubbing or even cutting. . . . Stahr had been his luck."

And his grief. He was totally dependent on Stahr. He sat with his henchman, Jacques La Borwitz, like a prisoner in his own office. "Stahr had ordered something or forbidden something, or defied Father or junked one of La Borwitz' pictures or something catastrophic, and they were sitting there in protest at night in a community of rebellion and helplessness."

Stahr was a popularist of the imagination, a tender of dreamscapes. He could assume only one condition, that he "take people's own favorite folklore and dress it up and give it back to them. Anything beyond that is sugar."

But Fitzgerald himself understood the power of that dreamscape, the magic behind the hollow walls. "Under the moon the back lot was thirty acres of fairyland—not because the locations really looked like African jungles and French châteaux and schooners at anchor and Broadway by night, but because they looked like the torn picture books of childhood, like fragments of stories dancing in an open fire."

*The fire of Plato's cave.*

Those torn picture books of childhood are what our dreams are all about. And Stahr was the master who delivered them to us without the least bit of complication. The dreams were just short of nightmare, as most films (and folklore) are. Because they suggest danger and desire. It's not what we don't want that frightens us. It's the terror of the "wish." We don't simply fall in love with those shadows, we lick their faces. And then we run home and fantasize. . . .

And Stahr, like Thalberg, couldn't hold the entire fabric together. "The old loyalties were trembling now, there were clay feet everywhere; but still he was . . . the last of the princes."

The prince was dying on his feet. "He was pale—he was so transparent that you could almost watch the alcohol mingle with the poison of his exhaustion." And he lived in a world of ambiguous romance, where ritual and nonsense often played together, right in the heart of movieland. "Everywhere floodlights raked the sky. On an empty corner two mysterious men moved a gleaming drum in pointless arcs over the heavens."

And to stay out of the darkness and those empty corners Stahr sought control. He was a frail sort of Byron from the Bronx who had pictures in his blood. He'd captured that crazy industry of shadow plays, yet couldn't seem to discern his own shadow on the wall. Like Jay Gatsby, Stahr had built a kind of make-believe career, a stepladder of dreams. And in the end, Monroe Stahr (and Irving Thalberg) were as sad and insubstantial as Gatsby's stepladder.

7 Neither Irving nor Monroe nor Louis B. Mayer was the last tycoon.

Of all the moguls, Jack Warner had the longest unbroken line of service. From 1923, when Jack and his brothers started Warners, until 1967, when he sold the company to Seven Arts. Jack was the youngest of twelve children, born in London, Ontario, on August 2, 1892, to Polish-Jewish immigrants. His dad was a tinker of sorts who settled in Youngstown, Ohio, where he fixed bicycles. Then the whole family bought a nickelodeon in Newcastle, Pennsylvania, the Pioneer. It was 1903, and that's how Jack got into the picture business. Soon he and his brothers, Harry, Albert, and Sam, went into film distribution as independent pirates. But they had to sell out to Thomas Edison's Trust. The brothers became tinkers themselves, wandering about, producing short subjects, until they acquired ten acres near Sunset Boulevard. Their first success was with a choleric dog named Rin Tin Tin, the most popular animal in pictures until Mickey Mouse. Warners was "just a shitty little studio then." But that changed with *The Jazz Singer*.

Mayer and Thalberg had scorned the idea of sound films. Why should they monkey with the profits? They had an international audience with their shadow plays. "Talkers" would bring about chaos. They'd have to reshoot their films in several different languages. It was an insane idea. In 1924 D. W. Griffith had said, "We do not want now and we shall never want the human voice with our films."

But D.W. hadn't counted on Jack Warner, with his white leather shoes, his hand-painted ties, and his Panama hat. Warners had nothing to lose. They didn't have an empire like Paramount and MGM. They were constantly in debt. So Jack and his brothers started that whole monkey business of the talking shadow play.

*The Jazz Singer* is a schizophrenic film, with its songs, its ad-libbing by Al Jolson, and its descent into silence, with title cards and the familiar mechanics of pantomime. It moves from silence to sound like a wanton child. But when Jolson sang, the audience went delirious. His shadow seemed to bounce right off the silversheet. There was an intimacy that no moviegoer had felt before. The shadows could talk. Sitting at the piano, the jazz singer tells his mom that if he's a success, they'll move up to the Bronx. "A lot of nice green grass up there. And a whole lot of people you know. The Ginsbergs, the Guttenbergs, and the Goldbergs and a whole lot of Bergs."

*The Jazz Singer* played to an endless audience at the Warner Theater in Manhattan. People would line up around midnight for the morning show. The brothers moved out of their little lot and took over First National Studios in Burbank. They'd become rivals to Louis B. Mayer. But Harry, Warners' president, was a notorious spendthrift and a junkman all his own. He'd walk through the sound stages at Burbank "picking up nails . . . and straightening them with his teeth."

Warners was successful with its gangster films and its tough, streetsmart musicals. It kept away from the classics, celebrating the city's rise to power. It had Cagney, Bogart, Robinson, and Raft. Raft was so popular that Bugsy Siegel, Hollywood's own member of Murder, Inc., began to dress like him, talk like him, until he looked like any gangster on the Warner lot.

The writers who did the crime melodramas couldn't really get along with Jack. He cursed them, called them "schmucks with Underwoods." He was contemptuous of his stars, though he was frightened to death of Bette Davis, who loved to give Jack a hard time.

He was FDR's favorite mogul.

"Jack Warner used to steal everything he could out of the property department," recalls producer Jules Levy. "If you picked up a vase [at his mansion], it had a number. He would go to the warehouse," which had "floor after floor of great stuff," and grab whatever pleased him. But the head of the property department was "an old railroader," Pat Quinn. One afternoon Jack arrived to plunder his own property department and parked in front of the entrance. A voice came out of the warehouse. It was Pat Quinn. "You cocksucking son of a bitch, get that fucking car out of the way."

Jack apologized and drove off. "He ran the studio like a prison. Everyone was fearful of him . . . nobody knew from one moment to the next whether they could keep their job." But he respected the old railroader and wouldn't interfere with him.

He prospered, turned into a superpatriot during the witch hunts, grew old. His three brothers had died. He sold the company and fell into a dark mood. It was around the time Arthur Penn had filmed *Bonnie and Clyde* for Warner Brothers. And Jack's lieutenants kept pestering Warren Beatty (the film's producer and star). "They kept saying, 'Show it to Jack, show it to Jack.' "

Beatty and Penn arrived at Jack Warner's house. Before the film was run, Jack said, "If I have to get up and piss, you'll know it's no good."

In the first ten minutes of *Bonnie and Clyde,* Jack got up, returned, and got up again. At the end of the film he told his lieutenants, "What the hell is this? How could you have put up our money for this piece of crap?"

Jack had already sold Warners and Beatty wasn't too perturbed. He said to Jack about *Bonnie and Clyde,* "This is really an *hommage* to Warners' gangster films."

"What's an *hommage*?" Jack asked.

And Beatty told him. "You really put a mark on American films with your gangster epics."

"Warren felt better by the end of the evening," according to Arthur Penn.

They were sitting in the library at Jack's house, where all the Warner Brothers' scripts were bound in leather jackets. And Arthur Penn asked Jack: "Of all these scripts which one are you proudest of?"

Jack pulled out a little pamphlet from between two of the binders.

It was a list of David Belasco's plays. Belasco had been the greatest theater impresario in the world when Jack had started Warner Brothers. Belasco could "sell" a play to any audience on the strength of his name. And he wouldn't deal with picture people.

Arthur Penn looked at the list.

"I don't understand."

Jack knew that Penn had directed *The Miracle Worker* on Broadway.

"When we first started out," Jack said, "you guys in the theater wouldn't sell us anything. I got down on my knees in front of Belasco."

And Belasco sold him a play.

It was "that little moment of acquiring legitimacy," fifty years before, that Jack decided to cherish, at least in front of Arthur Penn.

Warner Brothers released *Bonnie and Clyde*. Beatty hadn't gulled the old man. It was a kind of homage to the Warner gangster epics, filtered through the Sixties. *Time* magazine panned the film, then reversed itself, and put Bonnie and Clyde (Beatty and Faye Dunaway) on its cover. They were like a romantic death wish. And as the country fell deeper and deeper into Vietnam, Bonnie and Clyde made a perfect couple. The film introduced a poetics of violence that we hadn't seen before. It felt like a long, beautiful, deadly kiss.

But it awakened Jack's bladder. *Bonnie and Clyde* had sent him out to pee.

Jack became an independent producer for the new Warner Brothers. He was seventy-five. His first film was *Camelot*, an *hommage* to the only Hollywood he knew: a land of kings and principalities. The film was a flop.

Jack retired to Palm Springs. He got more and more depressed. "You're nothing if you don't have a studio. . . . Now I'm just another millionaire."

# six

# "Young Fellah"

1    "I'm the king of silent pictures," says Warren Beatty in Arthur Penn's *Mickey One* (1965). "I'm hiding out till talkies blow over." Mickey One is a comic caught in a paranoid dream, hiding from a mob that is everywhere and nowhere at once. The movie was financed by the moguls at Columbia, who were no more sympathetic to Arthur Penn's slanted image of America than Jack Warner was. Penn had a two-picture deal with Columbia. The second picture was never made.

But Beatty's words, tossed out as a melancholic riff, a means of disguising who he is (a comic on the lam from himself) have their own prophetic pull.

There *were* kings and queens of the silents, like Jack Gilbert and Clara Bow, Gloria Swanson, Lillian Gish, Francis X. Bushman, Colleen Moore, Buster Keaton, Ramon Novarro, Louise Brooks, Blanche Sweet, Mary and Doug, who took early retirement or played lesser and lesser roles until they reached the point of invisibility, where they weren't even shadows on the wall. The most frightening reenactment of that long, long wait "till talkies blow over" is Billy Wilder's *Sunset Boulevard* (1950), where Gloria Swanson plays Norma Desmond, a retired silent queen (essentially herself), who's making a phantom comeback, assisted by her butler and former husband, Max von Mayerling (Erich von Stroheim), who'd also been her first director. Von himself had directed Swanson's last silent film, *Queen Kelly,* which was never released in the United States. Gloria had fired Von because of his usual extravagance, and because he'd recreated a brothel with such authenticity, hiring a professional madam and a string of prostitutes, Swanson soon realized the brothel scenes could never be shown.

In *Sunset Boulevard,* Norma Desmond, like any "demoted" silent star, swears that movies have betrayed her. Joe Gillis (William Holden), a writer of B films who's become Norma's gigolo, tells her, "You used to be big."

"I am big," Norma Desmond answers. "It's the pictures that got small."

And as Norma goes insane, shoots Joe Gillis, and we're left with Stroheim's sad face at the bottom of the stairs, the whole history of the silent film sweeps past us like a relic from another time, another place, a world and a way of being that were obliterated by the talkies.

Norma Desmond becomes our image of the silent star, the madwoman of Sunset Boulevard, who lives in a "big white elephant of a place . . . the kind crazy movie people built in the crazy Twenties," the years of Valentino and Gloria Swanson.

I saw Valentino once. I must have been twelve. *The Sheik* had come to our neighborhood palace. I don't know why. Perhaps it was the bottom half of the bill, some mogul's idea of a B movie. I laughed at all the muggering, Valentino's big eyes. And I suppose I measured myself as a future lover against The Sheik. Valentino had bigger biceps, but he was ridiculous in most other ways.

The silents themselves drifted out of my memory. It was Brando's time. And I preferred his mumbling to the eyes of The Sheik.

Movieland wasn't pushing Valentino any more. "Hollywood is afflicted with total amnesia," said author Ezra Goodman, "a complete group blackout and loss of recall when it comes to anything that happened more than twenty-four hours ago."

The moguls had their own futures to promote, their latest film. The old stuff was stored in cans or melted down, because the silver content in the nitrate stock was more valuable than an *old* movie (and movies became old after six months).

But it wasn't only Hollywood that conspired against the silent era. America itself seemed a little ashamed, a little forlorn, about those lost faces. We're a country of amnesiacs. Maybe it's because our own past seems so ambiguous to us, so tentative. Yes, we have fond memories of the Pilgrims and all that. Pocahontas. Muskets. Thanksgiving feasts in the forest. And we sing of the Founding Fathers and the Bill of Rights. But where are the epics of the American Revolution? Or our images of George Washington on the screen? We have Ginger Rogers (Dolly Madison) and David Niven (Aaron Burr). But no George. D. W. Griffith did complete a silent film about the Revolution, called *America* (1924), with battle scenes as convincing as *The Birth of a Nation;* it's completely disappeared.

George was a gentleman farmer with a stomach ailment and rotten teeth. He was over six feet tall. He married a young widow, Martha Custis, with two live children. The widow was twice as rich as George. He had his ups and downs as a colonel in the French and Indian War. He lost more battles than he won. He retired to farming and would have had an uneventful career as a planter in King George's American colonies. But the two Georges clashed, not in person, of course.

George III never stepped outside his own beloved isle. He was a much better king than most historians like to admit. Pious, well-behaved, even if he wasn't brilliant. But he got into trouble over his American colonies, allowing his ministers to tax them too hard. The colonies rebelled and there was this little war. The Brits should have knocked the pants off those Sons of Liberty. But there was this stubborn general who had wooden teeth in his mouth and was plagued with the shits. He *was* the Revolution. He wove a mass of recruits together, retreated like a fox, and wore out those Britishers whose hearts weren't in the struggle. And suddenly there was something called a nation. It required a king, like that other George. But this George said no. He returned to his farm. Then he was called back into service as the president of his country.

That's where our confusion begins. We longed for a king, a touch of divinity, though the framers of the Constitution would have denied it, and we got Father George. He was only a farmer who knew how to fight. And fables began to build around him, a folklore about the boy who could not tell a lie. So every brat in the United States has this fib about young George and the cherry tree, as if we had to be very, very careful whenever we approached this man. He was the rebel *and* the father-king. And somewhere in this country's psychic heart is that irreconcilable wish that we could have "rebelled" and still not lost the Mother Country, our umbilical cord.

We've all had to suffer the consequences. That feeling of expansive power, masking a terrible inferiority. We've looked to the English and the French for our literature and our fashions. Until World War II *half* of American literature was created abroad. As if all those damn Yankees had to breathe in "culture" before they could learn to write. Fenimore Cooper was our consul at Lyons. Washington Irving was attached to the American embassy in Madrid. Hawthorne spent two years in Florence and Rome before he could write *The Marble Faun*. Melville, a phantom writer by his mid-thirties, visited the Holy Land and scratched out *Clarel,* a long, marvelous, unreadable poem about a pilgrim boy. Henry James knew more about Florence, London, Paris, Sussex, and Rome than the New York City where he was born. T. S. Eliot lived in London fifty years. And Gertrude Stein, the most radical of writers, discovered her own strange vernacular rhythms on the rue de Fleurus in Paris.

While all this happened, Hollywood sprang up and attached itself to Los Angeles, a dirty little pueblo during the Civil War. And why shouldn't Hollywood have inherited America's cultural "wounds," its obsession about bigness, its madness to buy—actors, writers, musicians, everything, and its belief that the future was all that mattered, since the past was so hard to find. It developed amnesia along America's own crooked lines, turned into a village of immigrants and cowboys who came down from the hills to act in motion pictures. Movieland developed so fast it could only afford a present tense. The street that was built for *David Copperfield* grew into "Andy Hardy town," and Tarzan's jungle at Culver City became some Civil War saga.

Hollywood couldn't allow itself to look back. The single memory that remained was the Civil War. And thus we have *The Birth of a Nation,* the one silent film that half the world still remembers, and *Gone With the Wind*. Of course, the mansion that David O. Selznick created for Scarlett "had no rooms inside." But millions of moviegoers couldn't have known about it and wouldn't have cared. MGM's picture-book Atlanta was all they'd ever need.

The Civil War was just as traumatic as the Revolution, even more so, because this time there were no Brits in the battle. It was North vs. South. And that crack in the United States has never healed. When the Ku Klux Klan rides to the rescue of the defeated South in *The Birth of a Nation,* most white Americans cheered. Griffith's own pappy was a colonel on the Southern side. And his version of the war was like a childhood fable, where only men in white sheets can undo what the wicked North had done. . . .

It's been a hundred and twenty years, and that war hasn't gone away. I'm not talking about the mock battles that are replayed, the sentimental songs, the illustrated books and manuals that relive every historical site. The North won the war, but the South won the nation. It had a deeper "culture," it seems, a belief in a chivalric past, a simpler way of life, without machines and modernism. And Hollywood yoked itself to that mythic land of the South, which was like a magnificent all-American baseball team (before Jackie Robinson appeared in 1947), with no blacks, a couple of Italians, Irishers, and Jews, and a whole lot of country boys (and girls in the stands).

This was the audience the moguls aimed at. And why not? It was as uncomplicated as America, the country of blue-eyed amnesiacs. Hollywood could show the big, bad city on the screen, the scoundrels, the jazz babies, because the audience loved a bit of danger as long as it could go home and believe that everything was all right. Moviegoers would listen to the sophisticated Northern folk with their strange talk and stranger places, like "Conneckticut." It was fun. But who the hell would want to live there?

They had their magic show, shadows on the wall. And as Woodrow Wilson said, after watching *The Birth of a Nation:* it was "like seeing history with flashes of lightning."

*History with flashes of lightning.*

That's what the moguls tried to deliver.


2 In 1979 Kevin Brownlow and David Gill produced, directed, and wrote a thirteen-part series about the silent film for Thames Television in London. It was called *Hollywood*. And it exploded the vision that most of us had of a simple, slapdash land of silly people and silly stars making funny faces on the silversheet. All of a sudden the silent film had a poignancy that went far beyond Chaplin and D. W. Griffith. *Hollywood* celebrated the silents and all the "technicians" surrounding them—players, directors, camera-

men and others who witnessed a world that was so easy to forget after the talkies arrived.

The whole series was narrated by James Mason in his marvelous, silky voice that lent its melody to those images on the tube. And I wondered to myself: Why the hell couldn't an American team have made the series? With Nicholson as the narrator. Or De Niro. We could do *That's Entertainment*, celebrate ourselves with a wondrous crowd of MGM stars. Nostalgia, but no heartbreak. Fatty Arbuckle doesn't haunt *That's Entertainment*. Or Jack Gilbert. Or Clara Bow. It took the Brits to reveal our past to us, to record what the silents had become, stars lost in a silver cocoon.

But they weren't lost sixty years ago, when Hollywood's faces were seen and felt around the world. "We had one language," said journalist Adela Rogers St. Johns, "and Hollywood was it."

Without the babble of spoken dialogue, the stars could romance an entire planet with the aura of how they looked. Cecil B. De Mille put his favorite actress, Gloria Swanson, into sunken bathtubs invented in some designer's closet at Paramount, and those tubs created an international style. They were copied *everywhere*. No woman of fashion, on or off the screen, would dare exist without a tub that wasn't the size of a living room. And when she wasn't bathing for De Mille, Gloria had her own tub of black marble and beaten gold, for the movie princess she'd become. She wore the craziest gowns in De Mille's bedroom comedies, with peacock feathers like wings on her back. America dressed the way Gloria dressed. She was "the most imitated woman" in the world. And it wasn't because De Mille had turned her into a clotheshorse.

Swanson's kind of sensuality had never been seen before on the silversheet. She was the first actress who literally made love to the camera. De Mille called her "young fellah," and she called him "chief." But De Mille's "young fellah" could hypnotize an audience. Swanson had a carnality mingled with grace. While you watched her, your eyes blooded over and you wanted to bite her neck. She was available *and* remote, a shadow whose eyes and arms and mouth seemed to send off sparks that were hot and cold. It's dizzying to watch her climb down a flight of stairs, like some illumination that can walk, a lioness let out of her cage (she even lay down with a lion herself in one of De Mille's pictures); we can imagine the orchestra playing at the bottom of the stairs (all the silent stars would act to their favorite piece of music), and De Mille with his megaphone, cautioning his "young fellah," conducting each of her movements like a benevolent dictator.

And when Swanson lay down with that lion, went into the bowels of his den (in *Male and Female*), with hot breath in her ear, who was in danger—Gloria or the beast? The lion clawed a man to death two weeks after the scene was shot.

Recalling that lion in a conversation with Kevin Brownlow forty-five years after the shoot, Swanson said that the animal's trainers "cracked their whips till he roared. It felt like thousands of vibrators. Every hair on my body was standing straight up. I had to close my eyes. The last thing I saw was Mr. De Mille with a gun."

And then De Mille got her a gift "for being a brave boy."

I wonder about that confusion of genders. Gloria was young. But she was hardly a boy. Was it De Mille's need to deny that sexuality he saw? Or his manner of distancing himself and diffusing Gloria Swanson?

She became the biggest star of the early Twenties. She went to Paris, made *Madame Sans-Gêne,* married a marquis, had an abortion, nearly died, and returned to America for the premiere. There were banners for her on Sunset Boulevard. All of movieland had appeared for Gloria's homecoming. The crowds yapped and roared. The orchestra in Sid Grauman's Million Dollar Theater played "Home, Sweet Home."

Swanson was depressed at the premiere. She knew that all the fury wasn't for her, but for that icon she'd become, the movie goddess, "the personality who came back like Lazarus from the dead, Cinderella who married the prince . . ."

And the icon sneaked home with her mother and the marquis.

It's a story she loved to tell. Other icons would relive their own versions of the tale. Rita. Marilyn. And more.

But Swanson had a toughness that Rita and Marilyn lacked. And an irony about herself, a sense of play. "I had a fit being so short," she said (Swanson was five-two). She liked to call herself the runt. And if Rita and Marilyn felt ambiguous about their bodies, Gloria didn't. They had a kind of schizoid streak that doomed them, but the Twenties was a different time. It devoured goddesses with less of an appetite. It loved Gloria and the lion.

3 Swanson had another advantage. Pantomime preserved her. A silver shadow couldn't be eaten up so fast. "When sound started," said King Vidor, "that's when popcorn began. . . . In silent pictures you couldn't eat popcorn and do drinks, because you had to watch the screen all the time, and you had to interpret what was going on."

The audience couldn't rely on words. It watched. It listened to the music. There had been experiments with sound long before *The Jazz Singer*. Actress Viola Dana remembered doing talkies in the Teens, when she spoke words into a horn. But audiences booed at the tinny voices. They preferred their silent ghosts. And movieland seemed to rise out of strange barns near all the Hollywood bungalows. It had no real beginning, no logic. It was suddenly there. At a time when "every picture broke boundaries," recalled Agnes de Mille, Cecil's niece and one of the original "movies," those odd characters who'd come to the lemon groves, like a gypsy caravan. While the caravan settled in, films had to grope for a vocabulary and a form. Cecil, according to Agnes, saw himself as a precursor, a clay man who would help the next generation of filmmakers discover and define a new art. But Cecil didn't seem so modest to Adela Rogers St. Johns. "I think he gave God top place, but under that was De Mille."

Movieland became this curious Xanadu that the whole world wondered about, as if a tiny civilization had simply announced itself. It was the movies, after all, where anything could happen. And Hollywood had become its own biggest star.

It sent emissaries around the world, picture people as ministers of state. Mary and Doug arrived in Soviet Russia in 1926. Whatever its upheavals, Russia had more moviehouses than any other nation on earth. Moscow mobbed Little Mary and the Black Pirate, who couldn't wander into the most meager alley without being recognized. The two most famous shadows in the world had suddenly appeared on the streets of Moscow: it was an extraordinary shock, as if shadows wore flesh and could come waltzing out of the moviehouses, like America itself, a stunt only Hollywood could produce. A Soviet film was built around Mary. It was called *A Kiss from Mary Pickford*. Mary kisses a movie usher who idolizes her. That kiss is seen by a host of other people. The entire population hungers over the little man who is part of Mary now, and he's worshipped like a star.

It was the lesson of movieland. Mary Pickford had come down off the screen, and anything she touched was also an icon. That was the Twenties. Highkicking beauties with bobbed hair, the Black Pirate, Mary, Gloria, Von, and Cecil B. De Mille.

The marvel of Kevin Brownlow and David Gill (with their thirteen little epics about the silent era) was all the digging they did. Now one could sense the full range of the silents, from the first nickelodeons to Garbo and Gilbert in *Flesh and the Devil* and Gary Cooper. I wouldn't have known that Coop had been a silent star, since so much of him seemed invested in his voice. But he steals *Wings* (1927) from Richard Arlen, "Buddy" Rogers, and Clara Bow, with his one scene (as a doomed airman). He was romancing Clara at the time. She'd been getting him parts in her movies. And it was funny to think of Mr. Deeds doing pantomime without his slow, deliberate drawl.

I watched moments from a hundred movies, thanks to Brownlow and Gill, and I could hear those shadows "speak" without memorizing the title cards. I wasn't a blinking magician. But I could enter into that landscape of the silents, seize the melody of those films, and suddenly Garbo and Valentino and Doug were talking to me with the motion of their bodies.

I'd been wrong about Rudy. Valentino moved like a knife in *The Four Horsemen of the Apocalypse*. He didn't smirk so much. He was married to Natasha Rambova, who bungled his career. She was also in love with the actress Nazimova, who retired from the movies, took her Sunset Boulevard estate and turned it into the Garden of Allah, where Scott Fitzgerald lived for a while like a Hollywood bedbug and began to dream of Monroe Stahr.

Valentino hadn't been illiterate, as his studio liked to advertise. He'd come out of the middle class (his dad was an animal doctor in southern Italy). He arrived in America seeking adventure and was soon a male taxi dancer. He spent some time in the Tombs as a petty thief. He got to movieland, danced in a couple of ballroom scenes, and like a lot of extras, he slept around (with women and men) to help his career. *Four Horsemen* made him a star. Women fainted wherever Valentino went. He traveled to Rome and was disappointed by the reception. "In Italy I was just another wop."

He had contract disputes, lost Rambova, and died of a perforated ulcer at thirty-one. He was that secret object of desire. Valentino suggested the violence of romance. But if his own sexuality was ambiguous (Pola Negri would get cross with him because he "preferred making spaghetti . . . to making love"), he was, on screen, the "dark eyes" of the 1920s.

Erich von Stroheim also had dark eyes.

He was probably the most brilliant of all the silent directors. But he couldn't dance around Irving Thalberg. He was "tired of cinematic éclairs," audiences fattened with Hollywood cream puffs. So he did *Greed*. And cameraman Karl Brown, who worked with Von, felt there was a deliberate sense of debacle behind Stroheim's forty-two reels.

"Why did he do it? Somewhere early in his life he was visited by such great humiliation . . . there came in him this insane desire to use his genius as a weapon." Is Karl Brown playing Sigmund Freud with Von's gift as a moviemaker? One can imagine the humiliation that *might* have visited the child of a Jewish hatter in the land of the Hapsburgs and the Hohenzollerns. A perilous wound perhaps. The simple fact of his Jewishness in an empire of Christian kings. And so he transformed himself into the very person who would have despised him the most: the Hapsburg horseman, Erich von Stroheim. And he also became a "nobleman" in his art. Forcing Hollywood to accept his purity of line. He failed. Still bitter about movieland, he told his biographer as he lay dying in Paris: "This is not the worst. The worst is that they stole twenty-five years of my life."

And then there was Jack Gilbert and Clara Bow, the two most talented picture people of the Twenties, according to Adela Rogers St. Johns. Clara was born in Brooklyn in 1905. Her dad was a Coney Island waiter and her mom was crazy enough to have tried to kill Clara. She had a girlhood out of Dickens. She starved until she was sixteen, when she won a beauty contest that brought her out to Hollywood. By her eighteenth birthday she'd appeared in twenty-three films. And then she hit gold.

That moonface of hers appealed to the whole country. Clara Bow of the banjo eyes. The "It" girl who had an electric appeal. Clara was the original sex kitten. The first of her kind. She didn't have Swanson's iron will, or sunken bathtubs and gowns of peacock feathers. She was a child of the back alleys, a waif who could fall in love with lots and lots of men. In 1927 she juggled three boyfriends: director Victor Fleming, actor Gilbert Roland, and the Coop. She was never invited to Pickfair. The crown princes of Hollywood wouldn't sit with Clara. She was always an outcast, like Stephen Crane's Maggie, a girl of the streets. But she represented that new creature of the 1920s: the shopgirl gone wild. She sat on her boss' lap in *It,* hung there like a crazy kitten.

She had four fabulous years. She gambled all the time, and Paramount let her go into debt. She became a chattel of the studio. The papers began to list the boyfriends Clara kept in her closet. She sued her secretary, Daisy de Voe, for stealing money. There was a trial. Daisy talked. About drink and drugs and all the men in the closet. Clara had a breakdown. The moonface had lost its appeal. "Clara didn't exist off the screen," remembered Louise Brooks, another defeated movie soul. "She manufactured this whole person." The kitten who'd climb on your lap.

But the talkies had come to movieland, and the "It" girl was out. Suddenly she was an actress who had to learn her lines. All her instincts meant nothing now. The studio whispered about Clara's "microphone fright." She babbled in a couple of films, sounded like a Brooklyn brat. The delightful motion of her body was gone. She married cowboy star Rex Bell and withdrew into the depths of his ranch. Clara disappeared from the screen at the age of twenty-six, had bouts of mental illness, like her mom. You can't go home again, said Thomas Wolfe. Clara did. Into the wasteland of her own childhood. That fragile charm, the popping of the eyes, the impetuous moves, were only short leaps out of the darkness for Clara Bow.

And what about Jack?

Born in Logan, Utah, in 1897. His mom was a minor actress who took him on the road. Jack had no friends. Didn't go to school. His mom never gave him toys. She locked him in a closet when it was convenient for her. He went from theater to theater with his mom. Jack himself had become a toy, his mother's own rag doll. She'd wake him in the middle of the night and introduce him to her current lover. He had daddies all the time. Jack considered himself one more waif, like Clara Bow.

He was an extra in the movies before he was nineteen. Had his first featured role in *Bullets and Brown Eyes*. Soon he was playing the "other man" in comedies, Westerns, and historical romances. But it was the age of Valentino, and Jack Gilbert was just another dark-eyed man. He switched from Fox to MGM and that's when his career started to fire. He was Irving Thalberg's friend. He starred in *The Wolf Man* with Norma Shearer. He was in *The Merry Widow* and *The Big Parade,* the two best films of 1925. And critics began to talk of Jack's brown eyes, how much more expressive they were than The Sheik's. He'd become the biggest star in movieland, the most romantic of all the male screen lovers (Valentino died in 1926).

In 1927 he starred with an obscure Swedish actress in *Flesh and the Devil*. Louis B. Mayer had found her in Berlin. The ugly duckling, Greta Gustafsson, who failed her first screen test at MGM. Thalberg said she was impossible. Who would fall in love with such an awkward girl? Thalberg looked again. Gilbert was so popular he'd "carry" the Swede. But not even the Boy Wonder could have anticipated that electrical storm between Garbo and Gilbert. And Garbo didn't seem to act at all. She'd stare out at you with her penciled eyes, and it was like looking into a mask. Together with Gilbert, she inhabited a landscape that hadn't been seen before. A lyrical station of shadows that seemed to suggest hysteria under some marvelous control. Garbo whirled around Jack Gilbert and he pulled at her with his brown eyes.

There were stories of a love affair right on the set. Jack would go pale whenever Garbo appeared. Garbo would later deny that anything had happened between them during or after *Flesh and the Devil,* even though she lived at Jack's estate. No one could fathom Greta. "She was man, woman, and child," said actress Eleanor Boardman. "You can't pigeonhole Garbo." She was "extremely selfish, beautiful, strange." Garbo would walk around naked in front of Jack's guests. "She was completely unconscious, being Swede."

Jack himself wasn't an easy man to live with. "Jack Gilbert was . . . was mercury," said Leatrice Joy, his second wife. "You touch him and he vanished."

The talkies came, and Gilbert's career spun down and down. Audiences tittered at Jack, and a myth began: Gilbert couldn't make that transition to sound because of his high-pitched voice. His voice wasn't high at all. A little somber perhaps. It was his style that had gone out of fashion, the deep, dark-eyed lover. Valentino "would have suffered the same death had he lived," according to King Vidor. Jack stopped dancing with his eyes. "You couldn't put that image he had established into words . . . it becomes funny."

MGM wanted to retire his contract, pay him off if he agreed to stop acting. Gilbert refused. His pictures failed. He was forgotten while he was still on the screen. A melancholy talking ghost, Hamlet's little brother. Garbo rescued Jack, put him in *Queen Christina*. But that storm between them was gone. He was just another actor, mouthing his lines, and Garbo was Garbo. Gilbert drank his life away. He willed himself to die "in a beautiful, beautiful place up in the hills . . . surrounded by some rather attractive women and a lot of empty bottles."

4   It was the great upset, as Fitzgerald said in *The Last Tycoon*. The talkies had destroyed an entire era and at least some of its stars. The fabric of silent films became a fossil in a couple of years. This new skittery language of talking heads overturned the art of pantomime. And Hollywood wouldn't look back. It converted its glass houses into gloomy caverns and called them sound stages. And the irony was that the glass houses had been full of sound and fury: orchestras playing for the stars, carpenters sawing at sets, directors shouting into megaphones. It was the caverns that had to be silent to let the actors act.

The Black Pirate looked into one of those caverns with his art director, Laurence Irving, saw its heart of darkness, and said, "Laurence, the romance of motion-picture making ends here."

Doug was right and wrong. That powerful lyricism of the silents had disappeared, the shadows in constant motion. But the talkies brought an energy and verbal wit that would have doomed the silents no matter what. America had fallen in love with the radio, and it wanted radio talk on the screen. Doug retired. Mary retired. Pola Negri ran off to Berlin to become Hitler's favorite star. Swanson retired after a few years, an "old lady" of thirty-six or -seven. She made her first "comeback" in 1941, with Adolphe Menjou (another silent star) in *Father Takes a Wife*. It did no business at all.

And then there was *Sunset Boulevard,* directed by Billy Wilder, an Austrian refugee who got to America in 1934 and lived in the basement at the Garden of Allah, where he began scribbling screenplays. He starved for a couple of years until he met Charles Brackett and worked with him on *Ninotchka* and *Bluebeard's Eighth Wife*. The team prospered. Brackett produced and Wilder directed the material they wrote. *Five Graves to Cairo* (with Erich von Stroheim as Field Marshal Rommel). *Double Indemnity. The Lost Weekend. A Foreign Affair. Sunset Boulevard,* Wilder's last film with Brackett.

Both had come out of the silent era. Brackett was a novelist and drama critic during the Twenties. And Wilder was a screen-writer and something of a gigolo (in Berlin), like Joe Gillis, the character William Holden plays. *Sunset Boulevard* has the force of myth, because Wilder himself had swum in Hollywood's ectoplasm. The film could have been conceived in the basement at the Garden of Allah. We feel Norma Desmond's madness firsthand. It's caricature deepened with nightmare. Swanson and Stroheim are parodying themselves, playing out pathetic versions of their screen lives, as if we'd arrived at some fourth dimension, where fact and fancy existed under a crazy quilt.

"We didn't need dialogue," Norma says about the silents. "We had faces."

She sits in her mansion with Max von Mayerling (Stroheim) writing a script about Salome, whom she expects to play. "I'll have De Mille direct it," she tells Joe Gillis. "We made a lot of pictures together."

"I didn't argue with her," says Joe. "You don't yell at a sleepwalker."

Max von Mayerling drives Norma and Joe to Paramount

(Swanson's old studio), with its Alhambra-like gate. A few of the old grips recognize Norma, and she gets in. De Mille appears. He plays himself, of course. He's shooting a picture on the lot. He takes the time to see Norma Desmond.

"Hello, young fellah," he says.

And Norma answers, "We'll be working again, won't we, chief?"

Suddenly we have a time warp, and the whole damn century seems to bend. Swanson plays a madwoman, and the madwoman is Swanson herself. She's Cecil's "young fellah" again, just as she always was. And we, the audience, are caught in Hollywood's web; we no longer have boundaries, some safe line between the real and the unreal.

Either we've dreamt Norma, or Norma's dreamt us.

As we watch *Sunset Boulevard,* we become that "young fellah" De Mille was talking about. Phantoms of the moviehouse, ghosts on either side of the silversheet.

# Cowardly Lions and Forgotten Men

**1** Those dark caves that worried the Black Pirate turned into golden gardens quick enough. Stars suddenly bloomed all over the place. The stock market crashed just after talkies arrived, but there were no Black Fridays on the MGM lot. Hollywood rode across the Great Depression with a verbal and visual style that had nothing to do with poverty and heartbreak. America wanted movieland, not its own sad reflection in the mirror. It loved success stories, the rise (and fall) of gangsters and gold diggers. It was obsessed with that fantasy world of the rich. It walked into movie palaces that could have been conceived by Kubla Khan and searched for some emerald city on the screen, like that Venice where Ginger and Fred danced in *Top Hat,* with seaplanes sitting in a glass lagoon.

Such style and wit had become the mark of movieland, that America of our deepest desire. Whoever we were, midgets, morons, "ladies from cold-water flats," we longed for love at the movie palace. Most of the palaces had already been built before the coming of sound. The two greatest impresarios of the picture palace were Roxy Rothapfel in New York and Sid Grauman in Los Angeles.

Born in Minnesota in 1882, Roxy was like a Bedouin boy, drifting all over the place. He would put up nickelodeons in different towns, using bed sheets as a substitute screen. Roxy landed in New York and managed most of the earliest palaces. The Rivoli and the Capitol weren't enough. He wanted a palace named after him. He got it with the help of movie mogul William Fox, who invested millions in the Roxy, a palace on West Fiftieth. It could seat six thousand two hundred souls, while another four thousand waited in the lobby. It had its own hospital and enough electrical power to light a small city. Its screen "floated in a luminous mist." It had a chorus line, the Roxyettes, girls of "blinding blondness," a symphony orchestra with four conductors, and a battalion of ushers that always marched to a bugle call.

"Being a Roxy usher was a serious business and there was no room in the corps for weaklings." The ushers' shoes "glistened like limousine fenders, and their faces shone with goodness." It seemed like the most important job in the world, and it probably was. Rothapfel believed that future captains of industry would "hark back to their early training at the Roxy Theatre and say, as they sit behind their desks, 'God bless you, Roxy.' "

Sid Grauman modeled himself after Samuel Lionel Rothapfel. He was "Roxy West of the Rockies," born in Indianapolis on Valentine's Day in 1889. Another theatrical child, like Jack Gilbert. But Sid's mom never locked him in a closet. Before he was sixteen he ran a nickelodeon on Market Street in San Francisco. But the nickelodeon vanished in the earthquake and big fire of 1906. Sid wasn't scared. He and his dad found a bunch of church pews, shoved them inside a tent, and created a new "dreamland" in the midst of the rubble.

In 1917 he opened L.A.'s first real movie palace, the Million Dollar Theater. Unlike Roxy, who always presented a vaudeville show with individual acts to "frame" whatever picture was on the screen, Sid invented the Prologue, a kind of pageant with the same theme as the movie itself, so that there was never chaos at Grauman's Million Dollar Theater; every performance was "a complete unit."

Sid went to Hollywood and opened his Egyptian Theater in 1922. Five years later he opened the Chinese, which would become "the movie capital's . . . hall of fame," as the stars left their hand- and footprints in the wet concrete of Sid Grauman's Chinese court. The whole structure, with its footprints and pagodas, was insane, but that didn't stop it from becoming the most celebrated picture palace on earth. If, says Ben Hall, the Roxy was the Cathedral of the Motion Picture, "the Chinese was its High Pagoda."

Roxy died in 1936, without a palace, but Sid remained a movie king. "God does all my shows," he said. But the managers of most movie palaces weren't as lucky as Sid. They lost much of their clout after the talkies arrived. They weren't impresarios bringing in live acts, worrying over musicians. They turned into "candy salesmen." And suddenly "there was popcorn in paradise."

But a curious thing happened. The stage shows moved right onto the screen. Sound brought a new phenomenon: the musical film. Those girls with their blinding blondness were now kicking their feet up on the wall. And with the musical came a particular piece of furniture, the *nightclub,* where whole societies could strut. "According to Hollywood, nightclubs were vast modern temples where passion and pleasure could be played out on a great scale. Here, love affairs began and ended; fortunes were made and lost. . . . Human lives might collapse, but the orchestra kept playing and the crowds kept dancing on and on and on," wrote Howard Mandelbaum and Eric Myers in *Screen Deco.*

Of course Hollywood's nightclubs were like no other nightclubs in the world. Forests of glass, done in Art Deco, or the "modern" style, as it was called at the time. They were "dream clubs," where "people who had been studiously trying to avoid each other would meet face-to-face" and live out their fantasies and fears. It was as if *all* the characters of the Thirties were one enormous family that could dance and argue and kiss and say goodbye in an endless living room with a glass floor on which they could read their own reflections.

That equanimity would never come again. Movieland was movieland, and if many of the films were mediocre, they were never mean. But the very best of them, like *Trouble in Paradise, My Man Godfrey,* and *Top Hat,* had a flair and a look and a playful innocence that no other period could recapture.

The Depression hadn't seemed to poison our lives. Because *everybody* was poor, America could romanticize (and poke fun at) the rich, long for Art Deco skylines, the gleeful modernism of the gold digger. And because there was no marketplace for women to move into, they could occupy the screen in a manner they would never do again. From Joan Blondell to Jean Harlow, from Garbo to Dietrich to Crawford and Lombard, the Thirties presented a landscape where women were wiser and funnier and much, much sexier than men.

All those lovers of Fred Astaire ought to look at Ginger again, the gold digger of *42nd Street* who grabs the rich producer and retires from the chorus. In *The Great Movie Stars,* David Shipman says about one of Ginger's stage appearances almost fifty years after *42nd Street:* "The fact that she could not sing or dance well seemed immaterial, for she was a legend—thanks to Mr. Astaire." Who knows? Without Fred, Ginger might have flopped on her ass. But Fred would have been lost without Ginger. She had a beauty and a grace that never interfered with Fred, but always excited him.

And the truth is, Ginger's anger at Fred provides the locomotion for almost every film they were in together. She loves him, she hates him, and when they first meet in *Top Hat,* he says, "Every once in a while I find myself dancing."

"I suppose it's some kind of an affliction," she says.

And it's this affliction that brings them out on the floor. A kind of divinity comes to them, a divinity that hasn't been seen since Ginger and Fred. " 'Fred and Ginger,' " says critic Arlene Croce, "as we speak of them, are all the characters created by Fred Astaire and Ginger Rogers while they are dancing." That is, they exist beyond the tangibles of any plot, beyond that constant play of cat and mouse, as if the world were one huge nightclub for "Fred and Ginger," or Ginger and Fred. There's an erotic pull between them, a lovemaking in their moves, that's unique in American films. We've had an awful lot of wrestling since the Production Code was revised in 1966, but very little romance. That strange woman who'd leapt out of the chorus at the Brooklyn Paramount with her blinding blondness, that ferocious girl, and the pandalike guy who looks like Stan Laurel had discovered the very style of love on a Bakelite floor. Tender and fierce, the two of them are like energized dreamwalkers who'd found that perfect trance state.

It's no lie when Ginger says, after she gets angry at him again, that he'd made love to her while they danced and now she pretends not to like it. Fact is, she's a great comedienne, and she knows how to get under Fred's skin. She didn't have Garbo's classic face. She was "the working-class princess," that fabulous creature of the 1930s, who had to try very hard to be nice. But an angelic sweetness would have ruined their dance. And if she'd been a blueblood rather than the ambiguous girl who really shouldn't have had a room at the Ritz, would we have fallen for Ginger? Would she have troubled us all these years? No other time but the Thirties could have produced a Ginger, the reformed gold digger who was ferocious *and* gentle with Fred.

He was an aristocrat with no credentials other than his lithe walk. The son of a brewery worker, he started dancing professionally with his sister, Adele, before he was seven. Adele was eighteen months older than Fred and the star of the family. He danced in her shadow until Adele retired in 1932 and married a British lord. And Fred was like a little boy lost. He took a screen test. The moguls thought his ears were too big. But RKO signed him anyway. He didn't have much of a career until he danced the carioca with a certain Miss Rogers in *Flying Down to Rio* (1933).

Fred had to lose a sister before he could become a movie star. Adele had her lord and Fred had Ginger to fight with. Later she would leave him too and win an Academy Award. And he would inherit other partners, sexier girls, like Rita Hayworth and Cyd Charisse, with their long long legs. But when he danced with Rita and Cyd, it was "a world of sun without a moon."

And what a moon Ginger provided. She was more than "a faithful reflection," as Arlene Croce says. She brought that shy little man out of himself. She was constantly slapping Fred in the face. She couldn't love him without a slap. But while she danced with Fred, bent around his body, "as no other woman in the movies ever did, she created the feeling that stirs us so deeply when we see them together: Fred need not be alone."

Nor Ginger. Because she's trapped in that same Art Deco landscape, with figures on every door: kings, harlequins, archers, and nymphs. She became a bigger star than Astaire. But around him Ginger revealed a softness and a sense of comedy that she could never have with another man. He wooed her in a way that reached beyond vanity or sexual prowess. There was never acrobatics between them, or even carnal delight. But an erotic ideal that was never too bitter or too sweet.

2   And that's what the best of the Thirties was about. The elegance of Fred Astaire or William Powell, and the blinding blondness of Ginger Rogers, Carole Lombard, and Jean Harlow. They walked on some kind of magnificent glass that was an image of movieland itself. *The Adventures of Robin Hood, Gunga Din, The Good Earth, Lost Horizon,* and *Top Hat* were all shot "on location" in or around Hollywood. RKO built their Big White Set (Fred and Ginger's Venice) on two sound stages that were joined to form one monstrous cavern with its own lagoon and crazy Venetian bridges.

All the major studios had their own New York, London, Paris, Chicago streets. They were the best magicians in town. "There's Paramount's Paris, and Metro's Paris and of course, Paris, France. Paramount's is the most Parisian," said director Ernst Lubitsch, Paramount's chief of production at the start of the 1930s. It wasn't an idle boast that Lubitsch's Paris was more provocative on the screen than Paris, France. Half the world agreed with him.

French director René Clair liked to say that an artificial street "artificially lit can create *an impression of reality* more striking than the real street, which, when photographed, presents excessive or arbitrary contrasts."

It was the real thing that felt like a forgery. Movieland didn't have to travel to Europe or China by canoe. All it needed was the right kind of paint. Hollywood ventured abroad in the Thirties by going deeper and deeper into its own lots. No actual city could compete with it. Hollywood had become the world. Its image fell everywhere. So what if Marco Polo (Gary Cooper) landed in an Art Deco Peking? What could the Chinese know about China that Hollywood didn't? The Imperial City looked much better with Bakelite floors.

But the *monster* of the 1930s, the city that provided the motor for film after film, was New York. Fritz Lang discovered that dream city from the deck of the *Deutschland*. He'd arrived at night and "saw a street lit as if in full daylight" with "oversized luminous advertisements moving, turning, flashing on and off, spiraling . . . something which was completely new and nearly fairy-tale-like for a European in those days, and this impression

gave me the first thought of an idea for a town of the future."
He left the *Deutschland* and drifted into that fairy-tale Manhattan, where the buildings "seemed to be a vertical veil, shimmering, almost weightless, a luxurious cloth hung from the dark sky to dazzle, distract and hypnotize. At night the city did not give the impression of being alive; it lived as illusions lived. I knew then that I had to make a film about all these sensations."

The film he made was *Metropolis,* a wondrous prototype of the modern city-state, which feels more and more like a plausible plan for Manhattan 2005, where the wealthy will live in hanging gardens of "luminous cloth" and the poor will inherit all the caves inside Manhattan's bowels. But Lang wasn't thinking like a Hollywood producer, even though that dream city he saw would have been recognizable to any mogul.

It was modernism's big black heart, where gangsters dwelled among the nouveau riche, where dancers danced and gold diggers searched for their ultimate daddy. It was the town of chorus girls and business tycoons, millionaires who muttered absently while their daughters played and their wives adopted artistes and their butlers spoke better English than they ever would. It had nothing to do with a literal New York, caught in the midst of the Depression, with apple peddlers everywhere and little cardboard cities in Central Park. Its shoreline housed shack after shack. There were Hoovervilles under every bridge. But most of the blight was ignored, or sugared over to suggest a kind of happy, singing, dancing hobo jungle, where bank presidents down on their luck always had a second chance. There weren't any women, of course, in Hollywood's Hoovervilles. Only men were allowed to be homeless, as long as they looked like William Powell. Women were too busy being chased after by Broadway producers to get stuck without an address. Guys like Powell could fall from grace and become a "forgotten man," but there were no "forgotten women" around.

And so we have a series of urban fairy tales, either gangster films, or backstage musicals, or romantic comedies about the rich, or Cinderella stories about shopgirls who marry the boss (or the boss's son); it was always a rise to power in that magical land of skyscrapers, the Hollywood "Manhattan." The most beloved character of the 1930s didn't even have a human face. He was an animated cartoon, King Kong, who stands on top of the Empire State Building with Fay Wray and swats airplanes out of the sky. *King Kong* was about beauty and the beast, but the beast wasn't Kong, who'd never have harmed Fay. It was New York City, monster town that could eat up love-sick gorillas. Kong was the big hairy child who couldn't make it in Manhattan. One more hick.

The film opened at the Roxy *and* Radio City, and filled eleven thousand seats every night. It's a fable that has never ceased to haunt us. It lives in the nation's blood. Kong is the pure American primitive caught in Manhattan's web. He was movieland's song to itself, all the magic that Hollywood could produce. In that strange war between movieland and Manhattan, movieland always won.

But Hollywood was only warring with itself. Because its Manhattan had no more substance than one of Lubitsch's Paris streets. It was conjured up in Culver City, or Burbank, or behind Paramount's gate. It was dreamtown, the cinematic village that represented all spectacular rises and falls.

In writing about the gangster, that archetype of the Thirties, critic Robert Warshow hints at the curious marriage among gold-digging, crime, and the modern dream city. America, Warshow reminds us, is the land of happy people, "committed to a cheerful view of life." An aristocratic place, like England or France, could afford a sense of gloom. Because the individual's fate didn't determine the country's politics. You were born into a class and died there. Whatever leap you made, whatever rise, was *always* within the particular order of things. The grocer's son could become a rich merchant, could even marry the daughter of a duke, but that didn't make him an aristocrat. There were boundaries, and it was almost impossible to break through such thick, invisible walls.

But there were no boundaries in the land of happy people. "Aristocrats" were created almost overnight. There was only one card to play, and that card was cash. A bootlegger like Joe Kennedy could manufacture his own kingdom of fabulous sons. Because America had no historical past. It was the first modern country. America had given birth to itself. It could celebrate the Marquis de Lafayette for his part in our little revolution, but it couldn't create a genuine marquis. It loved aristocrats: there were more uprooted barons and princes in Hollywood during the Twenties and Thirties than in any other town on earth. Most of them ate at Pickfair. Some of them entered the movies as extras and grips. A lot of them were fakes, like Mike Romanoff, the "prince" who started his own restaurant in the Thirties. His Imperial Highness Prince Michael Alexandrovitch Dmitri Obolensky Romanoff was also Harry Gerguson, a Lithuanian immigrant and a jailbird who'd been kicked out of several countries. But Harry/Mike belonged in movieland, where he was a fraud among frauds, who "became more widely admired, feted, and entertained as a famous impostor than he ever had been in the days when he was accepted as the real thing." And which of us is so different from Harry?

We've always been a country struggling to define ourselves. Ah, if only Father George had been a little less egalitarian and agreed to become America's first king. Then we might have had a chance. Aristocracies could have sprung out of nowhere. George could have knighted whoever pleased him. And we'd have developed a kind of cousinship with the British throne. But our gentlemen farmers chose the democratic way; it was a narrow democracy, reserved for landed gents. But the damnable idea began to spread. And without a real king, or at least a prince who could have ruled from some palace farm, the idea of a particular class could never stick. Oh, we could have the Sons and Daughters of the Revolution, and *Mayflower* parties, but what did it all mean? It was the purse that ruled from the very beginning. And our presidents, *even* George, were only middlemen between different power brokers who barked at them. And always in the background, lying there like a rotten wound, was the half-memory of that mad king, George III, our own little father whom we decided to forget.

And dynasties began, based on a Constitution and a Bill of Rights which declared that the pursuit of happiness was the privilege of every man, so long as he had the least bit of property and wasn't black. Things would have been fine if it hadn't been for the Civil War. The South, with all its ingrown habits, had managed to maintain the illusion of aristocracy. And then it was gone. America was thrust into a modern world of immigrants, with all their infernal babble. But the immigrants discovered how to read. And they went after the same pursuit of happiness, the same ideals that the Founding Fathers believed in. And so that terrible distance was created between possibility and dream, between those democratic ideals and the backbreaking need to survive and earn one's bread. And just at that time, the Wizard of West Orange, Thomas Alva Edison, helped invent this new machine that could hurl shadows on a wall, and America saw its own sad and ghostly face in constant motion.

The war came. Then Prohibition and the big crash. And out of this odd curl of events the gangster was born, that creature of the cities who had his own idea of happiness and knew how to get it. He was ruthless more often than not. He wasn't surrounded by romance. He was in hot pursuit of cash. But he did play upon America's belief in success, and he had a kind of anarchy that seemed to mirror that *other* side of our lives, the secret side that resisted law and order, just like Father George had done. George was our first and biggest gangster.

"The gangster," says Robert Warshow, "is the man of the city, with the city's language and knowledge, with its queer and dishonest skills and its terrible daring." But the landscape he inhabits is only another dream, "that dangerous and sad city of the imagination . . . which is the modern world."

But that dreamland, whether it's called Chicago or New York, is some Manhattan of the mind that took root in the 1930s, planted itself in celluloid. There'd been lots of gangsters in the silent era. But that mythical gangster Warshow mentions arrived with sound. The gangster has to talk, not because what he says is remarkable or eloquent or even necessary. It's because speech is his one identifying mark. What could Little Caesar have been without his snarl? "Mother of God, is this the end of Rico?" says Little Caesar after he's shot. No title card could have preserved that line. It needed the acid of Edward G. Robinson's voice.

Jack Gilbert could make love to millions of women with his dark brown eyes. The talkies doomed him; all his gestures seemed redundant now. But the gangster's menace could only come with the music of his voice. He was the first hero of the talkies. And part of him inhabited every other hero. Like most modern men, he was "without culture, without manners, without leisure," the way we often think of Clark Gable. But he's also "graceful, moving like a dancer among the crowded dangers of the city," a little like Fred Astaire. He pushes people around, bullies them, lies, like Julian Marsh (Warner Baxter), the musical comedy director in *42nd Street*. In fact, most of the backstage musicals featured impresarios like Warner Baxter, James Cagney, and Warren William, who were as ruthless as Little Caesar. They weren't dealers of stolen goods, hitmen, or beer barons in Hell's Kitchen and Chicago's South Side. They didn't fall in love with their own sister, like Scarface. None of them had time for love.

Julian Marsh works on Broadway, but he's an outlaw, and outlaws work alone. He has producers, assistants, stagehands, and stars, but he stitches a musical together with the force of his own will. Julian is dying, and *Pretty Lady* will be his last show. We never see him coughing in the dark. We don't know where he lives. He's the phantom of Broadway. He hires a thug to beat up Bebe Daniels' boyfriend, because the producer of *Pretty Lady* is in love with her and might abandon Marsh if he discovers that Bebe Daniels has a beau. But Bebe breaks her ankle and can't perform on opening night in Philadelphia. Peggy Sawyer (Ruby Keeler) is plucked out of the chorus. Julian becomes her jailer now. He locks her in a big closet and teaches her all the tunes. Of course Ruby Keeler dances her head off and saves the show. "Sawyer," Julian says, "you're going out a youngster, but you're coming out a star."

And Julian Marsh? We meet him in the alley after the show, exhausted, alone. He can't find any nourishment from his own success. His enterprise gets him nowhere. He can only live inside the "wilderness" of the show, as if it were some cruel animal that devours while it sustains, like that old American drive for success. Like Scarface and Little Caesar, Julian can't win. Because whatever "victory" he has pulls him toward his own doom.

3   Women in the Thirties often had the same subversive role—that is, they undercut that song of success America always loved to sing about itself. Harlow, Lombard, Stanwyck, Ginger Rogers, Dietrich, Myrna Loy, and Mae West seemed to wiggle around their men like snake charmers. The Thin Man, William Powell, would have been lost without his wife, Myrna Loy, who was always dizzy and getting in the way of the plot. She could create short circuits with her

cockeyed remarks. And it didn't matter that the Hays Office obliged Nick and Nora Charles to sleep in separate beds. Nora gave off a lot of sparks, and she had one of the few screen marriages that really worked. Nick and Nora didn't have to dance out their marriage on a Bakelite floor. A drunken lasciviousness surrounds their every move, so that *The Thin Man* exists in a state of constant turmoil. It's a film about chaotic play, and the "mystery" that Nick solves as all the characters sit around a table is only another form of chaos.

Myrna Loy wasn't the only partner Powell danced with. Watch him in *My Man Godfrey*. From the opening credits, delivered from a mock Manhattan skyline of neon letters and lights, the film is a Depression fairy tale with the wackiest Cinderella we've ever seen . . . and the most unconventional prince. Powell plays Godfrey Smith, a hobo who's minding his own business until his cardboard palace is invaded by Cornelia Bullock (Gail Patrick), a Park Avenue girl. Cornelia is looking for a "forgotten man" whom she can take back to the Waldorf-Ritz Hotel as part of a scavenger hunt. She offers Godfrey five dollars. "If I find a forgotten man first," she says, "I win."

Godfrey growls at her and Cornelia goes away. Then her sister, Irene (Carole Lombard), comes out of the shadows. She's recovering from a nervous breakdown. Irene has never won anything in her life. She explains to Godfrey that a scavenger hunt is like a treasure hunt, but the difference is, "you try to find what nobody wants." A forgotten man.

Godfrey agrees to go with her to the scavenger ball at the Waldorf-Ritz. The hotel is like a madhouse, crawling with millionaires. Irene presents Godfrey to the master of the hunt. The master is suspicious. He looks at Godfrey and asks: "What is your address?"

"City Dump Thirty-two, East River, Sutton Place," Godfrey says, and Irene wins the hunt.

"Can you butle?" she asks, and hires Godfrey as the family butler. "You're the first protégé I've ever had." Godfrey Smith turns out to be Godfrey Park, a Boston blueblood, and he not only "butles," he saves Irene's family from financial ruin and opens a nightclub called The Dump, where Dump Thirty-two had been. And Irene moves into The Dump and marries the man.

Everything is kosher, of course. Powell was an aristocrat even with a scruffy beard. And his metamorphosis from bum to butler to nightclub entrepreneur (he hires all the other hoboes from Dump Thirty-two) satisfies our sense of order. The film hasn't dated because it doesn't really judge. Godfrey isn't better than the Bullocks. And Irene would be just as wacky if she weren't so rich. We've entered a comic universe, not a proletarian dreamscape where rich and poor are obliged to battle it out. Godfrey calls the millionaires at the scavenger ball "a bunch of nitwits." And they are. But the scene at the ball isn't Marxist melodrama. It's funny and full of a maddening life. With animals and junk and one forgotten man being bartered for points by men and women who are out of their skulls.

And if Godfrey walks through the chaos of the film, Lombard is the whirlwind who surrounds Godfrey and captures him. She was, said Bing Crosby, "one of the screen's greatest comediennes and, in addition, she was very beautiful. The electricians, carpenters and prop men all adored her because she was so regular; so devoid of temperament and showboating. . . . The fact that she could make us think of her as being a good guy rather than a sexy mamma is one of those unbelievable manifestations impossible to explain."

She'd also been married to William Powell once upon a time, and that gave the film an added comic twist. She was chasing her own ex-husband through *My Man Godfrey*. And she startles us, because we've met a beautiful woman who isn't subtle or quiet. Lombard schemes like a child. She could play the gold digger or a millionairess with the same delicious feel for the madcap. It's almost as if the Marx Brothers had found a sister of their own, a beautiful sister with a blinding blondness and long legs. She tore through Hollywood's love of snobbery and high seriousness about itself and created a universe where anything, anything goes.

**4** I marvel at the "literacy" some of those Thirties films had, the machine-gun dialogue of *His Girl Friday* (released in 1940, but made in 1939), the wit of *Twentieth Century,* the surreal explosions of *Duck Soup,* the sexual play of *I'm No Angel,* the delightful doublecrossing of

*Trouble in Paradise,* the bordertown romance of *Destry Rides Again* (with Dietrich as the classiest whore of the Wild West), the deadpan fun of *Ninotchka* (where Garbo revealed what a comedienne she was), the utter lunacy of *Bringing Up Baby,* the endless chatter of *Gunga Din.* . . . . All this narrative intelligence, the faith in an audience's willingness to listen, disappeared soon after 1939.

Pauline Kael believes that the style of the Thirties didn't come from the moguls or their stars, but from their very own vassals, that tribe of invisible people, the screenwriters of MGM and Paramount and Warners and Fox, those bedbugs who lived at the Garden of Allah, worked in windowless rooms, punched their lives into a timeclock, sacrificed their own talents to prepare a diet of pages for the moguls every day, sunned themselves like lizards on a rock, turned into hacks. "Hollywood destroyed them, but they did wonders for the movies." Unappreciated and overpaid, such Hollywood bedbugs "may for a brief period, a little more than a decade, have given American talkies their character."

The best of them "brought movies the subversive gift of sanity." They sabotaged the old classics, until suddenly "all the Dumas and Sabatini and Blasco Ibáñez . . . had to compete with the freedom and wildness of American comedy."

But the bedbugs paid a price. A kind of self-hatred settled in, an understanding that much of what they did was fools' work. "They had gone to Hollywood as a paid vacation from their playwrighting or journalism, and screenwriting became their only writing. The vacation became an extended drunken party, and while they were in the debris of the morning after, American letters passed them by. They were never to catch up; nor were American movies ever again to have in their midst a whole school of the richest talents of a generation."

It's difficult to argue with Kael. "Raising Kane" is a marvelous elegy to the screenwriters of the Thirties, most of whom were underground men and women (bedbugs). And they did undermine the moguls in their own way and fashion a sense of high jinks that flavored so many films. But they couldn't have done it all alone. I'm not talking about the directors and the stars, who cooperated in this "sabotage," and whoever it was that approved their scripts and allowed all that horseplay to get on the screen. I'm talking about the moviegoers, who cared even less about writers than the moguls did. Audiences stopped reading the credits after the stars' names appeared. Herman Mankiewicz or Morrie Ryskind meant nothing to them. Ryskind had worked on *Animal Crackers, A Night at the Opera,* and *My Man Godfrey.* But who would have noticed? Hollywood needed writers once the talkies arrived, and despised them because of that very need. All of a sudden the screenplay mattered. Little Caesar and Julian Marsh couldn't function without dialogue. And the studios brought in writers like so many carpenters, practically paid them by the word. The moguls would have chopped them dead, cut off their hands and feet, if they hadn't discovered that audiences were laughing and crying at those lines the "carpenters" wrote.

Who the hell was this audience that jumped from twenty million a week in 1930 to over eighty million by 1939? Sixty percent of the population. They weren't college professors. They were no more clever than people are today. Yet they supported a visual style, a grace, a simple charm that makes us seem like children.

That movie Manhattan they feared and admired, that dreamtown where Ginger and Fred sometimes lived and danced, where Julian Marsh worked on his last musical, where Godfrey Smith rose up out of his ashpile to "butle" for the Bullocks, where Nick and Nora Charles romped with their cowardly little dog Asta, was much more vivid than any other Manhattan, before and after. Was it because, having so little themselves, audiences could enter into that night song of the movies, could go much, much deeper into the dream culture Hollywood had manufactured for them? It was a time when films were more than crucial; they held the country together with common icons, common ideals.

If the features provided a fairy tale of success, a magical curtain where kids behaved like grown-ups, and grown-ups could act out their most infantile wish, then there was also the newsreel, which had its own romance, as it looked out at all those peculiar events outside the grip of Hollywood and fabulated them, turned them into monsters of the moment. Lou Gehrig crying in front of the cameras on his last day in a Yankee uniform; Hitler "seducing" sixty thousand souls at some Sportpalast, with his dream of a thousand-year Reich; a giant balloon blow-ing up in New Jersey and disappearing in front of your eyes; and most of all, a president like a great fish out of water, crip-pled and godlike, because you never saw his crutches or his wheelchair, but he stood on a podium with his eldest son at his side, laughing, smiling, wagging that enormous head, and some-how you felt safe. He smoked Camel cigarettes. He had a dog named Fala and a wife named Eleanor, who'd descend into coal mines or visit Louis B. Mayer at MGM, even though Mayer despised the president. Roosevelt was the country's own movie star. He smiled just like Gable. And like Gable himself, there was nothing that smile couldn't win or erase.

And so a frightened country felt secure at the movies, whether it was a palace in Milwaukee or a bijou near the woods, with moldy pictures of half-forgotten stars behind the candy counter. It was hallowed ground, a piece of Hollywood itself. And be-cause the audience *believed* in movieland, it could accept more and more from those talking heads. It might stay home when Gable played Parnell, because he looked funny in Irish pants. It might fall out of love with Miss Shearer. But it was faithful to the movies. And an odd sophistication developed, an ability to intuit and slip into those psyches on the screen, join the ghosts up on the wall. It wasn't mindless adoration, though Crawford had fan clubs throughout the country that exchanged letters about the clothes she wore and the tiniest details of her life.

The Thirties had created a nation of movie addicts, forgotten women and men who visited moviehouses with such regularity they could follow the entire career of a favored star. The Roxy became a hangout and a home to half the population of Man-hattan. And you could find little Roxys everywhere, palaces that waltzed you right out of the Depression. Audiences gave them-selves to the movies, and expected more from them. They were, as *The New York Times* said of Gable after his death, as certain as the sun.

And it was within this bounty that movies flourished without the least sense of bile. There were few corrosive fairy tales. Being poor, America dreamed rich. If blacks and Jews and Italians were caricatured, or made invisible in the movies' magic lamp, it was because America itself wasn't ready to look. It lay in deep slumber, like some giant dozing in a tree, a big Protestant giant who climbed down once or twice a week to visit movieland. And in the movies that giant saw, the gangster was Italian or Irish, the porter was always black, and the Jewish lawyer had the loudest clothes.

The moguls themselves had bought the dream of some Middle America, where Andy Hardy lived with his dad, the judge, in a world of eager white faces. "The products of the dream became its creators," as the moguls packaged a mythic country, *movieland,* for a perpetual Kansas, their ideal American audience. They were their own Wizards of Oz, half fraud, half magician, who wanted to take all of us, including themselves, to that place Judy Garland dreamed of, "behind the moon, beyond the rain." The Emerald City of Oz, where tin men went looking for a heart, scarecrows longed for a brain, cowardly lions sought the courage they never had, and Dorothy, the bravest of them all, decided she'd had enough. The Emerald City was okay for a little while. But she was a Kansas girl. "There's no place like home," says Glinda, the good witch, and Judy Garland agreed.

She was sixteen when she made *The Wizard of Oz*. She'd come from Minnesota, but she might as well have been born in Kansas, like Dorothy. There was a sexiness to her that animated the film, like a woman who seemed to flower from an ordinary little girl. The whole film was about metamorphosis. Kansas becomes Oz. Miss Gulch becomes the wicked witch. The farm hands, Hunk, Zeke, and Hickory, become the Scarecrow, the Tin Man, and the Cowardly Lion. The huckster, Professor Marvel, becomes the Wizard. Dorothy goes through a dream storm with her dog Toto, wakes up, marches out her door, and arrives in Oz, as the film turns from black-and-white to Technicolor, and Dorothy herself becomes a witch much more powerful and sexy than the wicked Witch of the West.

All the little people, the Munchkins of Munchkinland, are in love with her. So are the Lion, the Tin Man, and the Scarecrow. She destroys the wicked witch, exposes the Wizard of Oz with the help of her dog, gets him to give a heart to the Tin Man, courage to the Lion, and a brain to the Scarecrow. Then Dorothy rescues herself from Oz and becomes a little girl again in a Kansas of good old black-and-white. "Oh, Auntie Em," she says, "there's no place like home."

And the moguls believed her.

Garland is the perfect woman-child in *The Wizard of Oz*. But the wonder of the film is Bert Lahr as the Cowardly Lion. His comic genius takes us outside Munchkinland. He growls at Dorothy when he meets her. She slaps his face. He starts to cry. "Is my nose bleeding?" he asks. And suddenly we've moved from L. Frank Baum to Samuel Beckett (Lahr would play another Cowardly Lion in *Waiting for Godot*). When his companions ask him why he doesn't count sheep to calm himself, he wags his tail and says, "That don't do any good. I'm afraid of them."

It's this that the Thirties provided. A comic bent inside the fairy tale. Lahr isn't a morbid, bitter lion. He's much funnier than any witch. He energizes *The Wizard of Oz,* much like W. C. Fields did as Micawber in *David Copperfield* (1935). Both performances lend an enchantment to each particular film, take us outside the normal boundaries of time. Looking at Micawber and the Cowardly Lion, it's hard to believe that they happened fifty years ago. They do not carry all the freight of self-importance, of an actor caught in a role. If Charles Laughton had played Micawber, as he was meant to do, it would have been another "memorable" performance, like his Rembrandt or the Hunchback of Notre Dame. But would we laugh fifty years later at Micawber's bulbous nose and skinny legs?

If the moguls had Kansas on their mind, if they shoved movieland into the heart of the heart of the country, there was, at least, a wealth of Cowardly Lions within their flattened America, a comic pull that livened the land of Oz.

# eight

# Dancing in the Dark (With Dick Powell)

**1** Almost two years before she played that sexy little witch who encourages the Cowardly Lion and exposes the Wizard of Oz, Judy Garland was a chubby child who sucks on lollipops in *Broadway Melody of 1938* (1937). Betty Clayton lives in a boardinghouse for all those untalented souls who hover around Broadway, looking for the big chance that never comes. *Broadway Melody* creaks along like some tired old horse. But the film has one incredible moment. Betty is in her room at the boardinghouse, writing a fan letter to Clark Gable. She looks at his photograph with such adoration we want to climb up onto the screen and comfort her.

"Honest Injun," she says, "you're my favorite star."

And suddenly she sings "Dear Mr. Gable (You Made Me Love You)," and it's as if she'd discovered the secret nerve of the whole damn country. It was Gable's time. He was the king who'd come out of obscurity with his big ears. His teeth were rotten, and MGM had to give him a new mouth. Women adored him, and men wanted to be like Gable. He was, as Paul Newman said, "a man of extreme relish." His first two wives were older women whom he'd called "Ma." He'd carried on a long, lazy romance with Joan Crawford in between her husbands and his wives. Then he married Carole Lombard in 1939, the year he made *Idiot's Delight* . . . and *Gone With the Wind*.

*GWTW* was no easy matter. Producer David O. Selznick had conducted a three-year campaign to find Scarlett O'Hara. A national hysteria had formed around the role. When Norma Shearer decided she didn't want to play Scarlett (she would have been stupendous as a cross-eyed Southern bitch), *The New York*

*Times* scolded her in an editorial. It was almost unpatriotic of Norma to remove herself from the race. The country was going out of its mind with Scarlett fever. "Who cared if Chamberlain appeased Hitler at Munich? The only important question was who would play Scarlett O'Hara."

But there had never been any doubt concerning Rhett Butler. The public "demanded" Gable get the part. When the king started to waver, feeling he couldn't live up to the expectations all of Margaret Mitchell's readers had of Rhett, the public itself "turn[ed] producer, assuming responsibility for the creation of the film."

The king was captive to his own subjects. It was movieland, after all. And the king of movieland was as problematical as the Wizard of Oz. He ruled with that smile of his, and his mustache, but he understood the territory he was in. "We all have a contract with the public. . . . They love to put us on a pedestal and worship us and form fan clubs and write thousands of letters telling us how great we are. But *they've* read the small print, and most of *us* haven't—they expect us to pay the price for it all . . . we have to get it in the end."

Yet nothing seemed to get at Gable in 1939. He played Harry, the song-and-dance man, in *Idiot's Delight,* and this time he wore an undershirt, so the haberdashers wouldn't get angry and have to consider any drop in sales when Gable was on the screen. He danced to his own rendering of "Puttin' on the Ritz." And there was such pleasure in his moves, such delight, people forgot he wasn't Fred Astaire. It was almost as if he were dancing to the decade. There were no cobwebs to the king. The world he inhabited was never gray. Mel Brooks delivered his own kind of homage to the king in *Young Frankenstein* (1974), when Peter Boyle, as the Frankenstein monster, also does "Puttin' on the Ritz," to a crowd of unfriendly scientists. It's the funniest moment in the film; the monster, witless, profoundly clever and dumb, is a movie addict, like the rest of us.

But I was talking of Gable and *Gone With the Wind*. It was Hollywood as high romance, that love duel between Scarlett (Vivien Leigh) and Rhett. Such obsessive clarity wouldn't come again. Tara was only a paper house, a mansion without rooms, but the whole film was peopled with marvelous children in a storybook South. There isn't a character in David O. Selznick's population who seems to have advanced much beyond puberty. Scarlett is a brat and a gold digger who finally can't get her way. And Rhett is a pirate who disappears to his own private kingdom. The blacks are all good or bad children. The white women are whores or wallflowers and belles. The men are scalawags or chivalrous fools with poetry in their blood.

*GWTW* has its own dumb energy and innocence that haven't dated at all. The film never doubts itself. Selznick had fifteen writers working on the script (including Scott Fitzgerald), and three directors, but that's only because an epic needs many, many hands. The South he presented was a dream world where a tarnished princess would lose her pirate prince out of greed and a lust to keep alive. Scarlett's emotions are so transparent, her desires so visible to us, that she becomes the beautiful, petulant child we've all hungered to be, where our only condition is to want, want, want.

Thalberg had turned down the rights to Margaret Mitchell's novel; no Civil War film, he said, had ever made a dime. The Boy Wonder was wrong. Civil War or not, the South was one of movieland's favorite subjects. And *GWTW* was our second great epic of the South. D. W. Griffith had traveled into that country long before David O. Selznick. But it was the same dark thicket, darker even, because *The Birth of a Nation* (1915) had to deal with the primitive psychology of its time. And it's a much more honest film. The Klansmen in *GWTW* don't wear masks. They simply ride out like aristocrats to save Scarlett O'Hara.

Selznick's dad hadn't been a Kentucky colonel during the Civil War, like D. W. Griffith's. D.W. grew up with that war in his head both as fable and fact. He was born in 1875, in the last years of Reconstruction, when the defeated South was still an occupied land. And in *The Birth of a Nation* Griffith wanted to show "the dark side of the wrong" that had been done to the South.

The entire film is suffused with sexual hysteria, as greedy blacks and mulattoes eye Southern belles in the Piedmont of South Carolina. The Northern radical, Austin Stoneman, with his clubfoot and peculiar, helmetlike hat of hair, becomes a virtual "dictator" after Lincoln's death, the uncrowned king of Reconstruction. Stoneman has a mulatto mistress, and his chief lieutenant is a mulatto named Lynch. Lynch would like to marry Stoneman's daughter (Lillian Gish) as soon as he turns South Carolina into his own vassalage.

Griffith takes us through "the last grey days of the Confederacy," where we meet "the little Colonel," Ben Cameron, who carries the Confederate colors across a battlefield and stuffs his flag into the bowels of an enemy cannon. And that's how the war ends for the little Colonel. He comes home to a town that's in the hands of black politicians and troops, with their mulatto overlord, Lynch. And it's the little Colonel who rescues the town with his own partisan army, wearing the robes of the KKK. He's the guy who gets to marry Lillian Gish.

Of course *The Birth* can be seen as racist melodrama. But it explores mines deeper than that. The "nation" that's born again is a new mythical South that's part of the U.S. and also has its own invisible boundaries, boundaries that cannot be touched by carpetbaggers or Northern blacks: some nation of the mind, like movieland itself, where little colonels can marry without the trouble of sex. In fact, Griffith was able to visualize the underlying fears of a country that was still caught in the slumber of Victorian times. The only sexual act the little Colonel performs is with that cannon. He never smirks or leers like the mulattoes in the film, who are *always* dangerous because they remind us of their own sexual origins, the "union" of white and black. They aren't characters; they're walking symbols of copulation, the somber side of American life.

Christ appears at the wedding of the little Colonel and Lillian Gish, and all the mulattoes have vanished from the frame.

But by 1939 sex was a commodity that David O. Selznick was allowed to sell. Hollywood had become the great American Babylon, which had to be controlled, or the country would fall into a huge libidinous well. Producers had to get around the censors and package sex. And Gable was the perfect dream package. The "mulatto" of Griffith's time had suddenly turned white. Rhett Butler could look at Scarlett and lick his chops. The forbidden had entered the movie palace. Gable wasn't lovesick, like Jack Gilbert. He didn't have moon eyes. He wanted Scarlett. He got Scarlett. And when he stopped wanting her, he went back to whatever pirate ship he'd come from in the first place.

"The only thing that kept me a big star has been revivals of *Gone With the Wind,*" Gable told Selznick. The king was perhaps a little too modest, but *GWTW* did remain America's number-one blockbuster for thirty years . . . until it was replaced in the country's ethos by *The Godfather* saga. Don Corleone was a new kind of pirate. But he couldn't kiss like Clark Gable.

Nobody could.

2 It was a happy marriage, the king and Carole. She wasn't constantly molding, molding her career, like Joan Crawford, who went from jazz baby to gold digger to shopgirl to sophisticated mama at MGM, and married the young prince of Pickfair, Douglas Fairbanks Jr. Carole was a comedienne. She wasn't so involved with the business of being a star. Lombard preferred her anonymity, even when she was promoting herself for Paramount. "She went shopping down Fifth Avenue with a studio publicist," William Holden recalled. "The publicist said, 'It's amazing. No one recognizes you.' 'That's simple,' she said. 'It's because I don't want them to.' Then she tossed her blond hair back and swung her mink coat and people started asking her for autographs. 'See what I mean?' she said."

But she wasn't so anonymous with Gable. She could move in and out of that manly universe of his; hunt, fish, and play. She was coming home from a war-bond rally in 1942 when her plane crashed into a mountain and Carole was killed. The king never really recovered. He joined the Army Air Corps, "and to many moviegoers that was a deprivation on a level with meat-rationing."

But he couldn't keep wooing Scarlett O'Hara again and again. Lombard's death had aged him. The old smile was gone. And something else was also gone. That powerful wit and energy that the Thirties had sprung upon America and helped make the king a star. The nation went on a sentimental journey for most of the war. It was the time of Betty Grable and Bing Crosby and Abbott and Costello: crooners and comics and pinup girls, and films about the Marines and the Seabees, where John Wayne could go back to Bataan and Errol Flynn could parachute over

Burma . . . and Judy Garland could take us back to St. Louis in 1903 and sing "The Trolley Song."

The gold digger had already been dead for a long time. Girls stopped chewing gum. They sat around the house and waited for their soldiers. The Andrews Sisters sang "Don't Sit Under the Apple Tree (With Anyone Else but Me)." Kate Smith boomed "God Bless America."

But something else was lurking under that thick patriotic pie. It seemed as if a couple of strange ghosts had crept inside our imagination. America itself was a haunted house. And it wasn't the simple vagaries of war, the doubts, the suspicions, the defeats. Hollywood could handle that. Hollywood had John Wayne on the home front, wearing a different uniform for every picture.

No. It had more to do with that guy in the White House. He'd been in office so long, a kind of magnificence surrounded him, as if there had never been a president before FDR. He was the king that George Washington should have been. His ancestral home was in the North, but he wintered in the South, at Warm Springs, Georgia, where he swam like a magical human fish, with his great body rising out of the water, and his thin, defeated legs hidden from the camera's point of view. But he began to look gaunt in the middle of the war. The whole of him turned gray. And no camera could hide that. He had Fala and Eleanor and Faye Emerson, the beautiful film star his son Elliott had married in 1944, but the president seemed shrunken under his cape. I'd caught him at the Loew's Paradise. He was with Churchill somewhere. It couldn't have been Casablanca or Teheran. I'd have remembered the landscape, looked for Rick's Café. . . .

It was on the ocean. The water was black. I heard the whoop, whoop of sirens, that crazy call of a battleship, like a big metal baby crying. Churchill wore a jumpsuit. FDR was wrapped in his long cape, an old tired merman who'd come out of the water to say hello to people. Fala must have been on board. It was hard not to notice a little black Scottie with hair in his eyes. He was the most famous pup in the world. But not even Fala could warm up the old merman. His smile was like a movie star's mask, *given* to the cameras.

I watched him under the stars in that endless ceiling of the

Loew's Paradise, where the clouds moved like enormous floating pillowcases. I shivered for Roosevelt. He was our president.
He was the United States. And when the newsreel ended and
the feature began—was it *Ali Baba and the Forty Thieves?*—I
couldn't closet myself in some Arabian den with Jon Hall and
Maria Montez. I was thinking how the pup would feel when
he was orphaned. Who would take care of Fala? Faye Emerson,
the Marines, or Mrs. FDR?

And who would take care of me? Because if General George
had been our first American father, after we broke with George
of England and rubbed him out of our minds, then FDR, whom
the Republicans liked to call King Franklin, really was our
father-king, with his appanage at the White House, where half
the pauper princes of Europe would visit his wife and be photographed with Fala, and his royal court, which followed him
to Warm Springs and Hyde Park. With his pince-nez, his old
hats, his cape, and his cigarette holder, he was the first cinematic
president. Neither Harding nor Hoover had been much to look
at. And Calvin Coolidge sounded like a bitter horn. But FDR
had arrived in the age of the newsreel and the talkies. He could
tantalize an audience with a throw of his head and his deep,
burning laugh. He was remote, aristocratic, *and* accessible at the
same time. He couldn't walk but he could swim. He had to be
carried on board a train but he could drive his own car (with a
series of ingenious pedals that he operated by hand).

He was the country squire who cared about cities, the rich man
who was preoccupied with the poor, the gentile who had a
kitchen cabinet of Jews, the "legless man" who loved to sail in
boats, the politician who wanted to "pack" the Supreme Court
with justices of his own persuasion, the Yankee who was at home
in the South. He hovered over the nation like some strange warrior in a wheelchair, riding across those special ramps that had
been built for him at the White House, with Fala in the wake
of the chair. He was a dreamlike man, loved and hated with
equal force. It was hard to be indifferent to Franklin the First.

As he grew grayer and grayer, the country seemed terrified.
And even before the grayness, there was an unconscious longing
that this crippled man wouldn't have to die, that he really was
a god somehow and could control the continuity and the design
of our very own lives; and there was also the knowledge, as deep

as desire, that the god would have to fall, that he could not stay with us term after term, heal our wounds, keep us out of every war.

And so *Gone With the Wind*, coming at the end of a decade, was also the end of that delirious optimism Hollywood had, the last "big bang" before that war in Europe crept into our bones. *GWTW* was almost a challenge that Hollywood was outside whatever narrative was "playing" in the rest of the world, that it was beyond the world's own confusions, that a make-believe Atlanta was all that mattered in 1939; Mussolini and Hitler could go to hell. But our absorption in Scarlett and Rhett, our belief in their eternity, was a childish thing.

Suddenly the decor began to shift. *Citizen Kane*, shot in 1940, introduced a shadowland that could never have belonged near Gable's mustache. It was a film about defeat—the defeat of ambition, ideals, and existence itself. Charles Foster Kane blunders through the film like some rich rhinoceros, causing damage wherever he goes, and winds up all alone in his castle, dreaming of the sled he had as a boy. It's almost as if those two great melancholics, Karl Marx and Sigmund Freud, had conspired to invent Charles Foster Kane, the tycoon who was torn from his home and couldn't complete himself. The film "reads" like a riddle without a real answer. . . . Charles would have been better off staying a boy.

Peter Pan had come to Hollywood in the clothes of Orson Welles.

Of course there were the Dolly Sisters (Betty Grable and June Haver), Kipling's wolf boy (Sabu), Maria Montez, who belly-danced her way through most of the war, and the Brazilian Bombshell, Carmen Miranda, with bananas on top of her head, taking us on some eternal trip to Rio, fabulated at Twentieth Century–Fox. "Miranda's superbly vulgar personality," paraded in outlandish costumes, seized the imagination of wartime America: "in fruit hats, frilly sleeves and swinging skirts, her eyes popping with excitement, the Brazilian Bombshell epitomized the period's energy perhaps more than any other star."

But it was energy that seemed to come from an odd source. Carmen's eyes popped a little too much. Her smile lasted a little too long, as if it were frozen into her face. The gestures were always frantic. The hat a little too high, like lost cargo. She was a frenzied creature in tutti-frutti colors. You felt she could never stop performing. She almost died in the middle of a dance. Long after her popularity fell, she appeared on Jimmy Durante's television show, collapsed after the performance, and died that night of a heart attack at the age of forty-six.

And Sabu? He'd been discovered at the elephant stables of the Maharajah of Mysore when he was twelve, and turned into a movie star. And like the Brazilian Bombshell, he had a sudden burst of fame. He could "handle the largest pachyderm" with incredible skill. After his first film, *Elephant Boy,* was released in 1937, he became a ward of the British Government. On a visit to the United States, he met Mrs. Roosevelt and rode on Carole Lombard's motor scooter. He fell in love with Carole, and when the press badgered him about it, he would only admit that she was his favorite star. He was fourteen years old at the time.

He wore a turban while he went to school. "Two bearded Indian turban-winders followed him about" to make sure his turban didn't unwind. The elephant boy was now a little maharajah.

He settled in the U.S. in 1941 and was soon one more Hollywood "immigrant," along with Louis B. Mayer, Thomas Mann, Brecht, and Billy Wilder. *The Jungle Book* was shot "on location," forty miles from Hollywood. The film's producer, Alexander Korda, created his own jungle for Mowgli, "the young man-cub," filling it with every sort of animal. "Elephants, tigers, black panthers, bears, pythons, cobras, water buffaloes, monkeys, and a pack of wolves were the boy's fellow-actors, and he moved among them with astonishing confidence."

Even as he was following his own call of the wild, Sabu fell in love with airplanes. He dreamt of buying one with eight machine guns that could shoot "thousands of bullets all over the place."

Sabu got his plane. He was a tail gunner on a Liberator bomber with the Army Air Corps. The elephant boy took part in forty-two missions over the South Pacific and won the Distinguished Flying Cross.

Staff Sergeant Sabu Dastagir returned to Hollywood in 1945. He played a young maharajah in *Black Narcissus* (1946). Like other "Hollywood" children, he was caught in his own image and couldn't really grow up. He was Mowgli or some kind of maharajah in film after film. He even played himself in *Sabu and the Magic Ring* (1957). He died of a heart attack in 1963. The elephant boy was thirty-nine years old.

3   And then, among the Dolly Sisters and Errol Flynn, Bing Crosby and Dotty Lamour, the Brazilian Bombshell, Scheherazade, Ali Baba, and the elephant boy—all the fluff and exotic pastry that Hollywood could produce—appeared a very odd animal, the dreamwalker, like Turhan Bey, Sonny Tufts, Paul Henreid, Alan Ladd, Veronica Lake, Lizabeth Scott, and Dana Andrews, whose face had a frozen quality and always looked half-asleep. It wasn't a question of lousy acting. So much somnambulism had never been seen before. The dreamwalker seemed to mirror all our own fears. His (and her) numbness was the underside of that crazed cinematic energy in the wake of the war. It was as if the country had cracked up in an underground way, had found a perfect species for its own crisis—ambiguous, asexual creatures who felt so narrow on screen they couldn't threaten us and hardly existed at all.

Veronica Lake was known for the lock of blond hair she wore over her right eye. Her long peekaboo hairstyle became a fashion symbol . . . and a national menace, according to the United States government. One of Uncle Sam's agencies asked her to pose with her hair caught in a drill, so that female factory workers wouldn't have to suffer a similar fate. Veronica laughed at the idea of being some sort of sex goddess. She called herself the "sex zombie."

She partnered Alan Ladd in a series of melodramas. Ladd and Lake were blessed with a marvelous blondness that made them the dream couple of World War II. Neither of them "occupied much screen space. Part of their appeal was in their essential stillness, their sculptured quality." They performed "as if from the end of a tunnel, phoning in their lines from remote control."

Stars had magical powers that made us more and more into children, often like themselves. They could speak directly to their fans from the posters advertising their films. "Kiss me or kill me . . . which will he do?" asks Veronica Lake. "Girls, mark down this name, because you're going to hear it plenty: *Alan Ladd!* When he looks at you, a girl just can't call her heart her own. Take my tip, that *Ladd*'s going places, so better see him first in 'THIS GUN FOR HIRE'!''

In spite of what the posters said, Alan never got to kill or kiss the girl. He was a hired gun with a crippled hand. There was something so mournful about him, such solitude in his face, that if he couldn't have Veronica (she belonged to Robert Preston), then dying was the next best thing.

Ladd was resurrected in *The Glass Key*. And this time he got Veronica Lake. I had no idea that their romance on screen was one of the earliest examples of *film noir:* that icy feel of the Forties, full of shadows and ambiguous boys and girls. Ladd and Lake looked perfectly natural to me. They were both short people, and even on the moviehouse wall, they seemed closer to children than adults: arrested in some way, frozen; Ladd, at least, never smiled. His earnestness felt so deep to a child that I could never imagine a life for him outside the roles he played.

I learned that he was married to Sue Carol (I'd become a big reader all of a sudden). I saw Ladd's house in *Modern Screen*. I'm not sure it was manly to read movie magazines, but I read them all. I believed the gibberish about George Raft eating dinner with Betty Grable every night of the week and then returning to his own little mansion, while Betty lived with her mom. What else did George Raft need than lamb chops with Betty Grable and a goodnight kiss? He ordered twenty glasses of champagne whenever he went to the barbershop, so the barber and all his helpers would have something to drink. That seemed right for Raft, who wore elevator shoes, like Alan Ladd, and had lots of trouble kissing tall women in the movies he made.

But the stories in *Modern Screen* about Ladd and Sue Carol took me much too far from *The Glass Key*. The only woman I wanted with him was Veronica Lake. They were the lovers who clothed my dreams. I was like a fortune-teller. I sensed their sad designs. They both turned alcoholic. Ladd was dead at fifty, a fallen star who'd survived an earlier suicide attempt and succumbed to a "cocktail" of alcohol and sleeping pills. And Veronica died in Burlington, Vermont, utterly forgotten, along with her famous lock of hair. "I will have one of the cleanest obits as an actress," she'd said. "I never did cheesecake like Ann Sheridan or Betty Grable. I just used my hair."

4 There was another actor who touched me more than Ladd and Lake. He wasn't handsome. He wasn't blond. He did all his dreamwalking with a weathered face. I never thought about his acting. He had "the kind of style that conceals style." He was just *there,* up on the screen, playing out my own phantom presence. Because he didn't look much like a star. He was always getting beaten and batted around. And the women he loved were spider ladies whom he sought out and then had to escape from. Even his name was funny. Dick Powell. He could have been your neighbor. Or the guy you went to school with. And he always looked like he needed a shave. Dick Powell.

He arrived near the end of the war. And he marked out a particular rite of passage for me. Because he wasn't a boy, like Alan Ladd. And the possibility of my own manhood seemed connected with him. If I ever grew up, it would be with the help of Dick Powell. He appeared in five films, *Murder, My Sweet* (1944), *Cornered* (1945), *Johnny O'Clock* (1947), *To the Ends of the Earth* (1948), and *Rogue's Regiment* (1948), that seemed to add extra ribs to my body. They were filled with such essential irony Powell himself seemed trapped. He *and* I had to climb out of the gloomy webbing each film proposed. It didn't matter if he was a private detective, a gambler, or a T-man. He was always rocking somewhere at the edge of the law. And if he didn't lose his life to the spider lady, he also didn't win very much. He was lucky to get out alive.

He was as muddled as the moviegoers watching him. Cobwebs appear on the wall in *Murder, My Sweet,* as Dick Powell, playing Philip Marlowe, falls unconscious. The film opens with Marlowe sitting blinded like a mummy, with bandages on his head, telling a murderous tale to the police. The good girl (Anne Shirley) leads him out of the maze at the end of the film, but Marlowe's heart seems to lie with the dead spider lady (Claire Trevor).

Powell turned television producer, and the cobwebs went

away. I stopped thinking about him long before he died, in 1963. He didn't inhabit any more rogue's regiments. He was like a lost father who couldn't get me out of any more jams. It wasn't until I became a ferocious movie addict and started seeking out films of the Thirties that I realized Dick Powell had a past. He hadn't simply appeared with *Murder, My Sweet*. He'd been a crooner, a stinking song-and-dance man, with a high-pitched voice, in *42nd Street* and *Gold Diggers* (*of 1933, 1935,* and *1937*). At first I wouldn't believe it. I wondered if that guy was another Dick Powell, or Philip Marlowe's effeminate kid brother. Because *my* Dick Powell only danced around in the dark and sang songs to get the bulls off his back.

Then I understood the metamorphosis he must have gone through. That high voice of his got him nowhere once the war began. He had to move from Warners to Paramount to RKO in order to play Philip Marlowe. He was an ex-crooner, forty-one years old. And he didn't have Bogart's deadpan dreamy manner. He wouldn't have fit around all the exotic souls at Rick's Café. He was a much plainer man.

How could I tell that he'd surface again as one of the heroes of *film noir*? I'd gone to the movies like a religious freak and no one had mentioned what *film noir* was supposed to mean. But certain French critics, like André Bazin and Henri Langlois, who'd been deprived of American films during the war and sat through the Nazi Occupation without their favorite stars, were startled by what they saw in 1946 when American films began to reappear in France. They noticed a peculiar patterning, a cultural pull, in American films made during and after the war that we ourselves were blinded to. Some of the films, the very best of them, like *Double Indemnity* (1944), *Laura* (1944), *Shadow of a Doubt* (1943), *This Gun for Hire* (1942), *Murder, My Sweet* (1944), *The Postman Always Rings Twice* (1946), *The Big Sleep* (1946), *The Woman in the Window* (1944), and *Scarlet Street* (1946), seemed submerged under a dark bubble, as if the landscape they delivered wasn't allowed to breathe.

That delirious Art Deco Manhattan, with vast painted skies and the electric billboards of Forty-second Street, re-created in the caverns of RKO or MGM with incredible panache, was now a somber, brooding place. And the optimism it suggested, that streamlined, sharply angled world where *anything* was possible, died with it. The "city" was now the home of the dead, filled with dreamwalkers and cadavers that wandered everywhere.

5 | *I Wake Up Screaming* (1941) could very well have been the war cry of *film noir*. It starred Betty Grable, who was no dark princess; nothing could defeat her, not even *noir*. But the other players, Carole Landis, Victor Mature, and Laird Cregar, were three of movieland's most spectacular zombies.

A heavy-lidded giant from Louisville, Mature seemed in a constant trance state, whether he was Doc Holliday in *My Darling Clementine* or Samson chasing Delilah. Hollywood billed him as "The Hunk." He had all the handsomeness of a beautiful ox. Rita Hayworth wanted to marry him once upon a time. She had a weakness for giants. She dropped "Vic" and married that other giant, Orson Welles.

Laird Cregar, "huge, glowing-eyed and silken voiced," had a much more interesting career. He wasn't a "beefsteak" hero. He moved with a slow, nimble menace, as if time could freeze around his enormous frame. His own body cradled the screen. He held you with his eyes and haunted every movie he was in. He could play Jack the Ripper, the devil, or a demented cop. Who knows what other phantoms he might have given us? He was "dead at 28 of a crash diet."

Carole Landis was as stunning as *two* Betty Grables. But she's an actress who's unremembered. She didn't have Grable's warmth, and she wasn't cunning enough to be a spider lady. There was a coldness about Carole Landis that was almost pathological, as if some essential part of her could never be reached. No matter what role she played, an absence registered on the screen. Like Marilyn, she "matured" much too quickly. She was married at fifteen. And stayed married for about a month. She married again. And again. And again. It was movieland, where marriages were as fickle as a pirate's flag.

She couldn't find much stability, but she did breed romance. While she was entertaining troops in the South Pacific, she fell ill in New Guinea, and nearly died . . . and a soldier "hacked his way through eighteen miles of jungle" to present Carole Landis with a couple of flowers.

She killed herself when she was twenty-nine. She was having an affair with Rex Harrison, who wouldn't leave his wife, actress Lilli Palmer. It was Harrison who discovered the body. "She was curled up on her side, her cheek resting on a jewel box," according to *The New York Times*.

Landis' life *and* death had all the particles of *film noir*. The frozen beauty who died for love. She wasn't one of the *femmes fatales* of the Forties, like Barbara Stanwyck or Lana Turner. But the territory she inhabited on the screen was much bleaker than Barbara Stanwyck's as the blond witch in *Double Indemnity*. Landis was a wild creature. She had anarchy in her blood and in her blond hair, a coolness that was outside any art. She belonged to no particular time or place. She danced with servicemen at the Hollywood Canteen. She sold war bonds in the rain. "You can't stop a war for the weather!" she admonished a crowd that was fleeing from the rain at a rally on Wall Street. But Carole Landis couldn't seem to gather much compassion for herself. She rubbed at our own raw nerve, the void that sits right under the American dream. She was a casualty of some secret war—the nightsong that says no, no to fame, money, and success.

She was like that lyrical breakdown the French discovered in the "closed society" of our films. Heartbreak without recompense. Bitterness in black-and-white.

# nine

# *Children of Paradise*

**1** Paris, October 1987.

A quarter of the French cinemas had closed. Newspapers were predicting that another ten percent would "die" before the end of the year. The cinemas along the boulevard Montparnasse looked like ghost towns. There was none of the ordinary queuing inside the metal gates that fronted the cinemas themselves. I saw stragglers here and there. Or a line that was no longer than a rat's tail. Some people were blaming the crisis on *canal plus,* the new cable network that was showing films into the middle of the night. *Canal plus.* I'd come to Paris to work on a comic book called *The Adventures of Billy Budd,* about a young KGB recruit with extrasensory powers. Comrade Billy could predict death and destruction like some perfect seeing-eye dog. *Billy Budd* was my *film noir* in comic-book form. But all I seemed to care about was *canal plus.*

I was red-eyed from watching films until the witching hours (after 1:00 a.m.). I caught the other channels too. I discovered American films on *le petit écran* that I had never seen in the United States. *They Won't Forget* (1937), with Claude Rains as the ambitious Southern D.A. who indicts a Yankee schoolteacher for the murder of a sexy student at Buxton Business College (Lana Turner in her first role that wasn't a walk-on). And *Three on a Match* (1932), with Joan Blondell, Bette Davis, and Ann Dvorak.

Both films happened to be directed by Mervyn LeRoy, and they had a fluidity of line, a sense of purpose and narrative space that would shrink off the moviehouse wall with the arrival of Carmen Miranda, Maria Montez, and all the casbahs and exotic creatures of World War II (in Hollywood), when "atmosphere" alone could determine the character and fate of a film.

There wasn't much room for Ann Dvorak among the different Bagdads. She went to England and drove an ambulance during the blitz. But she was marvelous in *Three on a Match* as a restless beauty married to a rich man (Warren William). She had enormous eyes and a dark, dark face that was a little too expressive for the alabaster look that Hollywood favored. But why the hell did I have to discover her in Paris on *canal plus*?

Her persona has disappeared from the American screen. One more victim of the old edict that Hollywood couldn't afford a past; it might compromise next year's crop of films. I had to fly to Paris to seek out whatever "history" Hollywood had. Because Paris itself was like an extraordinary museum that had collected our popular culture in ways we never could. The French had started a whole line of thrillers, the Série Noire, as an homage to American mystery writers of the hard-boiled school, like Dashiell Hammett and Raymond Chandler, Jim Thompson and Horace McCoy. And while we looked upon the crime novel as subliterature, a form of brainless reading to be shunned by all serious critics, the frogs were able to sniff out its very special aroma and to sense the crazy window it offered to the most hidden aspects of our culture—that crime was culture, and culture was crime. And so Hammett and Chandler were cherished in France, through the Série Noire, as their works went out of print in the United States.

And what was true of the American crime novel (the *roman noir*) was also true of American comics. Popeye and Batman, Blondie and Red Ryder, Captain Marvel and the Katzenjammer Kids, Little Orphan Annie and the Little King, Wonder Woman and Mandrake had seized the French imagination because they suggested a kind of reductive universe that stood for America itself—a land where anything goes. Red Ryder's carbine cuts across any cultural context or social class. Dagwood will always be at Blondie's call. And the Katzenjammer Kids undermine whatever authority is around them. The comic-book hero (or heroine) is most often an outlaw who has to fabulate his own society and reorder the world. He has the expectations and the dream vocabulary of a child. He may not always be a magician, like Mandrake, but stuck inside a frame, with nothing but a balloon of words to comfort him, he does seem magical, as if he (or she) were some phantom moving in and out of menace, like Little Orphan Annie, Captain Marvel, or Smilin' Jack . . . with all the strange democratic notions of the New World, where butlers talked like kings, where the worst slum could become an open plain in the width of a panel, and Red Ryder could plummet right off the page. The French saw a freedom in the American *bande dessinée,* a perverse, anarchic continent of line and color.

And while comics disappeared into some nether land in the United States, banished to the rear walls of candy stores and novelty shops, they began to flourish in France, where the *bande dessinée* was sold in every bookshop, and was as important to the French reader as Céline or Colette; a band of young French artists, writers, and critics, influenced by Hollywood, Hammett, and Terry (of *Terry and the Pirates*) was producing sexy, romantic comic books that were like films flattened onto the page. They had much more energy and fun than most of the recent novels I'd read.

And so I'd come to Paris to work on a *bande dessinée;* it wasn't a form I could have fooled with in New York, where serious comics for adults were like a cottage industry, so small that it couldn't be found in the phone book. I was curious about what drew me to France. Some longing to return to that territory of my first alphabet books? It was Walt Disney and his Donald who taught me how to read. The words inside a balloon had much more force than any kind of normal punctuation.

But I hadn't come looking for my literary roots. I wasn't going to unbury Donald Duck somewhere in the Champ de Mars. I realized who I was. A filmmaker manqué. I was here to direct a film in slow motion. Each panel of *Billy Budd* was like a frozen frame, and the artist I worked with, a self-educated brute from Lille, had an incredible knack to create flurries of activity between the frozen frames.

Ah, he was the genius, and I was the monkish man who scribbled words that bloomed on his drawing board, like an umbrella opening, opening onto its own peculiar habitat. And when I looked at his pages, that's what I thought of: flowers that had erupted from the designs in my own head. Just like a movie.

2 Jack Nicholson, Mickey Rourke, and Robert De Niro erupt on the walls of kiosks along the boulevard Montparnasse. Their faces are on the covers of all the French movie magazines, as if Paris were a province of Hollywood, one more outpost, a little movieland, like the Loew's Paradise, shorn of John Eberson's statuettes and twinkling skies. I wonder if Paris' own Cinecittà, the caverns at Billancourt, are becoming deserted barns. Does Billancourt need another Mussolini, or Louis B. Mayer, to revive French films? Or will the moviehouses continue to close until there's room only for De Niro and Mickey Rourke?

I pick up one of the French magazines, and I'm spooked, because the article on De Niro makes me feel as if American film culture were invented in France. I return to my flat on the boulevard Arago, next to La Santé prison, where Fantômas, the man of many disguises and France's fictional master of crime, was supposed to have spent a night or two. Fantômas disturbs my dreams. I imagine him in my next comic, looking a little like Tyrone Power or Turhan Bey. I imagine him in America, haunting the roofs of some metropolis, hunched over like a fat eagle, waiting to shed a widow's blood and steal all the jewels in the house.

I'm staying with a friend, Martens, who's known in the neighborhood as the Redhead, "Le Rouquin." Martens is a novelist and a screenwriter. His girlfriend's name is Marine. She looks like a beauty from another planet. I look again. It's a time warp, that's all. Marine belongs in the Hollywood of Ginger and Fred. She has the eyes and lips of Joan Crawford, the mouth of Alice Faye. And then I realize there's nothing peculiar in that. Marine is *très parisienne*. The whole bloody town is populated with women who could have been born on Louis B. Mayer's lots. *Marine a l'air de MGM.*

And suddenly I mourn that old junkman in a different way. Louis B. might have become one more Hollywood fossil after World War II, a mogul who was out of touch. But he hadn't been false to Leo the Lion. It was Hollywood that had betrayed him. Movieland wanted to go modern. But thirty years after he died a bitter man, his legacy could be found in the streets of Paris. Women he'd never dreamed about had the MGM look.

And Martens? He knew more dope about Hollywood than I could ever gather as a constant moviegoer since the age of five. It wasn't fair. I'd sat in movie palaces with Bagdadian walls and miracle skies. I'd seen Jane Russell in *The Outlaw,* I grew up with Danny Kaye, and Martens was only a frog. He couldn't have tasted the Three Stooges, or followed Don Winslow of the Navy from week to week, in those Forties serials that could drive a kid so insane he'd stop doing his homework. But I hadn't counted on the Cinémathèque.

Martens had been one of those children of paradise who sat in the shadows with Henri Langlois, founder of the Cinémathèque Française. The Cinémathèque was an extraordinary institution, as much a chapel as an archive, museum, and salon devoted to the films of the world; it came into being because Langlois began collecting films as a very young man and couldn't keep storing them in the family bathtub. He was a junkman who collected whatever he could. Langlois didn't believe in critics. There was no such thing as a bad film. What was out of fashion this year might become next year's masterpiece. He was, according to François Truffaut, "both unassuming and extravagant, a fabulous man, an obsessed man, a man animated by an *idée fixe,* a haunted man."

His only passion was to collect and catalogue films. He had his own idea of what cataloguing was about. He kept long lists in a child's scrawl that no one else could decipher. He was like some curious scribe who could produce cans of film whenever he had to. He created his own whirlwind and functioned within it. When the Germans arrived in Paris in 1940, Langlois began to bury all the American films he had in various backyards before the Boche could get their hands on them. It was Langlois himself who had to unearth the films after the war. He lived a spidery existence during the Occupation, sharing headquarters in the same building with the director of the Reichsfilmarchiv and also helping to smuggle Jews out of Paris. He was his own kind of commando.

And a wizard, a magical rabbi of the moviehouse. He's "one of the greatest French film directors, director and scriptwriter of a continuous film called the Cinémathèque Française," said Jean-Luc Godard. And for Bernardo Bertolucci the Cinémathèque was "the best school of cinema in the world. . . . And the best professor is Henri Langlois."

And what sort of school did the rabbi run? He didn't lecture, he didn't dictate. His only classes were the movies he showed to all the "children" who sat with him at the Cinémathèque. "I have not helped, I have not taught. I have put food on the table. . . . This is my work, to show films; to save and to show films, nothing more. Henri Langlois does not exist."

When he was young, Langlois was so thin he couldn't hold up his pants without the help of copper wire. And when he was forty, he got so fat he moved like a wheezing elephant. He lived in a world of orderly disorder. But he found a scheme to deal with some of the chaos he caused. Whenever he traveled, he carried two plane tickets, because he was forever losing one of them. And he had little concept of money. Even after he and the Cinémathèque had become world-famous, he was poor as a mouse. He died of a heart attack one night in 1977. He'd been sitting at his desk with a candle like some Robinson Crusoe, living without electricity or a workable phone. The rabbi had forgotten to pay his bills.

3    Henri Langlois was born on November 12, 1914, in Smyrna (now Izmir), a Turkish port city populated with Greeks. The Turks and the Greeks couldn't get along. They were constantly at each other's throat. Hemingway described the aftermath of one particular war between Greek and Turkish nationals in his short story "On the Quai at Smyrna." As the Turks sacked the city, women congregated on the piers and clutched their dead babies. "You couldn't get the women to give up their dead babies. They'd have babies dead for six days. Wouldn't give them up." And the withdrawing Greek soldiers couldn't take their baggage animals with them, "so they just broke their forelegs and dumped them into the shallow water."

That was Smyrna in 1922. A bit like old Shanghai, with its international quarter, where Americans, Germans, Italians, English, and French lived in houses that were considered part of their native soil. So Henri was a little colonial boy in a rather crazy town. His mother, Annie-Louise Braggiotti, was a woman of Italian descent. Her mother's mother was born in Charleston, South Carolina, where the Braggiottis had migrated before the American Civil War. It could have been a fable out of David O. Selznick's story pile. The Braggiottis left America after the defeat of the South, "because, Langlois thought, they had been on the losing side" of the war.

Ah, he'd missed his calling, this man who sat on miles and miles of film cans. He should have been a scenarist at MGM. . . .

The Langlois family got out of Smyrna during the siege of 1922, as mobs milled through the city and mothers held their dead babies. A French battleship brought them to Marseilles. The family settled in Paris on the rue Laferrière in the ninth arrondissement, a tiny curving street not far from the Place Pigalle.

Henri grew up in that mythic, dreamy period between the silent films of the Twenties and the coming of sound. He was fifteen when he saw *A Girl in Every Port,* one of Howard Hawks' last silent films, starring Louise Brooks. Louise mesmerized him. "As soon as she comes on the screen, fiction disappears along with art, and one has the impression of watching a documentary . . . she embodies all that the cinema rediscovered in the last years of the silent film: complete naturalness and complete simplicity. Her art is so pure that it becomes invisible."

And it was, in part, to *save* the silent film that this schoolboy began his own little cinémathèque. The moment sound arrived, silent films were doomed. Their silver content became more valuable than the films themselves. Like Louise Brooks, the films "fell into that black hole" between silence and sound and "disappeared from the world's screens," writes Richard Roud in *A Passion for Films*.

And so Langlois begged and borrowed and bought whatever films he could. His life was marked before he left high school. This bag of bones with the big, big eyes and the copper wire around his waist was building the oddest of empires: a library of films that no one seemed to want. He and another young *cinéphile,* Georges Franju, started their own film club, Le Cercle du Cinéma, renting a room on the Champs Élysées to screen silent films every Friday night in a tiny salon with gilded chairs. But Paris was bursting with film clubs. And Langlois didn't want to remain a simple showman, a barker of films. He and Franju established the Cinémathèque Française in 1936, when Langlois was twenty-one. They stored their films in an abandoned building behind an old-age home in Orly, a suburb of Paris.

A curious footnote to the "Orly affair" is that Georges Méliès, a former magician and one of the first and most remarkable of all film directors, was residing at the old-age home, and it was Méliès who guarded the archives, Méliès who kept the key to the Cinémathèque, as if the old magician had been able to conjure time itself in the film cans of Langlois and Franju.

Langlois wasn't a miser. He didn't hoard. He didn't squirrel his acquisitions away. He shared them with other archives and clubs. He became something of a godfather to the Cineteca Italiana, a film club in Milan that was frowned upon by the Fascists. He would smuggle into Milan films by Eisenstein, Pudovkin, and René Clair that had been outlawed by Mussolini's men.

Langlois loved Milanese ice cream almost as much as he loved films. As skinny as ever, he "discovered a particularly good ice-cream shop, and . . . devoured a dozen portions" while he was with Gianni Comencini of the Cineteca Italiana. Langlois had a terrible stomachache that night. Comencini's mother found her own magical cure. "Langlois was placed on his back on the kitchen table, and Signora Comencini began to *iron* his stomach. Her theory was that the heat of the iron would thaw out the ice cream." And somehow it did.

In 1938 Langlois and Franju helped form the Fédération Internationale des Archives du Film (FIAF), with Franju as executive secretary. One of the founding members and first president of FIAF was Frank Hensel of the Reichsfilmarchiv. Having a German bureaucrat (and member of the Nazi party) as a fellow *cinéphile* turned out to be an act of providence for the Cinémathèque Française.

Hensel was a major in the Wehrmacht during the war, director of the Reichsfilmarchiv, and chief of the cinema for the whole German army. He was also a very mysterious man. Little is known about Frank Hensel. He was "an early Nazi recruit," he had an English mother, and he was in charge of a circus once upon a time. Like other Nazis, he disappeared into the woodwork for a while once the war was over, went into business, and at least publicly gave up his "romance" with films. But during the Occupation of Paris Hensel had his own secret life. He was almost *hollywoodien,* like a benign Fantômas or Scarlet Pimpernel.

He found vaults for Langlois and Franju to hide their films. "Whenever there was a threat of a film being seized by any of the other German authorities, he arranged for a counterseizure," and got the film to Franju. He also secured a permanent home for the Cinémathèque at 7, avenue de Messine, which housed the Reichsfilmkammer (the German film office). It was the Cinémathèque's "nearness" to the Reichsfilmkammer that kept it alive.

And Langlois himself? He moved about like one of the ghosts inside his film cans, playing his own little game of politics to preserve whatever archive he had. "I have hidden films like *The Great Dictator* and some Soviet films in a castle which belongs to Mme. Jean Voilier, who is half for the Resistance and half for the Germans."

It was around this time that he began to live with Mary Meerson, who was as obscure and volatile as Langlois himself. "No one knows exactly where or when she was born." But she'd been a great beauty who posed for Oskar Kokoschka and Giorgio de Chirico. Her maiden name was Popov and she might have been born in Bulgaria. She spoke half a dozen languages, including Yiddish. And when pressed about her own past, she'd smile and say that there was no such creature as Mary Meerson. "I am Scheherazade."

When Scheherazade first met Langlois he was "thin, thin, with very big, prominent eyes." And they grew fat together. "After the war Mary began to put on weight, and so I decided to do the same—to keep her company."

**4** And the Cinémathèque began to flourish. It shared prints with archives around the world and showed movies seven nights a week at its little theater on the avenue de Messine. Critic Georges Sadoul had scoffed at the Cinémathèque, called it a "fragile fiction, a bizarre magma." But Langlois' *fiction* wasn't so fragile any more. If his theater only had fifty seats, that couldn't prevent him from mounting retrospectives or reintroducing Hollywood films. It was at the avenue de Messine that French moviegoers discovered Howard Hawks, Samuel Fuller, and John Ford, and the dreamy, atmospheric angles of *film noir*.

Because many of the films had no subtitles, Langlois' "children" could catch the choppiness or fluid motions of a director's visual style without the fuss or the bother of translating dialogue from one language to the next. And so Langlois' "children" discovered that someone like Hawks had an unmistakable signature, a nervousness and a pulse that went beyond the particulars of plot; for Langlois, Hawks was as much an "author" as Balzac, inventing a language and a density of purpose as he moved from film to film.

Langlois never disparaged the moguls. He understood how they had manipulated and abused his own favorites, Buster Keaton and Louise Brooks, but he felt that their "illiteracy" had lent a curious fervor to their films, as if they had hallucinated their own America, and this very hallucination was much closer to that wound of what America was all about . . . and the dreamscape of cinema itself.

For "children" such as François Truffaut, Langlois' little screening room was school and paradise. "The Cinémathèque was really a haven for us then, a refuge, our home, everything. There were only about fifty seats, and we had the habit of not sitting down, but lying on the floor in front of the first row of seats—especially for the popular films."

Truffaut was like that "orphan" he introduces us to in *The 400 Blows,* Antoine Doinel, a sad-eyed wanderer who can find his only comfort in the streets. Doinel's mother and father are caught in a loveless marriage and drift out of his life. *The 400 Blows* was a film that bothered my sleep, not because my circumstances and surroundings were the same as Doinel's, but because circumstances and surroundings mattered very little—we were both dream children, comrades of a sort, sleepwalkers who couldn't win. Whatever Doinel did turned out wrong. He couldn't even steal with much authority.

He haunts the screen because he has no real antecedents. His mom and dad don't count. Antoine Doinel is a cinematic child, "born" within the frame of the movie, as most movie characters are. But we feel his isolation more, his essential loneliness, like our very own century, which has made drifters and dreamers of us all—cinematic children, powerless in some profound manner—because we've tumbled into the world at a time of merciless migration, where countries have been created and doomed and created again, entire peoples have vanished, dictators have ruled and died, royal lines have come and gone, until the planet itself seems pulled out of shape, and we meet our own shadowed selves and haunted eyes over and over again on the walls of a hundred moviehouses.

Blame it on Jean-Pierre Léaud. He's the brat Truffaut picked for Antoine Doinel, and he plays Antoine with such infinite sadness that he leaves scars in our heads. He *is* Antoine Doinel. He became Truffaut's "double" in a series of films that took Antoine from the streets of Paris to a reform school to a military camp, where he was given a dishonorable discharge . . . like François Truffaut.

Truffaut dedicated *Stolen Kisses,* his second full-length feature about Antoine, to Henri Langlois and the Cinémathèque Française. He is the one director who seems closest to Langlois, not in terms of cinematic style, because Langlois had no preferred style, or the craziness they shared for American films, and *film noir* in particular, but because, unlike Godard and Alain Resnais and Claude Chabrol, those other "Children of the Cinémathèque," he had no home. He was like some *enfant sauvage* who lived in moviehouses and on the streets. He was sent to jail for juveniles "after stealing metal doorknobs" and worked in a factory when he was fifteen. He became a ferocious boy critic on *Cahiers du Cinéma,* attacking most current French filmmakers for having little substance and no signature at all. But it was at the Cinémathèque that he found his bearings.

When he joined the army in 1950 he willed all his movie memorabilia, including posters he'd swiped from different moviehouses, to the Cinémathèque, on the condition that Langlois would let him in free to the little theater after he became a civilian again. Langlois "said yes, so I rented a cart, and brought all my 'treasures' to the Cinémathèque." And that was the first time he ever spoke to Henri Langlois.

Truffaut's military career was as disastrous as Doinel's. He deserted, sat in the brig like some kind of convict, dreaming of films, I suppose, and his new "father," Henri Langlois, and he was lucky to leave the service with all his skin. He followed the Cinémathèque through its pereginations from the avenue de Messine to the rue d'Ulm (in the Latin Quarter) and the Palais de Chaillot.

The Cinémathèque was now a government "office," supported by the Centre National du Cinéma. And Langlois himself was a "librarian," serving under André Malraux, Charles De Gaulle's minister of culture. And Malraux considered Langlois a very poor librarian. Both were willful men with enormous followings. Malraux was a novelist, art historian, and hero of the Resistance. And Langlois was an ambiguous creature who'd been helped by a Nazi major during the war, an archivist who sat on rotting cans of film and couldn't even tell how big his archive was, who traveled here and there like some fat Flying Dutchman and created new cinémathèques wherever he could.

Malraux was disturbed by the disorder of the man. In February 1968 he removed Langlois from the Cinémathèque, had him and Mary Meerson locked out of their offices. It caused a big stink. Truffaut and Langlois' other "children" took to the streets. Half the city of Paris seemed to rebel against De Gaulle. But Langlois did nothing in his own defense. He stuck to his apartment on the rue Gazan "playing solitaire, or arranging to be driven to fortune-tellers, the only ones, according to him, who were capable of predicting the fate of the Cinémathèque."

There was an outcry from directors all over the world. Chaplin, Kurosawa, Rossellini, Buñuel, John Huston, Nicholas Ray, Samuel Fuller, Lindsay Anderson, Joseph Losey, Elia Kazan, and hundreds of others threatened to remove their films from the Cinémathèque. But it was Langlois' own unorthodox methods *and* the big American studios "that really saved him." During the German Occupation of Paris, when American films were considered contraband, Langlois played the pirate, burying whatever films he could. According to S. Frederick Gronich, head of the European office of the Motion Picture Association of America, the pirate returned all the American prints without much commotion. "There were no pieces of paper exchanged, no records; he just handed them back. He could have kept them, as some archives did . . . but with the prints Langlois had saved, the film companies were able to get back in business [in France]."

And the studios didn't forget Henri Langlois. Gronich visited Malraux at the time of the crisis over the Cinémathèque, and told him that unless the "librarian" got his job back, the American studios would pull their films out of the archive and boycott the Cinémathèque. Malraux capitulated, but he withdrew government support from the Cinémathèque. And Langlois found himself a beggar again.

But he lectured, traveled, mounted exhibits, and turned all his fees over to the Cinémathèque, while "he continued to suffer from gout, high blood pressure, and overwhelming fatigue." Langlois was like old Ahab. He was monomaniacal on the subject of films. He wanted cinémathèques everywhere on the planet. He might have had an American Cinémathèque situated under the arches of the Queensboro Bridge, in a glass house designed by I. M. Pei, but the plans were finalized during New York's fiscal crisis and the glass house was never built. That didn't stop Langlois from shuttling between Paris and New York, with that crazy dream in his head, as if he could pull the finances out of his own thickening pants.

He was always, always on the move. Hollywood presented him with a special Oscar in 1974. He'd been the "conscience" and the preserving angel of film. But Langlois needed a tux to attend the Academy Awards. A tailor arrived at the Cinémathèque to measure Langlois for his "Oscar suit." Langlois was suffering from the gout and wouldn't stand up for the tailor, who had to measure Langlois while he was sitting in a chair. But not even an Oscar could keep Langlois alive. Truffaut believed that Langlois died of a great sadness. No one man, young or old, could be the constant curator of his own house of film. "His heart was bruised by a feeling of powerlessness: what a man alone has created he cannot preserve."

 I loped through Paris after learning about Langlois. I had to wipe that man from my head. I had pictures of him in his magic tux. He was enormous. He looked like a character actor out of the Forties, "Cuddles"

Sakall, who'd played Carl, the maître d', in *Casablanca*. The whole world had become a movie palace. It was Black Monday, October 19, the day of the big crash, or *le crack,* as the French called it. And I walked around in a dream, wondering if America would disappear into a sea of worthless paper. Suppose I became marooned in Paris. I didn't care. I visited my agent, Madame L, who lived next to the Eiffel Tower. I had to borrow a few thousand francs.

Old men were playing *boules* in the brown fields of the Champ de Mars. I listened to the clack of the balls and looked up at the Eiffel Tower. Its metal ribs were substantial enough, but I was the phantom of my own film library, and I could only see that tower in cinematic terms. It was the most recognizable movie icon in the world. It *was* Paris. It had become the establishing shot of a hundred, hundred Hollywood films. One blink of the tower and you could tell right away where you were. The entire film could be studio-bound after that, created in one of the caverns at MGM, or the "Paris street" on a different lot. But that first glimpse grounded you *forever* . . . during the length of the film.

I studied the real thing, an enormous spike on the Champ de Mars that would remain a marvelous totem because of the movies. It no longer mattered that it had been an incredible feat of engineering once upon a time, the tallest man-made object in the world, the brainchild of Alexandre Gustave Eiffel, built for the Paris Exposition of 1889. The citizens of Paris were ambiguous about what they saw. Three hundred artists, writers, and composers, including Guy de Maupassant, François Coppée, Charles Gounod, and Dumas *fils,* signed a petition against the assault of Eiffel's tower on the city they loved. It would leave Paris, they said, in a land of perpetual shadow. Of course public taste began to soften a bit. And when the tower was scheduled to be torn down in 1909, other artists and writers, such as Maurice Utrillo, Raoul Dufy, and Guillaume Apollinaire, insisted that the tower was a fixed piece, a permanent part of Paris. But they didn't have to insist too hard. The tower was already valuable as a radio telephone terminal. What was all this historical hullabaloo compared to an image on the moviehouse wall? The tower had become *hollywoodien,* like the Empire State Building and Big Ben, an artifact that could define a place in half a second. Millions of people who'd never seen Paris *knew* the Eiffel Tower.

It was some kind of cultural tyranny. I was convinced of that.

I returned to the boulevard Arago, thinking of Fantômas, wondering if he had red hair like my friend Martens. *The Untouchables* had come to Paris—Eliot Ness and Al Capone had knocked French films into the suburbs somewhere. *The Untouchables* played on every boulevard. Paris itself seemed like a gorgeous set in some Hollywood jungle—a grounded pirate ship with many, many decks, a haven for Fantômas . . . and Eliot Ness. I was all mixed up. That old American myth of the gangster and the good guy was as powerful as it had ever been.

I talked to Martens. "Hollywood," he said, "was the fabulous creation of monsters, a mythical town in a mythical country, producing myths. Here we don't produce myths. Hollywood was the kingdom, the womb of it all."

I was curious if Martens mourned Louis XIV, if he was a monarchist at heart.

"We don't have a king and queen in France," he said. "We use Monaco as our royal family."

And wasn't it perfect that our own Hollywood princess, Grace Kelly, Gary Cooper's fiancée in *High Noon,* should have become Princess Grace of Monaco? "Instead of publicity shots, her delicate [and icy] face now appeared on postage stamps," wrote Ephraim Katz in *The Film Encyclopedia.* But didn't we feel that Grace had never left us, that Monaco was an extension of Hollywood itself, a satrapy of MGM and Paramount, one more movie set . . . that just happened to be on the French Riviera? As if God were the ultimate *auteur,* parceling out people and places from His house in Beverly Hills. Or was that what Hollywood wanted us to believe?

"Who created the movies?" Martens asked, and answered with a Chaplinesque shrug. "Hollywood established the landmarks, established the signs from A to Z. America mastered an art and invented it. For the whole world at a certain time in its history the cinema was America. From China to Patagonia everybody knew Charlot [Charlie Chaplin]. There was no TV, no radio. . . . Chaplin was Charlot, the movies' first phenomenon. It wasn't sound that established Hollywood, but silent films. You didn't need much equipment. You could watch silent films on a white sheet—a funny little man and funny little images, coming from a land where everybody knows where to go when you had nowhere to go.''

"But we're a barbaric tribe of people," I said, like some cultural commissar, trying to pierce Martens' mythomania about the United States. "We took Charlot and turned him into one more barbarian.''

"Perfect," he said. "A noncultural country produces noncultural art. You don't have to read, you don't have to write, you don't have to be literate. That was the way Hollywood became the imperial city.

"Everything merged at the same time. The First World War ruined Europe, and the growth of the U.S. was so quick it couldn't develop at a human pace. The mastery of movies was an extraordinary event. In which other art could you master the signs so quickly? Who else but the Americans who can relate to nothing culturally could master the signs of this art? Who else had the power and the naiveté? The first paintings were naive. You mastered your world by recreating it. . . . Every empire had its capital, and Hollywood was the capital of America.''

We had to laugh, because Hollywood, the home of Paramount, the Garden of Allah, Schwab's drugstore, and Grauman's Chinese, had become a mythical country for both of us, a kind of *fiction* and magic kingdom, where the infinite overshadowed everyday life. We thought of Jorge Luis Borges and all the libraries of Babel he created, those labyrinths and problematic countries with "transparent tigers and towers of blood," illusions which had overwhelmed the ordinary until we questioned our own lives and our sense of time, believing "that while we sleep here, we are awake elsewhere and that in this way every man is two men." Isn't that the condition of the moviegoer, who is asleep *here* and awake *elsewhere,* inhabiting at least two lives? The somnambulists we admire are our very own selves, and the movies, rather than bring us close to other people, enforce our sense of isolation and our ghostly presence on the screen.

Hollywood was only another dreamtown, as perverse as Borges' Tlön, a labyrinth that is slowly replacing our world, until in a hundred years ordinary languages and shapes "will disappear from the globe. The world will be Tlön.''

**6** We had other questions to consider, like the Ciné-mathèque, and why it rose up in France with the maniacal devotion of Henri Langlois. "France is the most centralized nation in Europe," Martens said, "and the scheme and politics of centralization is concentration. The Bibliothèque Nationale was the first library in the world. I don't know which king decided that everything written [and engraved] in the kingdom of France should be on deposit. It works as a memory of things, but it also works politically as surveillance. Once you centralize everything that's created, you know what is happening: no writer or engraver can exist on his own, no artist can create without sending copies of his production to the central library. It's exactly like a totalitarian country. Nothing created is external to political life."

I felt like Borges stuck with an encyclopedist from the land of Tlön, as Martens continued to talk. "Only France could give birth to this crazy idea of collecting and preserving all the films that had ever been made. Everything must have its copy somewhere [its ghost]. The Cinémathèque could only develop where archivism was a political fact for centuries. Langlois' isolated genius found in the substructure of the country the means of creating the Cinémathèque. . . . He had a crazy idea. But he could put it through. And only someone external to the 'empire' [Hollywood] could create the Cinémathèque, on the borders of the empire."

We talked about that mysterious Nazi major who helped Langlois in the middle of World War II. "Langlois' actions were heroic," Martens said. "He was trying to keep films out of the Germans' reach. He wasn't a collaborator, he wanted to save movies."

And Langlois himself, as reflected in Martens' eyes, began to look like a figure out of Borges, "Man, the imperfect librarian," who tries desperately to hold on to the memory of this world in a universe of "divine disorder." And Martens? He could have been some god who wore the red hair of wrath. And I? The only listener that was left.

"People conglomerated around Langlois, crazy people like him, the Christopher Columbuses of a new art. Truffaut, Godard, Rohmer, Chabrol were apostles who made films afterward. The real author of a film, they said, is the director. 'I belong to a new faith. Everybody is wrong about the cinema.' But who is the real author of *Casablanca*? The war? The script? The actors?' "

"What about Bogart's face?' "

Martens laughed. "No. The Cinémathèque would say Michael Curtiz [who directed *Casablanca*]. And once the apostles stated that the author of a film is the director, they then said: 'I am going to be a director.' You can't do films without megalomania . . . or terrorism, effective terrorism."

I asked Martens when he became a child of the Cinémathèque.

"I was fifteen, sixteen," he said. Martens had lived in the U.S. during the war and returned to France with his mother in 1946. He was like "a little American. . . . I was geared to the lingo." One of the first movies he remembers is *The Picture of Dorian Gray* (1945), MGM's idea of an Oscar Wilde novel. It was a film about an unforgettable face. Dorian, the young English dilettante, is played by Hurd Hatfield, who looked like a corrupted angel on the screen, male one moment, female the next, so that any child would have been confused by Dorian's identity.

In the film Dorian stays young while his portrait "ages" for him. It's doubly confusing, because not only do we have a "ghost" on the wall, with a masculine and feminine side, but *our* ghost, Dorian Gray, also has a ghost, who ages for him and for us. Most of the movie is in black-and-white, which highlights the perverse, sensual shadows of Hatfield's face, and we can feel the corruption in him, the mannered, doll-like gestures, the "monochrome" voice. The final sequence is in Technicolor: Dorian, sick of his "youth," slashes the portrait and falls to the ground. He "ages" instantly and dies, and now his portrait becomes young again. Martens was scared to death of that dual conversion. He was only five or six, and all that lurid color terrorized him.

In the late Fifties Martens met "a movie buff from Luxembourg, Fred Jung, a blondish fatso . . . a real nut from the North. Luxembourg doesn't exist. No one's been there. It's so small a country nobody has ever met somebody from Luxembourg [except Fred Jung]. It's more mythical than Monaco.

Jung geared himself into movies. He found his way, his way was to watch movies. How can you go through life watching movies? What did Fred Jung do? He created the Cinémathèque of Luxembourg. He went to see the prime minister of the ghost city of Luxembourg. 'We have museums,' he said. 'We need a cinémathèque.' He built his own cinémathèque. He watches movies and travels around the world six months a year. He exhumes old reels. Now he harbors some of the rarest treasures of the movies. He went to the Klondike, came across a ghost town, and discovered still frozen some films of Hollywood from 1915, 1916, and 1920, films that had disappeared. He was engraced by some frenziness of compulsion. There's always one more film to find for the smallest richest country in the world.''

Fred Jung is only ''another one of the monstrous children of Henri Langlois. You describe a person by his symbolic children. Langlois himself was monstrous. His empire was made out of celluloid, but it was an empire. He created the boundaries. He was Mr. Cinema.''

Langlois was ''an egocentric bastard maniac, a mogul in his way, a crazy mogul, so fat he couldn't fuck anyone. His only pleasure was to reign in the dark night of the movies. . . . He was monstrous like Orson Welles, with the voice of a castrato, a grotesque elephant, conveying to us why John Ford was a genius. He would present one or two films of Ford, the most obnoxious films that Ford did. Langlois was perverse.''

He began preparing homages to individual studios in the late Fifties. ''His homage to Paramount lasted nine or twelve months.'' Sometimes he would say that ''an American picture owes more to the studio that begot it than to its director or stars. Langlois was delirious about the difference between [the sound of] thunder at RKO and MGM. . . .

''The New Wave owed him everything. Neither Truffaut nor Godard went to film school. They never worked on a set. Here we have an emperor with his disciples . . . Saint Henri, Saint Langlois. He was always penniless. He bought too many films. He ruined himself for his museum. He himself lived in a museum. He slept in Cleopatra's bathtub [he'd acquired the bathtub from De Mille's *Cleopatra* for the Cinémathèque]. . . . He was a sadistic bastard at the end of his life. He would project an Italian picture with Japanese subtitles, and would say, 'It's the only copy I had. I bought it in Manila.' " Or else he would show "a Russian film in Danish. . . . He didn't have a life. All over the world there were tributes to his genius. But he made me feel uneasy. He did a monstrous thing, but did it with genius. His boundaries stretched too far, so he died."

7 We kept coming back to Borges, who had written detective novels and published scripts with Adolfo Bioy Casares for a pair of gangster films. Borges had understood that peculiar presence of film, its ability to diffuse time and enter those mysteries of mind and space that have troubled our imagination ever since we first began to articulate who the hell we were. A man has no life, Borges tells us, "not even one of his nights exists; each moment we live exists, but not their imaginary combination." But it is this *imaginary combination* that floods our dreams . . . and our films. Borges speaks of Chuang Tzu, the Chinese Taoist writer, who "more than twenty-four centuries ago, dreamt he was a butterfly and did not know, when he awoke, if he was a man who had dreamt he was a butterfly or a butterfly who now dreamt he was a man."

We are all Chuang Tzu, drifting into the flow of the century as we dream a path for ourselves through a universe that may or may not exist, like lost children in some ultimate movie palace with an infinite ceiling and very narrow walls. . . .

# Two-Headed Man

**1** Borges brings me to another labyrinth: those half-humans at the Garden of Allah who sat around a pool that looked like the Black Sea. Writers they were, men and women of real wit, who often wore two or three heads, as they collaborated on film after film and drank themselves into a stupor.

Several of them had been refugees from the Algonquin Round Table, that smart set who wrote for *Vanity Fair* and begot *The New Yorker,* almost as a parlor game for their own kind of people, and had a long, ten-year lunch at the Algonquin before they drifted out to Hollywood and fell into one of the cubbyholes and closet-cribs at Paramount and Warners, where writers had to clock in and out, in and out, while they swam in their own little Black Sea. They were "expatriates without leaving the country," a legion of the lost who "adapted each other's out-of-date plays and novels, and rewrote each other's scripts . . . and within a few years were rewriting the rewrites of their own or somebody else's rewrites."

They arrived in the Twenties and Thirties, and they've been abused ever since. Almost every writer of worth, from Dash Hammett to Faulkner to Lillian Hellman to Scott Fitzgerald to Dorothy Parker, joined that club of expatriates, at least for a little while, and lived in the sun like salamanders and high-salaried rats. Held in contempt by the moguls who hired them, they cobbled on this or that, were fired and hired and fired again, until their very existence was like a Marx Brothers movie. There was something absurd about the screenwriter, with his two heads, scurrying here and there inside those walled cities with a guard at the gate, vassals in a kingdom that couldn't start a picture without their help. They were little children who could graduate by becoming producers and tyrannizing other two-headed men. But most of them never got that far. They couldn't solve the simplest riddle of studio politics: the moguls had bought their services, like carpenters and shoemakers, and could ask them to write by the page . . . or by the pound.

Composers like Erich Wolfgang Korngold, who wrote the music for *Captain Blood* and *King's Row* and over a dozen other movies, fared much better than any two-headed man. The moguls loved music, and besides, Korngold was a genius. A child prodigy from Czechoslovakia, he'd composed an opera before he was ten and was conducting orchestras in his teens. Jack Warner had to kidnap him from the Vienna Opera House.

Korngold was movieland's own Mischa Elman, Brahms, Berlioz, and Bruno Walter, packed into one man. He could "play piano, fiddle, conduct and come up with thirty-two bars of *schmaltz.*" By 1938 his salary at Warner Brothers was $1,041.66 a week. He was " 'Doctor Korngold' or 'Professor Korngold' to strangers, fellow musicians," and movie moguls. Professor Korngold was passionate about his scores. If other composers on the lot tried to pinch from him, he would shout, *I steal from Richard Strauss. You can steal from Richard Strauss. But don't steal from me.*

At rehearsals he would often wear a Viennese hunting jacket "that hit him just above the hips." And he scorned knives and forks at the dinner table. He liked to eat dumplings and Sacher tortes with his hands. When Jack Warner and the junkman, Louis B. Mayer, had to give a party, they would invite Korngold, sit him down at the piano, and beg the maestro professor doctor to play one of his own compositions. But all a writer could do was saw at a script and "sew the dialogue into the action."

2 It was Scott Fitzgerald of the Garden of Allah, alcoholic, suddenly poor, with his wife in an asylum and Scott in the middle of his own blue midnight, his handsome profile gone, his novels earning nothing, his stories unsalable now, one more two-headed man working with other teams of writers, assigned to scripts that evaporated on him, guzzling Coca-Cola to keep his hands from shaking,

like some mogul's pet bear, it was Scott who sucked in his surroundings with all the Coca-Cola and revealed the foolishness and the heartbreak of the Hollywood writer as no one else had been able to do. Like Gatsby, he believed in romance and the golden sound of money. Movies meant success, and there wasn't much place in the "heights" of Hollywood for cobblers and two-headed men.

"I grew up thinking that writer and secretary were the same," says Cecilia Brady in *The Last Tycoon*. "They were spoken of the same way when they were not around—except for a species called playwrights, who came from the East. These were treated with respect if they did not stay long—if they did, they sank with the others into the white collar class."

Cecilia had as much contempt for the writer as any mogul did. "Writers aren't people exactly. Or, if they're any good, they're a whole *lot* of people trying so hard to be one person."

Her dad, Bill Brady, had offices in a building that resembled Louis B. Mayer's "mansion" at MGM. Brady's building had "long balconies and iron rails with their suggestion of a perpetual tightrope." And his own collection of two-headed men walked that tightrope six days a week.

But it was his partner, Monroe Stahr, alias Irving Thalberg, who dealt with the writers, "put them on an idea in pairs," and then put other pairs behind them, so that the writers and their closet-cribs became a series of Chinese boxes, and they were part of some labyrinth they could never follow.

"Through the years," Borges said, "a man peoples a space with images of provinces, kingdoms, mountains, bays, ships, islands, fishes, rooms, tools, stars, horses, and people. Shortly before his death, he discovers that the patient labyrinth of lines traces the image of his own face."

**3** Daniel Fuchs was one such writer who lived inside the labyrinth. He arrived in Hollywood in 1937, the year I was born, and a year after Thalberg lay dying, "a small thin figure in an enormous bed." Fuchs was a twenty-eight-year-old novelist. He hadn't been involved with the Algonquin crew. He wasn't a member of any Round Table. He was a "permanent-substitute" at a public school in Brighton

Beach, earning six dollars a day, his own kind of invisible man. He'd published three novels, a trilogy about Williamsburg that was poorly received and had sold *altogether* two thousand copies. No one in his neighborhood recognized him as a writer. And the Williamsburg he wrote about was hardly a ladder to success. Philip Hayman, the protagonist of his first novel, *Summer in Williamsburg,* is on the way to nowhere. The novel opens with a suicide and ends with suicide, as if the boundaries were forever fixed. The telephone wires across from Philip's tenement "looked like long, black fingers of a skeleton." And the cats in the street had "bulky faces, crude, like fists." Philip, the novelist-to-be, understands his Williamsburg. "Everything here was petty. Love was a hot joke. . . . Poetry and heroism did not exist, but the movies did. People in tenements lived in a circle without significance. . . . People were born, grew tired and calloused, struggled and died."

And Fuchs left his teaching job, his life as a "permanent-substitute," walked out of his classroom one day, and went to Hollywood, where he worked mostly on gangster films. It's no surprise. His trilogy is thick with gangsters and lowlifes, like Papravel, and his little band of two Italians, one Negro, and three Jews. Papravel controls the bus routes from Williamsburg to the Catskill mountain resorts. And as he drives out all the other bus companies, he says "it is only a beginning, because, remember, there is still a God over America."

Papravel is much more convincing than his own nephew, Philip, precisely because he's not a poet. He has the stink and fury of fuel oil, the smell of boardinghouses, the aromas of a man on the rise. And it's that kind of tension that Fuchs captured in his screenplays, whether he worked alone or as a two-headed man. *The Gangster,* with Barry Sullivan, was about a guy who came out of the slums, like Daniel Fuchs. In *Hollow Triumph,* Paul Henreid was a killer with a scar on his face. *Criss Cross* had Burt Lancaster as a thief among thieves. And Fuchs won an Oscar for *Love Me or Leave Me,* with Doris Day as actress and singer Ruth Etting and James Cagney as Moe the Gimp, the mobster husband who managed her career.

I'd seen every one of those films. *The Gangster* had all the sadness of myth. I remember the striped suit Barry Sullivan wore, his quiet manner, as if he were Philip Hayman turned into Papravel. And *Love Me or Leave Me* haunted the hell out of a kid from the Bronx. I cried when Cagney had one of his mad fits. He was crazy about Ruth Etting. "Ruthie," he would say, "Ruthie," and destroy the furniture of a nightclub. But I didn't remember Daniel Fuchs' name. He belonged to that quiet army of people who "crafted" the film. He wasn't Cagney, for God's sake. He was one of the screenwriters.

And then, in 1971, as if he'd risen from the dead, Fuchs published his fourth book, after a lapse of thirty-five years. It was one more Hollywood novel, *West of the Rockies,* about an aging actress. Fuchs couldn't go home again to Williamsburg. But I should have realized that Hollywood was his home. He'd dropped Williamsburg from his dreams. He was like an immigrant who'd gone to some magical West of the Rockies.

The points of his voyage grew much clearer when I read "Days in the Gardens of Hollywood," a little memoir he wrote for *The New York Times Book Review* in 1971. He talked about that hallucinatory afternoon when he disappeared from P.S. 225. "I'm going to Hollywood, Frank," he told the cop on the corner. And he did.

Fuchs was like a conquistador. He'd gone out to some undeveloped country called Southern California, "fresh and brimming and unawakened, at the beginning . . . everything in this new land [was] wonderfully solitary, burning and kind."

*Burning and kind,* like the Hollywood sun.

And the people themselves? "It is amazing how they cling to the studios here, how the studios dominate all their minds and lives. The studios exude an excitement, a sense of life, a reach and hope, to an extent hard to describe."

Ah, it was like Kafka's castle, only there were eight or nine of them in movieland, and they could be "broken into" if one had the right credentials. But nothing worked without these castle-kingdoms, Paramount, Warners, MGM . . . either you were part of their labyrinthian ways or you didn't exist.

Fuchs would roam the back lots on sunny afternoons, visit "the Western streets, the piers, the empty railroad depots, the somnolent New Bedford fishing village of 150 years ago. I watch the studio bravos in their costumes at their perpetual play."

But it wasn't as idyllic when Fuchs himself had to dive into the dreamscape. He'd gone "through the holocausts at Huntington Park and Long Beach, those sneak previews [for his own films] when the audience goes flat."

And once, on the fourteenth week of an assignment during which he hadn't written a word, he wonders if he can "think up some way of committing suicide without dying." He offers to go off salary, but his bosses look at him as if he's a crazy man. "How can we let you work for nothing?"

Fuchs discovers his answer "in a dazzling rush of clarity that scares me: all I have to do to commit suicide without dying is to murder the producer."

He has a curious affection for that "thug, harsh and ruthless" Harry Cohn of Columbia, who catches Fuchs walking around Beverly Hills with a box of candy, and gloats "that the crazy sums his company pays . . . go for chocolates" and the blue dress Fuchs' wife is wearing.

And the conquistador himself, Daniel Fuchs? Williamsburg was another life ago. Critic Daniel Golden sees a kind of Jewish angst in Fuchs' journey. "Fuchs's work has followed a segment of his people from their initial financial and physical destitution in Brooklyn to a more metaphysical impoverishment in modern, affluent California." How nice and neat a line, from Dostoyevskian novelist, rich in spirit, to a "bankrupt" character in Beverly Hills. But I see a different journey. I'm not so sure Fuchs would have become a better writer had he remained a "permanent-substitute" in Brighton Beach. It was the kind of drudgery that could have broken a horse. I ought to know. I was a "permanent-substitute" in a later era, a gypsy high-school teacher.

How many Williamsburg tales did *our* Daniel have in him to tell? He was looking for new territories. And he had a thirteen-week contract with a Hollywood studio, in the heart of the Depression. He could raise his children next to the citrus groves, the bougainvillea, and the Joshua trees. "The bones in their bodies are dear to me." And Beverly Hills couldn't have been any more harmful a *shtetl* than Williamsburg or Brighton Beach. If Fuchs was "caught up in the acquisitive dreams and centripetal isolation of Jewish immigrant culture," so were Jack Warner and Harry Cohn and Irving Thalberg and Louis B. Mayer and Darryl F. Zanuck, who wasn't even Jewish.

And if he clung to those walled cities, the castle-kingdoms, and sat down with Harry Cohn in the Columbia dining room, it wasn't Hollywood that "killed" Daniel Fuchs. When old friends asked him why he'd fallen into silence, Fuchs would insist: "I write, in collaboration or alone, from my own original material or from other source material, in the morning and in the night, on studio time and on my own time, until I fill shelves and prize Reticence as the rarest of jewels."

A two-headed man in the gardens of Hollywood who gave us *The Gangster* and *Hollow Triumph*. Screenplays rather than the further romances and fruition of Philip Hayman and the twisted routes of Papravel on the Williamsburg-to-Catskill line. Perhaps in another age we will have an *auteur* theory for screenwriters that will give them greater due. Meanwhile, Daniel Fuchs is a writer who wed himself to castle-kingdoms, not the Williamsburg Bridge. And why? "For the boon of work, for the joy of leisure, the happy, lazy days; for the castles and drowsy backlots; for the stalwarts I've come to know, John and Bob and Sam; for the parties at Barney's, the times at Phil's; the flowers, the sycamores, the blessings of the sun."

It's rather a sad credo, it seems. The end of an inner, imaginative life for a "station" in Hollywood, a key to all the little kingdoms. But it has nothing to do with the particular metaphysics that Daniel Golden describes, and more to do with fright. The novelist is a natural isolato who has to play one-on-one with what little talent he has, whether he (or she) lives in Southern California or the wilds of Brooklyn. He cannot collaborate. He cannot "sit" in the sun. And what makes Fuchs' words so poignant is the knowledge that he needed the *collaboration*—friendship and flowers within the walls of the labyrinth.

4 Raymond Chandler was another man of the West. His fictional detective, Philip Marlowe, has his office right in movieland, near the corner of Hollywood Boulevard and Ivar Avenue. And like many of the people around him, Marlowe is rootless and alone. He continues to haunt us and disturb our sleep, because in spite of his bravura and deep distrust of women (which would define ninety percent of all movie heroes), he has the quality of walking amnesia that describes the arc and fall of our lives in a century of sleepwalkers

and psychopaths. Marlowe, according to Raymond Chandler, is "a lonely man, a poor man, a dangerous man. . . . I think he will always have a fairly shabby office, a lonely house, a number of affairs, but no permanent connection. I think he will always be awakened at some inconvenient hour by some inconvenient person to do some inconvenient job. . . . I see him always in a lonely street, in lonely rooms, puzzled but never quite defeated."

He is the creature many of us fear we will become—a part of society, yet detached from it, without family or real friends, a phantom self we might meet on the moviehouse wall: the survivor as an urban animal. Perhaps this is why we've had so many renderings of Marlowe in the movies, so many faces for a single detective, as if no one character could contain him, capture who he is. Dick Powell, Humphrey Bogart, George Montgomery, Robert Montgomery, James Garner, Elliott Gould, Robert Mitchum . . . Marlowe has no definitive face. He exists at the edge of our dreams.

Chandler thought Cary Grant would have made the ideal Marlowe, but what does a writer know? Grant would have been one more face on the wall. Chandler aficionado Edward Thorpe envisions Marlowe as an American archetype. "Hollywood recorded and romanticized, distorted and developed every aspect of American—and world—history; yet no American folk hero, even the cowboy, owes his existence to one man, Chandler . . . as does the private eye."

The ghost of John Wayne might argue with Edward Thorpe, but it doesn't matter. Marlowe is in our guts, whether he looks like Elliott Gould or Dick Powell. And in Chandler's "Hollywood" novel, *The Little Sister,* Marlowe has a lot to say about movieland, California, and the City of Angels. He calls California "the department-store state. The most of everything and the best of nothing." And Los Angeles, he tells us, "has no more personality than a paper cup." Real cities, he says, have "some individual bony structure under the muck. Los Angeles has Hollywood—and hates it. It ought to consider itself damn lucky. Without Hollywood it would be a mail-order city. Everything in the catalogue you could get better somewhere else."

Marlowe is an ornery man. Whatever he hates, he also loves. In *The Long Goodbye,* he looks "at the glare of the big angry city" with its "night of a thousand crimes." But it's Marlowe's city, "no worse than others, a city rich and vigorous and full of pride, a city lost and beaten and full of emptiness."

For Philip Marlowe, Los Angeles is one more part of the American dream. "We're a big rough rich wild people and crime is the price we pay for it, and organized crime is the price we pay for organization."

And *film noir,* noticed and catalogued by the French, could only have come from this wild people, in the golden country of California. Los Angeles had been a forlorn little pueblo in Spanish colonial times, founded in 1781, and named after Nuestra Señora la Reina de Los Angeles. Its first building was a jail. Even after the Yankees grabbed California, Los Angeles was "the worst frontier outpost in the West." Its entire population was only eleven thousand in 1880. Like Hollywood, Los Angeles invented itself. It had the first Chamber of Commerce in the United States. It created its own myth, and "developed the puffing of cities into an art form." So even before Hollywood existed, the *idea* of it had come to California. And L.A. burst upon America, "sparkling like an overgrown movie set."

And into that movie set ventured Raymond Chandler, Chicago-born, "a boy whose father had gone to the bad." Chandler was raised by his mom, Florence Thorton, and a series of uncles and aunts. Florence abandoned America when the boy was seven and took him across the Atlantic to live in South London. He attended an English prep school, Dulwich College, where one of his classmates was Boris Karloff (Frankenstein meets Philip Marlowe!). Chandler had decided to become a poet. He scratched out mournful lyrics about ladies who yearn to die . . . and their lovers who lost themselves in some garden of the dead. But he couldn't make much of a living and he returned to America in 1912, a defeated poet at the age of twenty-three. He settled in Southern California to seek his fortune. He strung tennis racquets for a while. He became a bookkeeper at a creamery, moved out of whatever boardinghouse he was in, rented a place on Loma Drive in one of the "older" sections of Los Angeles, and soon Florence arrived from England to live with her bachelor son.

America's entry into the First World War interrupted Chandler's idyllic life. He joined the Canadian army, wore the kilts of his regiment, the Gordon Highlanders, and served in France as a platoon commander. His entire outfit was blown to bits during an artillery barrage. Chandler was the only one who survived. He was sent to England, became a cadet in the Royal Air Force, but the Armistice ended his career with the RAF. He got his discharge, knocked about in the Pacific Northwest, then returned to his mother in L.A.

He fell in love with Cissy Pascal, a woman who was seventeen years older than "Ray," but he didn't dare marry her until after his mother died. Mrs. Pascal was a buxom beauty with strawberry-blond hair. Twice-divorced, she'd been an artist's model in New York before she'd ever married. She was a passionate woman devoted to Ray, who was now in the oil business and had given up all attempts to write. But he was as restless as Philip Marlowe. "I have lived my life at the edge of nothing," he told his London solicitor after Cissy died.

He was a very formal man, bound by the strict codes of Dulwich College. Chandler wouldn't walk into the street without a jacket and a tie, but he was also a Bedouin in his ways, often moving once or twice a year. He had over seventy different addresses in Southern California. And he was an alcoholic. He lost his job in the middle of the Depression because of the drinking he did. And the failed poet started writing fiction for the pulp magazines. "I had to learn American just like a foreign language."

He saw himself as "a man without a country," neither English nor American, but some kind of cultural half-breed caught in the crazy quilt of Southern California, where men and women had to reinvent their lives. And Chandler, a good Dulwich boy who longed for tradition, had come to a place without a past, where whole peoples had to define themselves against the deserts, mountains, valleys, seas, and citrus groves. Chandler was one more anonymous soul who'd become "a mystery writer with a touch of magic and a bad feeling about plots."

His apprenticeship wasn't easy. He didn't publish his first novel until he was fifty-one. And even after Philip Marlowe was world-famous, Chandler grumbled about his own status in the United States. English intellectuals idolized him, adored his work, and Chandler "tried to explain to them that I was just a beat-up pulp writer and that in the USA I ranked slightly above a mulatto.''

When Cissy died, Chandler fell apart. He became more and more of a nomad. "She was the beat of my heart for thirty years. She was the music heard faintly at the edge of sound.''

He'd cheated on her, of course, would disappear for weekends with some little secretary when he worked as a screenwriter at Paramount. But it was Cissy who held him together, who provided the only fabric he had other than Philip Marlowe. When he closed up the house he'd shared with Cissy in La Jolla, he "felt a little like the last man on a dead world.''

He tried to kill himself and couldn't succeed. He sailed to England, stopped at the Connaught Hotel on Carlos Place, and was greeted like a celebrity. He wore white gloves wherever he went because of the skin allergy "that made his fingers split.'' He'd become a little cuckoo. He'd meet young women and propose marriage at first sight. And suddenly he had new ambitions for Philip Marlowe. He wanted to marry him off, as if Marlowe's "marriage" could assuage his own bitter loneliness.

The alcoholism grew worse. He'd forget to show up for dinners in his honor. "Chandler the celebrity ceased to be someone to celebrate.'' There were other suicide attempts. He'd lost the feel for magic that he believed was so necessary for a writer, "the distant flashes of insect wings" that could only happen on a page.

He died of bronchial pneumonia on March 26, 1959, after days of heavy drinking. He was seventy years old.

**5** What is there about Chandler's life and death that moved me in such a powerful way? He didn't have the high poetry or the vision of Faulkner and Scott Fitzgerald or Nathanael West. He couldn't write a story half as good as Ernest Hemingway. Yet I found myself reading Frank MacShane's biography of Chandler again and again and again. It doesn't really investigate the tones of Chandler's fiction, the particulars of his syntax, the melodies he produced, the originality of Chandler's "alphabet," his ability to enter into the psychic climate of California and give us the deep weather of a certain time and place.

Hammett had been a Pinkerton man. He understood the argot and specific gravity of detectives and thieves. Chandler, the oil executive, had never been near a sheriff's office. He was an amateur in matters of crime. And in spite of Marlowe's own misogyny, there is a great deal of romance to Chandler's writing, the lilt of modern, rootless California. Hammett had a geometry of purpose that fixes his characters clearly in our minds. His prose is crystalline and almost brutal in its plainness.

"Samuel Spade's jaw was long and bony, his chin a jutting v under the more flexible v of his mouth," begins *The Maltese Falcon*. "His nostrils curved back to make another, smaller, v. His yellow-grey eyes were horizontal. . . . He looked rather pleasantly like a blond satan." That's more than we ever get to see of Marlowe, who hides within the mirrors of his own voice. In fact, we might never have known what Marlowe looks like if an English admirer hadn't written to Chandler, attempting to puzzle out a portrait of Marlowe from Chandler's own books.

He's slightly over six feet tall, Chandler wrote back. With brown eyes and dark brown hair. He smokes Camels some of the time, lighting them with kitchen matches. "He will drink practically anything that is not sweet." Unlike Sam Spade, Marlowe had never had a secretary. He couldn't afford one. "The date of his birth is uncertain," according to Chandler. Marlowe might have been thirty-eight years old, "but that was quite awhile ago and he is no older today." He's a native Californian who comes from a town north of San Francisco. And he reminds us of Cary Grant. Is that because Ray imagined Grant to be another Dulwich boy, like himself? Did he know that Grant had been born in Bristol as Archie Leach, with a mom who was half-mad? That Cary Grant was as "fictional" as Philip Marlowe? When Robert Montgomery played Marlowe in *Lady in the Lake* (1946), he had the camera itself "pose" as Marlowe's face: Marlowe is invisible for most of the film, except when we catch him in the mirror.

Chandler himself was invisible most of the time. Perhaps that's why I was so involved with his life story, as told by Frank MacShane. The boy without a father or a country who was educated to be a little gentleman, a poet of lugubrious lines who became some sort of nomad in Southern California . . . and a pulp writer with his own peculiar sense of art, as if Chandler were not only inventing a face for Philip Marlowe, but a mask for all of us to wear, in a century of masks. And the twists of Chandler's life, the constant moving about, the wondrous marriage to an older woman, the strange survival in France, that flirting with the RAF, the sterile knights of his early, childish poems transformed into a detective with Chandler's code of chivalry, the alcoholism, the skirt-chasing, the white gloves worn to protect his fingers, the suicidal bouts, seemed like a very long movie, a voyage that began and ended in the dark, an outline of all our lives, a *shared* biography. . . .

6 And then there was Chandler the screenwriter, who toiled at Paramount, worked with Billy Wilder on *Double Indemnity,* wrote *The Blue Dahlia* while he was in an alcoholic daze, and fought with Alfred Hitchcock over *Strangers on a Train.* Chandler walked away from Hollywood, quit the movies altogether, denounced producers, directors, cameramen, actors, and actresses, including "Miss Moronica Lake," yet he had more to say about the movies than almost any other writer. He understood that film was "*not* a transplanted literary or dramatic art . . . it is much closer to music, in the sense that its finest effects can be independent of precise meaning, that its transitions can be more eloquent than its high-lit scenes, and that its dissolves and camera movements, which cannot be censored, are often far more emotionally effective than its plots, which can."

And he also knew that the writer in Hollywood could never be more than a hired gun. The studios "destroy[ed] the link between a writer and his subconscious. After that what he does is merely a performance. His heart is somewhere else."

For Chandler, the movie business was a "magnificent but childish colossus" that tossed upon the screen "some male idol" with "the build of a lifeguard, and the mentality of a chicken-strangler." He saw the Academy Awards as Hollywood's "tribal dance of the stars and the big-shot producers." Not even all the cops in L.A. could protect "the golden ones" from that numbing cry of the mob that sounded "like destiny whistling through a hollow shell."

And that cry also revealed the futility of the screenwriter.

"What Hollywood seems to want is a writer who is ready to commit suicide in every story conference. What it actually gets is the fellow who screams like a stallion in heat and then cuts his throat with a banana. The scream demonstrates the artistic purity of his soul, and he can eat the banana while somebody is answering a telephone call about some other picture."

And so Chandler withdrew from movieland. "I don't care how much they pay me, unless they can also give me delight in the work. They can't." Of course, part of this was Chandler's own pique. He couldn't get along with Billy Wilder or Alfred Hitchcock. But he also understood that even if he had been able to "dance" with Wilder and Hitch, his own scribbling on the page couldn't satisfy that sense of dreamwork the writer needs to survive. In the cribs of Hollywood, Chandler had "a sense of exile from thought, a nostalgia of the quiet room and the balanced mind. I am a writer, and there comes a time when that which I write has to belong to me, has to be written in silence, with no one looking over my shoulder, no one telling me a better way to write it. It doesn't have to be great writing, it doesn't even have to be terribly good. It just has to be mine."

The creator of Philip Marlowe couldn't exist as a two-headed man.

7 I never toiled in the gardens of Hollywood, or had to cut my throat with a banana, but I knew exactly how it feels. I worked in Hollywood-on-the-Hudson, Otto Preminger's offices near the roof of the old Columbia building on Fifth Avenue. Sigma Productions. I was Preminger's court jester and clown. It was 1976, and Preminger, one of the first independent producers, a man who'd fought the Hollywood blacklist and the Production Code, had just come off the biggest flop of his career, *Rosebud*, a film about Arab terrorism that was both infantile and incoherent. *The New York Times* called it "consistently idiotic." *New York* magazine said it was "a bloodless bore."

John Lindsay, New York's former mayor, had become a movie actor for *Rosebud*. He played a U.S. senator whose daughter was kidnapped. He was so wooden on screen, so full of fraudulent passion, that one forgot time, place, and plot and marveled how a human being could turn himself into a puppet. It was almost as if the very idea of cinema had broken down, and Lindsay's face took on the frightening tones of a man without a persona. He wasn't a phantom on the wall. His ineptness brought him laughingly close to the audience. And "Otto the Terrible," who'd been as powerful as any mogul, who could rescue a major studio with the receipts of one of his films, hire a blacklisted writer, tell Hollywood to go to hell, pick away at his budgets like a czar, find the perfect logo for *Exodus* or *Anatomy of a Murder,* rage whenever he wanted, fire half his crew or a star like Lana Turner, couldn't seem to finance his next project.

Hollywood had suddenly turned deaf to Otto. And he hired a novelist like me, who didn't have a movie credit, to work on some obscure television play about Justice Hugo Black of the Supreme Court. The maestro was marking time, dawdling with one of the TV networks, while he was dreaming up a multi-million-dollar deal, sculpting all the facets in his head. He was seventy years old. His eyes were as blue as Paul Newman's had ever been. He had a marvelous waltzing gait, as if the ground itself had to give in to Otto Preminger. His suits could have been tailored for a Persian king. They hugged his body with a silken feel. Everything around him or on him seemed stamped to his own measure, from the white letters of his name on a bare black wall, to the thick creamy carpets, to the blue veins in his skull. He was *hollywoodien,* like Orson Welles, a character larger than any movie he could make.

And I had to consider what had possessed him to hire me. He'd read one of my novels, or so he claimed. It was about a Jewish homicide detective who gets himself killed. But Otto never referred to the novel. He talked about Truman Capote. He talked about Thomas Mann. Otto's father had once been attorney general of the whole Austrian Empire, the first Jewish chief prosecutor Austria had ever had. "My father was very wise," he'd said in an interview. "We had a wonderful relationship really, like two brothers." His mother had been a "warm-hearted woman, but she did not really play a large part in the formation of my character."

Otto was a stage actor in his teens and he started to direct while he was still a university student. Max Reinhardt, Germany's most adventurous producer-director, put him in charge of the

Josefstadt Theatre in Vienna before Otto was twenty-five. And Preminger became the young prince of producer-directors. But he left Vienna three years before the Anschluss, when Hitler annexed Austria to Germany as if it were some kind of paper province.

Preminger arrived in Hollywood in 1936, met Irving Thalberg and all the other moguls and goddesses and gods. Cooper, Lombard, Gable, and Darryl F. Zanuck of Twentieth Century–Fox, who was now Otto's boss. But Zanuck had his own bag of Austrian prodigies and he didn't bother himself with Otto, who was idle most of the time. Like a museum piece. In the Thirties, Hollywood resembled "the great museums of the world: there was always considerably more talent in the warehouses than there was on display."

Finally Zanuck put Otto to work on a B picture and the "new Max Reinhardt" found himself confined to the back streets of Twentieth Century–Fox. And when Zanuck fired him, Otto discovered that none of the other moguls would go near Otto Preminger and risk Zanuck's wrath. The moguls might have been fiercely competitive, but they were also a community of kings.

Otto couldn't find work again at Fox until Zanuck was away in World War II as a lieutenant colonel in charge of documentary films. When the dictator returned, he demoted Otto again, forced him into his little club of producers, and wouldn't allow Otto to direct. "He always walked up and down with a polo mallet in his hand, and a long cigar." But after Rouben Mamoulian was fired from one of Otto's own projects, a film called *Laura* (1944), Zanuck allowed Otto to direct the film.

It's about a detective (Dana Andrews) who falls in love with the portrait of a murdered woman, Laura Hunt (Gene Tierney). The film is like a somber and romantic parody of *Dorian Gray*. Laura Hunt comes alive again halfway through the film, and the detective is confronted with the "double" of that dead woman he already loves. *Laura* is one of the first and very best examples of *film noir*.

Otto was suddenly Zanuck's "darling," a star producer-director at Fox. He stayed with Fox until he turned independent with *The Moon Is Blue* (1953), a harmless little film that proved controversial because Otto defied the Hollywood censors and dared have David Niven and William Holden use such obscene language as *virgin* and *seduce*. One has to recall how far the country had regressed. The witch hunts had frightened the pants off Hollywood. There was nothing really "sexual" about *The Moon Is Blue*. Twenty years earlier, before the Production Code was tightened and enforced, Hollywood had produced comedies and melodramas with Mae West, Clara Bow, Barbara Stanwyck, and Jean Harlow that were funny, perverse, and full of sexual play. But of course that had nothing to do with Otto the Terrible.

He kept defying the censors and toying with Hollywood's taboos. He revealed a junkie's paraphernalia on screen in *The Man With the Golden Arm* (1955), hired an all-black cast for *Carmen Jones* (1954), and brought one of the Hollywood Ten, Dalton Trumbo, back from the dead to write the screenplay for *Exodus* (1960).

Otto loved to dance around in controversy. He hired Joseph Welch, the Army's chief counsel during the McCarthy hearings, to play a small-town judge in *Anatomy of a Murder* (1959). Welch was terrific. And Otto was still fighting censors, still destroying shibboleths. He showed Lee Remick's underpants in that same film. He dealt with the subject of homosexuality in *Advise and Consent* (1962), offered us a heroine with a deformed face in *Tell Me That You Love Me, Junie Moon* (1970). Looking back now, there's little that was innovative or truly daring in what Otto did. He was a showman who tested himself against the tempers of his time.

Otto the Terrible loved a good fight. His father's years as chief prosecutor of an empire seemed to mark Otto in the best of ways. Rather than dodge the censors, he attacked. He took film studios, television networks, and cities to court if they interfered with the making or the showing of his films. And as an independent producer, he helped destroy the old studio system. Not even Darryl Zanuck could compete with the whirlwind that surrounded most of Otto's films. But what remains ironic is that Preminger did his best work while he was in bondage to Zanuck and Fox. *Laura* and *Fallen Angel* (1945) have a dreamlike quality, a disturbing psychic pull, that his later films lacked. Without ever being aware of it, Otto thrived in movieland's last golden years, before the witch hunts, before TV, before the stars rebelled, before antitrust legislation divorced the film companies from their own movie palaces, before the age of the independent producer. . . .

But it was 1976, the bicentennial of America's birth as a nation. There were tall ships standing in New York harbor while I toiled for Otto the Terrible. He had a white marble desk in his office and a telephone speaker that permitted him to shout into his phone from any corner of the room. My office was next to Otto's. He could enter it from a side door, and he often did, coming upon me while I scribbled words at my own desk.

"Write colloquial," he would shout, meaning that I should give each of the justices on the Supreme Court a distinctive flavor, a pattern of speech that could delineate them. I worked like a bloody carpenter on those voices, but I was never "colloquial" enough.

There was a tribal instinct to Otto. In 1971, after the death of novelist and burlesque queen Gypsy Rose Lee, Otto revealed that he was the father of her son, Erik Kirkland, who was his casting director at the time. Otto adopted him, and Erik Kirkland became Erik Lee Preminger. He hovered around his father's office, working on some project, I imagine. There was a continuity between them, a playful silence, even though Otto and Erik, who'd written the screenplay for *Rosebud,* must have been in mourning over that film.

John Lindsay arrived one afternoon, looking like a movie star. And somehow I couldn't grasp why that tall, handsome alertness, his mayor's smile, had been missing from the screen. His image, reflected in Otto's camera, seemed stuck in some black hole, without illumination or life. Yet sitting in one of Otto's black chairs, he had all the resonance that human flesh would allow.

It was my birthday and Otto took me to lunch at an Italian restaurant where the entire kitchen could be glimpsed through a window. I watched a cook in his tall hat beating eggs in a silver bowl. The restaurant boomed around Otto. *Rosebud* didn't matter. The maestro could have his flops. He'd also been a movie actor. He'd played a Nazi in four films, including *Stalag 17.* He ate and drank with more gusto than his scriptwriter-clown.

Otto didn't like to talk about his past films. He fell into a convenient amnesia. But his face bloomed like a little boy's when I brought up *A Royal Scandal* (1945), starring Catherine the

Great (Tallulah Bankhead) and a member of her royal guard, Alexis (William Eythe), who rises in her favor and then sinks. Alexis is an opportunist who just isn't clever enough. I saw the film when I was eight, and it seemed to embody all the politics of a public-school boy. William Eythe was like my own pathetic mirror. I rose with him . . . and also fell at Catherine's court. The film had bothered me more than Bela Lugosi ever could. It had all the cynicism of the Bronx.

"Lubitsch," Otto said. "It was Lubitsch's film. He had a heart attack . . . he asked me to direct. My friends said, 'Stay away, Otto.' But I couldn't. It wasn't a success . . . everyone was waiting for 'the Lubitsch touch.' They wanted another *Ninotchka*. I gave them something else."

"I loved it," I said. "Whatever happened to William Eythe?" He was my hero, that shifty, colorless man, handsome in his way, who seemed to live in the shadows.

"Alcohol," Otto said. Eythe had died of hepatitis at thirty-eight.

We took a walk after lunch. People stared at his familiar skull. Otto sailed into the traffic. We went to his townhouse on Sixty-fourth Street. Part of the teleplay was about the Supreme Court's reversal of a decision by the Regents of New York to block the showing of *Lady Chatterley's Lover*, a French film based on D. H. Lawrence's novel.

"Ah," I'd said to Otto, "if we're going to have Black and all those other crows on the bench ponder the immorality of *Lady Chatterley's Lover*, why not include a scene of them watching the film?"

Otto hadn't loved the idea. He'd never seen Marc Allégret's film, starring Danielle Darrieux and Leo Genn. There wasn't the least bit of pornography about it. But I thought I could milk a little drama from a gang of crows in black gowns looking for bits and pieces of Danielle Darrieux's behind. And so Otto had rented the film. And we watched it together in his screening room on the top floor of the townhouse. Danielle Darrieux was beautiful, of course. But the scenes I liked best were with Leo Genn riding around in his wheelchair.

Otto fell asleep after the film. He lay down on a divan near the window and started to snore. "Mama," he said in his sleep. "Mama." And beat on his forehead with one red fist.

8   "Films are not made out of the minds of screenwriters," said director Werner Herzog. And Herzog's right. Otto had given me a play in skeleton form, and I felt like a child with a coloring book that he hadn't chosen for himself. I'm not sure how many writers had worked on the teleplay before me, but I had a heap of bones to contend with: pages that were half-complete. There'd been a brouhaha during the time I sat behind Otto's idiot desk. Paintings had disappeared from the office. Detectives scuttled around on Otto's carpets, measuring the walls. They looked enchanted to me: caught in their own solemn spell. The whole operation stank of metaphysics. I wondered if I was in the middle of some time warp, a dreamer on the planet of Tlön. Whatever was going on, it was profoundly more interesting than my preoccupation with the Supreme Court, and much more *fictional*.

The culprit turned out to be the ex-boyfriend of a secretary at Otto's office. I'll call her M. Otto wouldn't press charges. He confronted the ex-boyfriend on a rainy afternoon, invited him up to Sigma Productions, as if he were interviewing an actor for our teleplay. He didn't shout. There was almost a musical lilt to his voice. He knew M hadn't been involved, and he wanted to protect her from any scandal. It was a curious kind of practice for an independent producer. He wasn't particularly close to M. But she worked for him. She was part of his little tribe.

The paintings reappeared. I continued to scribble. I felt more and more like a two-headed man. I liked my collaborator, Otto Preminger. I'd become one of his tribesmen, but I couldn't give him what he wanted, a docudrama of the high court, like a perfect line drawing. I was involved with empty spaces, subversive planets of the soul.

I ran from Otto Preminger, but it's a funny thing. I missed the office, drinking tea from Otto's china, the blueness of Otto's eyes, his mad quest for the "colloquial." I'd hear rumors about him from time to time. He'd been hit by a car. He fell into some kind of constant amnesia. And he died in his eightieth year.

# eleven

# *Wildies*

1 Mack Sennett died a poor man. But in his glory years, from 1912 through most of the Twenties, he was "King of Comedy" when comedy itself was king. There wasn't much use for Sennett when the talkies took over. He had a genius for absolute motion, and words got in the way. Chaplin had started with Sennett, and Fatty Arbuckle, Gloria Swanson, Carole Lombard, and Wallace Beery worked for him once upon a time. Sennett brought a kind of rhythmic mayhem to the silversheet.

The son of Irish immigrants, Mikell Sinnott was born in Quebec and moved with his parents to East Berlin (in Connecticut) when he was seventeen, and labored in an iron mill while he dreamt of becoming an actor and an opera singer. In 1902 he had a meeting with David Belasco, who discouraged him from seeking a career on the stage. But the boy entered burlesque and became a movie actor in Manhattan at the Biograph Studios. He worked for D. W. Griffith and soon was directing his own Biograph shorts. In 1912 he formed Keystone, a production company with financing from two ex-bookies, and the world of films has never been the same. Sennett introduced the Keystone Kops, bumbling acrobats of disorder, and his Bathing Beauties, "those dizzy sexpots" who were alarmingly beautiful and dumb. Sennett's films defied Sir Isaac Newton's laws of gravity. They seemed to exist in their own private field. They were, according to James Agee, "faster and fizzier than life."

The kid from Quebec hadn't invented comedy. He was part of "that great pipeline of horsing and miming which runs back unbroken through the fairs of the Middle Ages at least to ancient Greece." But what he did seemed funnier on film. He could bend time itself with the cranking of his camera and create a storm of movement that couldn't have been found in any other medium. Whatever else happened, a Sennett film "built up such a majestic trajectory of pure anarchic motion that bathing girls, cops, comics, dogs, cats, babies, automobiles, locomotives, innocent bystanders, sometimes what seemed like a whole city, an entire civilization, were hauled along head over heels in the wake of that energy like dry leaves following an express train."

It was as if the world itself was only one more prop for Sennett's people to play with.

Most of his scenarios were invented on the spot, while the Keystone Kops were in the middle of their mayhem, ripping up half of Hollywood. Movieland had become their own malleable thing. But Sennett did have story conferences. He'd invite a "wild man" to sit in, "an all but brainless, speechless man, scarcely able to communicate his ideas," someone with "a totally uninhibited imagination" who could think up "wildies." The wild man was a shaman of sorts, a primitive "priest" who connected Sennett's gagmen to their own particular roots. He "functioned as the group's subconscious mind."

But the "wildies" didn't last very long. As Sennett's company grew and grew, Hollywood itself seemed to resist those destructive Kops who would derail a whole trolley line, coming out of nowhere with cotton billy clubs and crazy hats. The comedies became quieter, and movieland divided itself into little walled kingdoms with an order of their own. And Mack Sennett's Kops disappeared from the streets.

Yet the disorder Sennett had dredged up, that nihilistic play, was the very stuff of our own century. How could Sennett have understood that the antics of his Kops and Bathing Beauties were close to the meat of psychopathology and modern physics? All along, without knowing it, Mikell Sinnott had been dancing with Einstein and Freud. When Sigmund Freud, an obscure physician with lunatic ideas, published *The Interpretation of Dreams* in 1900, few people took notice of the fact. Freud's little dream book sold 361 copies in six years. Articulate as he was, Freud must have seemed like Mack Sennett's "wild man," gesturing in the dark. He was trying to tell us that dreams were the architecture of our lives; they formed whatever psychic face we had; they outlined our heart's desire in a language that was deceptively simple and deceptively deep. We all arrive in a state of amnesia. Birth comes to us like a blow on the head. We dream our way out of amnesia, bit by bit, recovering memories of what might or might not have happened. It's our waking life that seems more and more like a shadowland, and at least in this century, when God feels as remote and meaningless as some celestial clock, we've clung to our childhood as that magical time when we were all "spacemen," discovering whole worlds as dream and fact, with very little distance between them.

And then some little clerk in a Swiss patent office, Albert Einstein, discovered that time wasn't absolute—that each of us recorded it as our own personal music, that we were all isolated beings inhabiting a very private planet, where chaos ruled most of the "time," like a Mack Sennett comedy.

2 The first nickelodeons, storefronts and barns with big white sheets tacked to a wall, were often called "Dreamland." The shadow plays on that silversheet were shunned by most people of quality. They were for an immigrant culture, illiterates and wild men who could learn from ghosts on the wall. The actors and actresses were as anonymous as the audience, pitiable as themselves. The audience fell in love with their silver presence, scribbled fan letters to the fictional characters they portrayed, the very first stars, who were still anonymous, like Broncho Billy and The Biograph Girl.

In 1910 The Biograph Girl was revealed as Florence Lawrence, and now the stars had legitimate names and could be worshipped as more than ghosts. And with this new star system came the first fan magazine, *Photoplay,* and the first of the movie palaces. But as Terry Ramsaye, chief chronicler of the silent film, noted in *A Million and One Nights:* "Neither the great names of the stage nor of literature could make an impression on the motion picture mind. . . . This world of the illiterati had to create its own stars," who were much more popular "than the late Mr. Homer of ancient Greece, or Sarah Bernhardt, of modern France."

But even if the stars had given up a little of their ghostly aura, and the movie palaces were not attracting the middle class, that sense of a *dreamland* hadn't gone away. And some of the pull

of entering that dreamland was a recall to childhood wonders
. . . and terrors too. Because there was always a terror after waking from our infant amnesia into a world that had no familiar
marks. And the movies seemed to recapture for us all the splintered signs of our earliest memories, when past, present, and future had no real distinction for us and time was like a long silent
spill of images in black-and-white, as anarchic as our own lives.

Ah, but it was also lots of fun, like Dreamland and Luna Park,
those two great "atmospherics" at Coney Island. Architect and
urban planner Rem Koolhaas called Coney Island "a foetal Manhattan," powered by all the marvels of the nineteenth century
to produce a magnificent dreamscape. The introduction of the
light bulb and the harnessing of electrical current brought about
a delicious disturbance, "false daytime" in the middle of the night,
with all its attendant magic. "If life in the metropolis creates loneliness and alienation, Coney Island counterattacks" with its own
"Barrels of Love." And suddenly we have "electric phantom cities" that seem far more exciting than the ones we live in.

Lunar landscapes proliferated around the country, boardwalk
after boardwalk, from Atlantic City to Long Beach and Ocean
Park, with its Dragon Gorge that could hurl you into the womb
of time, let you play the unborn child, and Venice (California),
with the world's biggest roller coaster and a grand canal that
carried you to Italy without having to cross much of an ocean.
Or, as George Tilyou, one of Coney's builders, promised: "If
Paris is France, Coney Island, between June and September, is
the World."

They were all preludes and preambles to Hollywood, the ultimate amusement park, where borders shifted with every film,
entire countries could be reproduced, and empires developed
from year to year with the arrival of glove merchants and junkmen who made themselves into moguls. Their influence was felt
in moviehouses which were like replicas of a dream park, tiny
Venices with interior canals. That's how the "common man"
voyaged at the beginning of the century, into dreamlands that
had been prepared for his pleasure.

And Dreamland itself? In May 1911 a fire started in the electrical circuits outside "End of the World" pavilion. Firemen-
clowns from "Fighting the Flames," who'd staged fire after fire,
fled from their dormitories, and the whole of Dreamland burned

to the ground. Some of the trained animals from Dreamland's menagerie managed to escape. No one bothered to collect them. "For many years after the holocaust, surviving animals" could be seen in the heart of Brooklyn, "still performing their tricks."

I wonder what Freud would have made of those animals— archetypes of the unconscious *and* pathetic beasts, they haunt the imagination like a kind of mad, educated anarchy that could be found in films. Sennett's comedies were like holocausts. And perhaps that's why they had to be tamed. Because there's something nihilistic in the American character that most of us would prefer not to see.

We love to declare how we "tamed" the West, as if we were all frontiersmen in coonskin caps. There's been such lawlessness throughout our history, such deep plunder in our past, that we've had to surround ourselves with myths of America as the relentless bringer of justice and civilization, celebrated in our notion of that man of the West, the lone ranger, the good bad man, who was both murderer and modern knight. He lives alone. He often dies alone. His only real furniture (and companion) is his horse. Women are strange animals who want to tie him to one spot, unless they're drifters like himself, dancehall girls who are the only creatures he's allowed to kiss. He fights bushwhackers and railroad men (usually from the North) and rogue Indians, heartless Comanches who attack infants and old ladies and might have scalped his kid brother or stolen a sister of his. Of course he avenges his brother and gets his sister back, and, like Natty Bumppo, he clears a path for farmers and preachers to come—all those civilizing people. But he cannot live among them. He can only ease their rite of settlement, their passage out of the wilderness.

D. H. Lawrence has a different tale to tell. "The world is a great dodger, and the Americans the greatest. Because they dodge their own very selves," he wrote in 1923. Lawrence didn't believe the Pilgrims arrived in America to escape religious oppression. "England had more freedom of worship in the year 1700 than America had." The Pilgrims "came largely to get *away*. . . . Away from what? In the long run, away from themselves. Away from everything. That's why most people have come to America, and still do come. To get away from everything they are and have been."

Wanderers, dreamers, madmen, rabbinical priests, sailors, prostitutes, farmers with some unholy vision in their heads, looking for some final continent: America, a land much too large to incorporate one king. Our fathers, whoever they were, arrived "in a black spirit. A black revulsion from Europe, from the old authority of Europe, from kings and bishops and popes."

And this black spirit is what we inherited from our original dads. "Somewhere deep in every American heart lies a rebellion against the old parenthood of Europe." That rebellion was internalized, taken under the American skin, so that it existed as a kind of constant tic, a disorder of the soul. And the old British lion, George III, my favorite king, was the sign and signal of that disorder. He seemed to stand in America's way, as if he could devour a continent.

The colonists rebelled against George, but they were a little lost in a brand-new country without a king. And so they had to escape "to some wild west" and become pilgrims all over again. The new American pilgrims were called pioneers. And that Wild West, no matter how vast it was, was mostly metaphoric, a mind country, populated with Indians and buffalo herds these pilgrims had to destroy in order to justify the madness of such a long trek. There was nothing heroic about that destruction. The good bad man was just another ghost invented to gloss over the brutality of that mission to "tame" the West. He belonged on a movie screen, like Broncho Billy (alias Max Aronson of Little Rock) and William S. Hart, a Shakespearean actor from Newburgh, New York, who became a cowboy with leather cuffs and a pinto pony named Fritz.

No matter how much the pioneers etched their own image upon this continent, they discovered that the "spiritual home of America was, and still is, Europe." And some of our nihilism comes from that—the desire to tear away our own feeling of illegitimacy, which is also reflected in our art.

For Lawrence, that art had an "inner diabolism." And like some detective of the American psyche, Lawrence sensed the duality between our "deliberate consciousness . . . so fair and smooth-spoken, and the under-consciousness so devilish. *Destroy! destroy! destroy!* hums the under-consciousness. *Love and produce! Love and produce!* cackles the upper consciousness. And the world hears only the Love-and-produce cackle. Refuses to hear the hum of destruction underneath. Until such time as it will *have* to hear."

And no other cinema but ours had that curious mix of poison and peaches and cream, sentiment, myth, the farmer's lovely daughter, and the blackness at the bottom of the well. Shirley Temple and W. C. Fields. The Marx Brothers and Sonja Henie. Margaret O'Brien and Mae West. Lassie and Boris Karloff. The Keystone Kops and the Goldwyn Girls . . . and we mustn't forget historical creatures, like General George Armstrong Custer, that Hollywood has taken out of its own little pantheon and turned into one more vivid wax doll.

Look at *They Died with Their Boots On,* that childhood classic of mine, made just before World War II. Custer is colorful enough, with his long hair and beautiful scarves, as only Errol Flynn could have played him. There isn't a hint of his nuttiness, his megalomania, the mad fits. The general graduated from West Point "at the foot of his class," according to my old faithful edition of the *Encyclopaedia Britannica.* But he distinguished himself during the Civil War. He was the youngest general the North ever had. And we watch Custer in his glory, leading his men in charge after charge. He doesn't fare so well at the end of the war. He's demoted to the rank of captain and left without a billet. But with the aid of his wife, Olivia de Havilland, he's sent to the Dakotas as a lieutenant colonel to put down Indian uprisings and help the white man colonize the West.

There's a bit of Marxism in his blood. He denounces crooked white traders and politicos for exploiting the Indians. He loses his command (Ulysses S. Grant never liked him). But Olivia intercedes for him again. He gets his old command back. The crooked traders have stirred up the Indians. He goes into battle against half the Indian nation and dies with all his men at Little Bighorn.

And the legend of the brave Indianfighter is upheld by Hollywood and Warner Brothers. We weep for Custer's widow. We remember the flamboyance of his coats, the long scarves, the long hair. And we can't help but make some transference. America is about to go to war. It will need generals like George Armstrong Custer, good-looking and gallant, slightly wicked perhaps . . . the way we imagine Errol Flynn, our very own Robin Hood and Captain Blood.

Custer has always been a controversial figure. We celebrate him for Custer's Last Stand, a perverse bit of soldiery, during which Custer divided his command, attacked the Sioux at Little Bighorn, and was wiped out with all his men. He was, like a later general, George S. Patton, a man of the West and a brilliant hothead, given to taking risks. And both were a little crazy. Custer had been one of Patton's heroes. And he turned his own tank divisions into a kind of cavalry, driving through the German lines like a band of horse soldiers. Both men believed in America as a land of conquistadors. Custer would have destroyed the Sioux and the Cheyenne to bring civilization to the West. And Patton, with his two pearl-handled revolvers, would have taken his army and turned it on the "Russkies," the new barbarians, the new Cheyenne.

Patton would get his own movie picture. But it wouldn't come until twenty-five years after his death. Franklin Schaffner's *Patton* (1970), starred George C. Scott as "Old Blood and Guts." It's a poignant study of a man who was fighting Germans and chasing the white whale of Communism. Scott is marvelous as the white-haired soldier with a short coat full of medals, buttons, and stars. Part Hannibal, part Caesar, and part little boy, howling at a world of generals that won't give him his way, he has some of the force and frozen, pitiable grandeur of Welles' Charles Foster Kane.

Scott declined the Academy Award he won for playing Patton. He didn't want to be involved in any horse race with his fellow actors, he said. There was a hullabaloo. But it didn't matter. Patton's popeyed face had haunted the screen. The nation needed a hero. Its soldiers were mired in Vietnam, fighting a war that couldn't be won. And the public superimposed his presence, with the pearl-handed guns, onto that insane war in the South China Sea. All we needed was another Patton . . . or General Custer.

Hollywood itself was much too chickenhearted to deal with Nam. It might lose half its audience. Only the Duke, John Wayne, would dare risk his reputation with *The Green Berets* (1968), a cockeyed homage to the Special Forces as horseless soldiers in the new Indian country. The film, directed by the Duke himself, was a flop. But there was a special kind of wisdom to what the Duke had done. He was only furthering the pioneer spirit, seeking other boundaries, a psychedelic West, America's final frontier: Saigon was Dodge City filled with "friendlies" and "unfriendlies," otherwise known as gooks. The war "was steeped in western imagery," as numerous critics have noted: "Dangerous areas were 'Indian country,' a South Vietnamese scout was a 'Kit Carson,' cutting the ears off dead enemies was equated with taking scalps, and more than a few grunts emblazoned their flak jackets with the slogan 'The only good gook is a dead gook,' " writes J. Hoberman in *Artforum*.

But that new Indian country did seep into our movie culture, in spite of Hollywood. One feels it in Robert Altman's *M\*A\*S\*H* (1970), a film about the Korean War, with all the mythos and absurdities of Nam. It was also there in *A Clockwork Orange* (1971), Stanley Kubrick's nihilistic glimpse of a violent, sleepy London of the future, borrowed from Anthony Burgess' book. And perhaps most of all, it was in *Little Big Man* (1970), Arthur Penn's adaption of the Thomas Berger novel. Once again we meet General George Armstrong Custer. And in that horrible looking-glass of the Vietnam War, Custer's extremes are monstrous now. He has the same long yellow hair, and his own kind of dash, delivered to us by Richard Mulligan. He wears a yellow coat when he goes to war, as if he were staging some sort of epiphany. He's histrionic and quite insane. He rages at Ulysses S. Grant for ruining his career. And that horse soldier of *They Died with Their Boots On* becomes a killer of Indian ponies. He can see only as far as his red scarf.

Of course it's overcooked. And this psychotic Custer is no more historical than the Custer of Errol Flynn. But it does seem closer to some kind of truth. The Indians were *at least* as human as the white man. They had a poetics and a civilization; they weren't pioneers seeking an unfathomable West, and they weren't running away from themselves.

And what's most remarkable about *Little Big Man* is that it doesn't preach. The Cheyenne are brutal, funny, kind, as ethnocentric as any of us. They call themselves "the Human Beings." The white man *and* the black white man seem worthless to them. And Jack Crabb (Dustin Hoffman), the single white survivor of Little Bighorn, moves between the Human Beings and the white man like a Ping-Pong ball with a physics all its own, as if he were occupying some Indian country in outer and inner space.

Arthur Penn is a director who's often given us a viewpoint that slants away from the official culture. *Bonnie and Clyde* (1967) was the first American film to probe our spooked, Vietnam-riddled psyche, to reveal the violent ghosts who inhabited the country's dreamscape. Bonnie Parker (Faye Dunaway) and Clyde Barrow (Warren Beatty) float past us, as familiar as our own cousins, funny, sad, with Clyde's sexual problems and Bonnie's desire for death and fame.

Warner Brothers despised the film. The head of distribution at Warners called it "a piece of shit. . . . What kind of movie is this? The two leads end up dead?" Warners tried to dump the film. "We lost our bookings after three days," Arthur Penn recalls. "But the theater owners were screaming to have the picture back. They [Warners] were dropping it, and the picture wouldn't drop. Warren [Beatty] came up with the advertising campaign [about Bonnie and Clyde]. *They're young. They're in love. They kill people.*"

The film had captured the internal beat of the country. "It was an apocalyptic moment." Hollywood had become a faltering farm. And directors like Truffaut and Godard had grabbed hold of the cinema, and seized it for themselves, with a style and a vision borrowed from Hollywood B films of the Forties and Fifties. The New Wave had appropriated America, turned it upside down, like some mock Normandy invasion, and was producing films with a nervous, contemporary lilt that was like an America we no longer had. And we, the *Ricains,* had gone to bed. Even Hitchcock, our own giant, was involved in cold-war dramas, like *Torn Curtain* (1966), that were almost feeble-minded. And suddenly America awoke with *Bonnie and Clyde,* a film that had a European flavor, but wore American pants. *Bonnie and Clyde* was the beginning of our own New Wave.

**3** Arthur Penn was born in Philadelphia in 1922. He's the younger brother of photographer Irving Penn. He had a childhood that seems cinematic in all its crazy shifts—with Charles Dickens as the screenwriter . . .

and puppeteer. His parents were divorced when Arthur was
three. He moved to Plainfield, New Jersey, with Irving and
their mom, Sonia Penn. The three of them formed a family
unit. The family would move every six months, covering the
entire map of the Bronx like a little wagon train. It was the start
of Arthur's life as a gypsy. Jack Crabb's peregrinations suddenly
feel familiar when compared to Arthur Penn's. Perhaps that's
one of the reasons Arthur was drawn to *Little Big Man*. He must
have seen the shadows of his own face.

When Arthur was nine he was sent to live in New Hampshire
in a sort of summer camp. But Sonia couldn't take him back at
the end of the summer. Irving had a rheumatic heart, and Sonia
had to care for him. Arthur remembers "all that poverty and
my brother's illness." And the phantom camp run by "a kind
of quasi-missionaries." He lived with the caretaker and went to
school in town. He was "a strange New York street kid . . . the
tough of the school." But something happened. "We were pee-
ing. The kids saw I was circumcised. They made fun of me."

Ah, Jack Crabb, Jack Crabb, the white man's Indian.

Arthur was brutally alone. "I never anticipated being there
that long." In the meantime, his mother had become a nurse.
He moved back in with her. She worked at a hospital and also
had a corset shop in Brighton Beach. She'd open the store in
the morning, close it around noon, and run to the hospital,
"and then I would open the store after I came from school."
Arthur was a corset salesman at eleven and twelve. "Here are
the girdles, here are the corsets," he'd tell the customers, ma-
tronly women who went behind a curtain to try on his mother's
merchandise.

During most of his childhood Arthur would make friends and
then have to move again. He went from Neptune Avenue in
Brighton Beach to another part of Brooklyn, where Sonia had
a candy store. But Arthur was "too wild." Sonia sent him to
live with his father (and Irving) in Philadelphia.

Harry W. Penn was a watchmaker and an engraver. He had a
shop on Sansome Street, where all the jewelry shops were. And
Arthur was apprenticed to his dad. He'd come home from high
school and work as an engraver in his father's office. His brother
was living with an English girl, Nonnie, whom he later married.
She'd been a costume designer with Michael Chekhov's theater

company in England. "She started taking us around to art museums. . . . We had a wonderful time."

But it grew into "a very bad period." His father got sick while Irving was away in Mexico with Nonnie. Harry's illness began to incapacitate him. He'd been "a brilliant engraver" who repaired watches for Bailey, Banks, and Biddle, "the Tiffany's of Philadelphia." And when he got sick, "we were trying to fake it," pretending that Harry was still available for Bailey, Banks, and Biddle. "Money was going like crazy, whatever little money there was." And with his father in the hospital, Arthur had to give up their apartment "on Eighth and Pine" and move into a boardinghouse.

Harry had cancer of the bladder and developed uremic poisoning (like Jean Harlow). "It threw him into a psychotic state. . . . Now he determined that I was stealing from the business. He was delusional. . . . He would turn on me, certain that I was stealing. He didn't know I had sold the furniture. Finally one day he took my hand and said, 'I'm so afraid, I'm so afraid.'

"It was the only time I'd held his hand or seen him weep. It was the first time I'd seen any demonstration of feeling toward me. He thought I was a terrible failure, a lousy watchmaker."

Harry Penn died when Arthur was eighteen. "It was at the end of high school. By now the war was on [in Europe]. I tried to go to England. . . . I was so infatuated with Nonnie, who was British. I wanted to work in precision instruments. I wanted to get over there."

But he was drafted instead. "The only action I saw was during the [Battle of the] Bulge. I ended up in Germany and by some crazy fluke I was invited into the Soldier Show Company," a kind of army acting troupe, a band of soldier minstrels and mimes.

"All the guys in the outfit were vets. The whole construct was about to come tumbling down" when Arthur was asked to be "the civilian head of the program for the new army of occupation."

Arthur was "a corporal or sergeant" one day and "the next day a civilian in charge of the unit." He'd become the little *Meister*. Arthur would put on plays to keep the [American] soldiers from fraternizing with the women. "I worked in the opera houses of Wiesbaden, running, flying from place to place, in artillery-spotting planes."

"Like a gypsy," I told him.

Arthur smiled. "A gypsy with terrific status."

But soon Arthur was caught up in all the mad machinery of an occupation army. His whole staff disappeared one day. "Now I was desperate to get home."

After a good deal of wandering and working on TV, Arthur found himself in California, directing his first film in 1958. It was about Billy the Kid. *The Left-Handed Gun* looks at Billy's life in a brooding, "left-handed" way. Paul Newman seems hysterical half the time as Billy, a lost son searching for his dad. He has his own shadow, Hurd Hatfield, who still has the features of Dorian Gray. Hatfield idolizes Billy and then betrays him. The film wanders a lot, with its own jerky motion, as if the camera eye can't seem to settle on one thing . . . except Billy the Kid. It disturbs the ordinary "sleep" of the moviegoer. I wondered if Arthur himself was left-handed, like the Kid.

"No," he said. But the film had an eccentric quality, "a left-handed twist that stays in all of my work. The film is so strange it disappeared. . . . It was edited by the studio. That was a shock. In live TV, we did it all. I had shot it exactly the way I wanted it. I made it in twenty-three days." And then Warners took it away from Arthur. But it still had his signature, that "left-handed twist."

"In live TV, we had been doing these skewered things. Orthodoxy was not our strong suit. *Left-Handed Gun* was dismissed in this country." But critics like André Bazin of *Cahiers du Cinéma* "were reacting to the movie the way in my darkest dreams I thought someone would respond to the movie."

Arthur didn't make another "skewered" film until 1965. "People were interested in Truffaut and Godard. That's how *Mickey One* got made."

Godard's *Breathless* (1960) and *Band of Outsiders* (1964) were low-budget films done with a kind of anarchic, consciously amateurish artistry that hadn't been seen before. Godard's handheld camera created a schizoid universe where almost anything could happen. The old romantic City of Light was now a land of gray streets, filled with petty hoodlums who wore funny hats on their heads. Godard had turned Paris into his own B-movie set, had sabotaged time and space to give us a series of disconnected dreams. Truffaut wasn't nearly as perverse, but he was radical and inventive in his own way. With *The 400 Blows* and *Shoot the Piano Player* (1960), he was able to mix heartbreak and delight, and introduce a catalogue of sad, urban clowns, orphans under the skin. The whole of Paris had become an orphanage in Truffaut's eye.

It wouldn't have mattered much to Hollywood, but these "little" films were making money. And so Columbia Pictures decided to look for an American Godard or Truffaut in Arthur Penn. "The only way I could get a picture made," Arthur recalls, "was to make a deal with Columbia: two pictures, not to cost more than a million each." And Arthur took a naturalistic play by Alan Surgal and livened it with his own "left hand."

We first meet Warren Beatty fully clothed in a steam room, wearing a derby. He's a comedian in Detroit, working for Rudy Lap of Lapland: Franchot Tone with a completely ravaged face. It's not the Tone we remember from *Mutiny on the Bounty* or *The Lives of a Bengal Lancer* (both 1935), the young and handsome second lead, slightly in the shadow of Gable or the Coop. Lap is a reminder of how even Hollywood shadows can decay. But he wields a certain power over the comedian, who owes money to some nameless, all-encompassing Mob. The Mob has been feathering his life, paying his bills through the personage of Rudy Lap. "Who owns me?" the comedian asks. "What did I do?"

He runs away, burns his Social Security card, all his ID, becomes a bindlestiff, a bum on the road, and lands in Chicago four years later, in the middle of a hobo jungle. He picks up a Social Security card from a man who's been mugged, but even his new identity is flawed. He has an unpronounceable Polish name. He goes to Rent-A-Man, Inc., a hiring agency for hoboes like himself. The manager takes one look at his Social Security card and dubs him "Mickey One."

Mickey gets a job as a dishwasher, moves into a boardinghouse, and starts to do one-night stands at clubs in the Tenderloin district. There are no Hollywood faces here; they have that ravaged, dusty design of the streets. Mickey One picks up an agent and a girlfriend (at his boardinghouse). His agent, Georgey, goes to one of Chicago's top clubs, the Xanadu, and tells the club's manager, Ed Castle (Hurd Hatfield), about the

new comic in Georgey's own little stable. "A golden talent,"
he says.

Once again we discover Dorian Gray. Hatfield's broken, brittle handsomeness seems out of another time and another film: he cannot escape his own screen image, and Arthur uses him remarkably well. Ed Castle looks as if he's about to corrode in front of our eyes. He watches Mickey perform at The Pickle Club and wants to hire him. But Mickey can't afford to be spotted in a big-time Chicago club. Castle tells him of the wealth he will have if he comes to the Xanadu. "Al Jolson had a hundred and fifty overcoats in his closets when he died."

But Mickey is still an orphan on the lam. "My mother was a waitress on a fast streetcar line."

His girlfriend ask him, "Are you frightened, Mickey?"

He answers. "As long as I live."

He still can't find who owns him. "How do you turn yourself in?"

When his shirt gets filthy, he wears the collar inside out. He's Mickey One, the man who's left his identity on the sidewalk somewhere. "I'm guilty . . . of not being innocent."

Like Kafka's K.

This is not the world of Louis B. Mayer. There are no more safety nets. Arthur Penn forces us to look into that dark chaotic well where our "personalities" come from. It's not entertainment in the MGM manner. We're no longer in movieland.

I asked Arthur how Warren Beatty felt about the film.

"Warren had a sense that he wanted to go with the really original directors. He said, 'I don't understand this fucking picture, but if you're happy with it . . .' But in point of fact, he did understand it." The relationship Arthur had with Beatty in *Bonnie and Clyde* "was cemented from *Mickey One*."

I reminded him that *Mickey One* had the feel of both our childhoods. It was an "orphan's" tale, filed with notions about being unwanted and unloved, about some nagging guilt that wouldn't go away. We were both "boardinghouse" brats. "I lived in a boardinghouse like that when my father took sick," Arthur said. "That was the texture of living for me." It was also the curse of our century. We were all Mickey Ones, amnesiacs with false identity cards, trying to find some central myth for all the fragmented selves each of us carries around.

4 Arthur fell into "a deep pessimism after *Little Big Man.* I couldn't find the right film, the string I wanted to be attached to."
    He found that string in *Night Moves* (1975), Arthur's own *film noir* about an L.A. private detective (Gene Hackman) who discovers his own particular fate as he tracks a gorgeous little runaway brat (Melanie Griffith) to the Florida Keys.

The movie captured the dream state we were in at the end of the Vietnam War. The action almost seems to take place underwater. "It was a dark picture," Arthur said. "The Kennedy assassinations were painful to me. I was in a foul deep depression at their terrible losses, and that's what *Night Moves* is really made of."

Arthur had worked with both Kennedy boys. He did two radio spots with Bobby, and he and producer-director Fred Coe "had been in the control room of the third Nixon-Kennedy debate. We designed the idea of a close-up for Jack . . . close-ups would ruin Nixon."

Ah, I can still remember Nixon sweating under his make-up, looking like an Alka-Seltzer salesman. But in spite of Arthur's "night moves," Nixon nearly beat Jack.

I asked him about Melanie Griffith, an actress I adored. She had a powerful craziness in most of her films. She was wonderful as the grown-up nymph in Jonathan Demme's *Something Wild* (1986) and the very best thing in Brian DePalma's *Body Double* (1984). She danced to her own sense of danger, as she'd done in Arthur's film. There was never that false, artful control.

"She was living with Don Johnson" (now of *Miami Vice*).

"Arthur," I said, like one of D. H. Lawrence's Pilgrim Fathers. "She was just a kid" (she was, in fact, sixteen).

Arthur laughed. "Here we had her tutor on the set . . . her mother knew about Don."

We talked of Gene Hackman, the ultimate "ugly" star of the Seventies—a genuine actor who'd become a movie idol. The shock of Vietnam had created new heroes, actors who looked and behaved like grunts; they weren't exactly rebels, as Brando had been in the Daddy Warbucks years of Dwight David Eisen-

hower, but "singularities," male actors who disturbed our unconscious minds because they pulled us away from that
uninterrupted dream of movieland, and obliged us to take a
longer look. Hackman was "pound for pound the best actor on
the screen. Gene is shy . . . he's a wonderful stage actor." But
some of our best stage actors had "suffered" because of the
movies. "It was our terrible American destiny [for stars like
Hackman] not to continue two careers."

Arthur's next project was *The Missouri Breaks* (1976), one of
the most anticipated films of the Seventies. Brando had just
come out of a "retirement" of four years. He'd been extraordinary in Bernardo Bertolucci's *Last Tango in Paris* (1972); he'd
stopped hiding behind costumes and accents, didn't wear a
rubber lip, and played a broken-down American with all the
insufferable bother of Brando himself. And the idea of Brando
*and* Jack Nicholson, directed by Arthur, ought to have been
movie heaven. It wasn't. I couldn't believe what was happening
up on that wall. Brando and Nicholson seemed to inhabit two
separate universes. They'd bump into each other from time to
time and then go about their business, Brando as the "regula-
tor" and Nicholson as the horse thief.

"*Missouri Breaks* was more a sociological event than a cinematic event. . . . We had no script."

"Shame on you, Arthur," I said.

I'd been working with Arthur on a screenplay, and he "sat"
on me for months, obliging me to reconsider the characters and
find a much better weave from scene to scene. I hadn't realized
how autobiographical the whole thing was. The film was about
a dead Russian engraver who'd forged counterfeit ruble notes.
That engraver could have been Harry W. Penn, or my own dad,
a retired furrier who'd "engraved" mink collars with his own
hand. But nobody's dad could have helped *The Missouri Breaks*.

"It was supposed to be the richest deal ever made," Arthur
said. "Two actors making more than a million each, figures now
that seem like eye drops. It took months and months to structure the deal. During this period I could not work with Mc-
Guane [novelist Tom McGuane had written the screenplay].
We're six weeks away from shooting, and McGuane goes off to
England to reedit *92 in the Shade*. If the sets for *Little Big Man*
hadn't been standing in Montana, we wouldn't have been able

to make the shoot. . . . Nicholson and I called Bob Towne [screenwriter Robert Towne]. He dropped whatever he was doing and came up [to Montana]. He rewrote a few scenes. We were making it up as we went along, pulling rabbits out of a hat, throwing snowballs here and there . . . we were beguiling instead of following conflict. Jack knew it. It was driving him crazy."

"But you had Brando," I said. "For Christ's sake. Couldn't he have done anything?"

"Brando's deal was for twenty days . . . Marlon and two creatures, a mule and a horse. We knew we were tap-dancing to save our lives, because we didn't have a movie."

5 I'd expected too much from *The Missouri Breaks*. I'd wanted Brando to redeem the film, to waltz with Nicholson in some marvelous way. And I wondered if the film hadn't been doomed from the start; a Western, in 1976, would have seemed quaint no matter how good it was. The Western's "whole elaborate mythology—its codes, rituals, and ancillary merchandise—has become obsolete," writes J. Hoberman. "It used to be that each western, no matter how banal, was a little Fourth of July." But that long, long holiday ended with the fall of Saigon in 1975.

The whole dream of the frontier, with the world as an endless prairie for America to play upon, collapsed overnight. The past, mythological or not, was no longer a prism that could enchant us. We developed amnesia about the war *and* its connection to the old frontier. We'd suffered a national disgrace much worse than Korea; we'd never really involved our psyche in *that* war. Seoul wasn't Dodge City, the way Saigon had been. We didn't go out on scalping parties along the 38th Parallel, and there were no Last Stands on the Yalu River.

Suddenly Saigon, which had obsessed the nation, dropped out of our vocabulary. Yes, there was talk of Agent Orange and MIAs, but Saigon itself wasn't even a ghost town. It didn't exist—past, present, or future.

And then came *The Deer Hunter* (1978), the first of the "war" films to deal with Nam in a metaphorical way. Half the film has a completely naturalistic setting in a Pennsylvania town. The other half opens out onto an hallucinatory Nam, where the Viet Cong and ultimately Vietnam itself are obsessed with the game of Russian roulette. Director Michael Cimino takes us into Cholon, the Chinese quarter of Saigon, for a final game of Russian roulette, between two Americans now, a soldier (Robert De Niro) and the friend he'd come looking for (played by Christopher Walken).

*The Deer Hunter* didn't moralize about the war. It revealed Nam as a black hole that had sucked us all in and was impossible to grasp in conventional terms—we had no language for it other than that crazy visual sign of Russian roulette. Nihilistic and patriotic at the same time, the film deals with our cultural schizophrenia, that wound of being American, a wound we'll always have, because we cannot locate ourselves in history. We have our myths—Custer, the Wild West—but they collapse under any real scrutiny. We're the somnambulists who've fabulated a New World for ourselves—a democracy of the possible that was codified in our speeches, our Constitution, and our books, and later thrust upon a hundred thousand walls, in film after film, presided over by furriers, jewelers, and junkmen who were hungry for that America they'd heard about, the land of unforgettable faces. . . .

It's 1989, and we've been deluged with films about Nam.

It was all quiet after *Apocalypse Now* (1979), Francis Ford Coppola's excursion into the heart of darkness, otherwise known as "the asshole of the world." Saigon is "civilization" compared to the edges of Cambodia and Nam. Most of the film was shot in the Philippines. Coppola found himself in the middle of an earthquake. Half the Nam he'd reconstructed was destroyed, and Coppola had to begin all over again. One of his stars, Martin Sheen, suffered a heart attack during the shoot, and Coppola himself seemed to be riding a nervous breakdown. The making of the film was a lesson in entropy—one of nature's meanest laws. With time enough, any system collapses into chaos. But somehow Coppola endured. *Apocalypse Now* is the ultimate frontier movie. It takes us across all the forests and jungles America had, all our visions of Manifest Destiny—that sense of ourselves as the Chosen People who could clear any wilderness—and into the underbelly of the American dream. General Kilgore (Robert Duvall) is another Custer, with his air cavalry, flying horses that can deliver music and napalm with the same dramatic flush.

*Apocalypse Now* was as disturbing and technically brilliant as *Citizen Kane*—both films tear at the fabric of our most cherished myths. If Charlie Kane is the American apostle of success, then it's a success that ends with a hollow fall. Kane dies alone in his castle, longing for the "sled" of childhood, his Rosebud that no one else (except the audience) can uncover. We become Kane's secret sharers. And the journey that Captain Willard (Martin Sheen) goes on to kill that crazy man, Kurtz (Brando), that ride upriver into the unknown, where dead bodies hang from trees and mountain warriors wear the spotted colors of their tribe, is a descent into the empty spaces of our own non-history, smothered with patriotic gore. If Brando ruins the last part of *Apocalypse Now,* it's because he gives it a bloated, histrionic feel that belongs in another movie.

It didn't matter. The nation had had enough of Nam. We moved from silence to the slow gathering of myth and the start of the Hollywoodian war, with *First Blood* (1982), *Missing in Action* (1984), and *Rambo: First Blood Part II* (1985); the grunt, maligned for so long, misunderstood, and half-forgotten, as most casualties are, was suddenly transformed into the superhuman scout and Indianfighter, Rambo, who, ironically, had the same-sounding name as the French symbolist boy poet, Arthur Rimbaud. Rimbaud stopped writing poetry at nineteen and became a gunrunner in North Africa. And our Rambo lives his life in reverse: he's the soldier turned "poet," the forgotten man who articulates the pain and forlornness of every other grunt and Green Beret.

And now Vietnam was one more movieland. Oliver Stone's *Platoon* (1986) was the ultimate World War II movie with slightly different collateral: the grunts had blacker faces and the rotten habit of killing each other rather than the Comanches in the bush. Saigon itself was becoming a piece of Hollywood furniture. In Barry Levinson's *Good Morning, Vietnam* (1987), Saigon was the setting for situation comedy. The Viet Cong were "good guys," people one could bargain with. And *Off Limits* (1988), starring Willem Dafoe and Gregory Hines, was the first police procedural set in Nam: Saigon looked like Hollywood's idea of inner-city Detroit.

Of course, the new landscape, Saigon, USA, might disappear any second, or become a permanent addition to the culture. And then, who knows? We could have Rick's Café near the old Presidential Palace and the Saigon zoo. The point is that the distortion is always one more figment of an unhistorical past, a journey away from nightmare, into a familiar, lulling timescape, with its own weave.

And yet, underlying that safe border, there's also a hinterland, with a pull toward chaos, like Mack Sennett's wild man . . . and a deeper pull perhaps, into a rejection of all our cultural props, the signs and signals of America's own divinity. Before Irving Thalberg tamed them, Groucho, Harpo, and Chico Marx were full of "wildies." *Duck Soup* (1933) is as near as one can get to a kind of cultural breakdown. Groucho is Rufus T. Firefly, prime minister of Freedonia, a "postage-stamp" republic floating around somewhere in the middle of a lost Euro-American continent. Rufus plays jacks in the Chamber of Deputies, and that's how business gets done in Freedonia. He dons a coonskin cap and Civil War uniforms of the North and South, while Harpo is dressed in Napoleonic gear. The Old World and the New have collapsed into the little storm of Groucho's painted mustache, and history is nothing but a toy for the Marx Brothers to play with.

The film was a flop. America was in the midst of the Depression, and Franklin Roosevelt's New Deal had become one more sacred cow. The Brothers' nihilism cut a bit too deep into the bone of American feeling. After the Brothers moved from Paramount to MGM, their furor was curtailed. *A Night at the Opera* (1935) and *A Day at the Races* (1937) had a lot of classic nonsense, but the boundaries were enclosed, and the nihilistic universe that the Brothers inhabited grew smaller and smaller. The Brothers could ruin an opera or fix a race without disturbing our dreamtime at the movies. And they had Allan Jones to sing a couple of songs and provide a bit of superfluous romance. All the romantic interest the Brothers ever needed was Margaret Dumont, Groucho's screen "mistress," who was a perfect foil to his libidinous and lunatic one-liners.

And then there was W. C. Fields, deeply misanthropic, with a verbal wit that almost had the force of a visual style. Fields was so distrustful he had over seven hundred bank accounts, under different names, scattered all over the world. He hated families, doctors, bankers, children, and dogs in his films. But his energies wore down with all the alcohol he consumed, and his wit wouldn't have survived the patriotism of World War II. You couldn't have Rosie the Riveter and W. C. Fields.

There was also Howard Hawks. Comedies like *Bringing Up Baby* (1938) and *His Girl Friday* (1940), and thrillers like *The Big Sleep* (1946), seemed to defy logic and conventional film grammar in their machine-gun dialogue and madcap situations. We wander in and out of chaos, as Hawks takes us on one rollercoaster ride after the other. There is no real center to *The Big Sleep*. Bogart, as Philip Marlowe, walks on the peripheries of a sliding landscape. He learns less and less as the film moves along. *All* the characters are amnesiacs.

And then there was *The Maltese Falcon* and *Murder, My Sweet*, films that "grope boldly for that image of disorder which most films struggle to gloss over as quickly as they can." Because Hollywood couldn't deal with too much damage. "Movies preserve our moral slumber in the way that dreams are said to preserve our sleep." Movieland had an "excess of style," which, according to Michael Wood, was Hollywood's own signature. "This is not life, the signature says, and it is not art, not realism, not even fantasy. It is *the movies*, an independent universe, self-created, self-perpetuating, a licensed zone of unreality," often with "interchangeable plots, characters, patches of dialogue, and sets."

And that little paradise began to falter in the Fifties and the Sixties. "It was not that popular films had suddenly become false, for they had always been false. Just that they had become *too* false." Hollywood was still our national dream park, but it couldn't comfort us the way it once did. The "reality" around us seemed to shatter movieland's crystal sleep. The decay of our cities, the ugliness of Vietnam, the murder of Malcolm X, the Kennedys, Martin Luther King . . . *"Voici le temps des Assassins,"* as Arthur Rimbaud once said, with all the prophecy of a brilliant child.

Suddenly America *was* the Wild West, as if our mythical past awoke in us, squeezed our guts like an accordion box. And out of that rumbling life we had our own New Wave: *Bonnie and Clyde*, Noel Black's *Pretty Poison* (1968), John Boorman's *Point*

*Blank* (1967), Peter Yates' *Bullitt* (1968), Sam Peckinpah's *The Wild Bunch* (1969), films that incorporated violence into the frame, like a new kind of character.

And in the Seventies we had Terence Malick's *Badlands* (1973), Coppola's *The Conversation* (1974), Roman Polanski's *Chinatown* (1974), and Martin Scorsese's *Taxi Driver* (1976), which revealed the fug and foul stink of our rallying cries and hymns to the heartland. Americans had become a murderous tribe.

Ah, it wasn't much of a revelation. We'd cleared the prairies by killing people. We'd involved ourselves in a suicidal engagement called the Civil War. We owned more handguns than any other people, had the highest rate of homicide in the world. When Mark Twain took us down the Mississippi more than a hundred years ago, in *The Adventures of Huckleberry Finn,* we discovered enough violence to populate twenty novels. Most of it was senseless—family fights that continued from generation to generation. Huck's only refuge was his raft; there was less killing on the water. He and Nigger Jim float right past society for a little while, removed from the laws of "civilization." Huck and Jim were probably the last American innocents, a tribe of two. . . .

We entered the Eighties in a kind of regressive stance, with children's classics from Steven Spielberg and George Lucas. *Star Wars* and *E.T.* They were our prophets, our singers of palatable songs. And yet Lucas himself had given us one of the most nihilistic films ever made: *American Graffiti* (1973), a "road" movie about being on the way to nowhere . . . except death in the Nam. But in the Star Wars saga we had Princess Leia and Han Solo and Luke Skywalker and Chewbacca (who looked like the Wolf Man *and* the Cowardly Lion) and C-3PO (a cantankerous Tin Man who didn't have to go out searching for a heart). Lucas had recycled myths from several different genres and given us a Western–outer space–Wizard of Oz.

E.T. was Bambi and Dumbo with a very long neck. Spielberg's film satisfied our deepest wish at the movies: to become the child again, to be restored to that state of innocence when we first saw Bambi, or whatever magic animal occupied our dreams. Politics was gone from the table. We were at peace, despite the little witches who tortured us to "death" in Spielberg's gardens of delight.

The whole planet fell in love with E.T. and Chewbacca. But I preferred a couple of films that went unadored. Alan Parker's *Angel Heart* (1987) and William Friedkin's *To Live and Die in L.A.* (1985). Pauline Kael called Parker's film "a lavishly sombre piece of hokum—'The Exorcist' for people who haunt book-shops specializing in metaphysics." She talked of "Parker's fu-nereal, loony style. He edits like a flasher." And it bugged her that Parker's hero, Harold Angel (Mickey Rourke) never changes his clothes. Rourke "wears baggy pants that might have been used to wipe the grease from a ship's engine."

But those pants seemed important to me. Our first image of Rourke is that of a wrecked man blowing a bubble in the street. It's 1955. Harold Angel is a private detective on the Lower East Side. He doesn't have much of a clientele. He works out of an office that Philip Marlowe himself might have been squeamish about. Angel is adrift in his own dirt. His pants literally corrode around him until the cuffs disappear and he looks like a ragged pirate. And, says Pauline Kael, "there's no indication that this is meant to be funny." It isn't. Harold Angel is the ultimate amnesiac. He thinks he knows who he is. But his psyche starts to shed like his pants. He's been hired to track down a crooner, Johnny Favorite, who thrived before World War II. "Johnny Golden Tonsils" has disappeared, and his trail leads Mickey Rourke from one murder to the next. As with Hawks' Mar-lowe, Harold Angel's education is a matter of memory loss, of *unlearning* who he is. The more he discovers about Favorite, the more he begins to unravel, until he's completely ragged at the end of the film.

Of course, he has a partner in this escapade, Monsieur Louis Cyphre (Robert De Niro), better known as the Devil. Seems that our Johnny sold himself to the Devil to further his career . . . and then slipped away in another man's soul to beat the Devil out of his due. And Harold Angel is the shell of that man, the ghost of Johnny Favorite. He's a walking zombie, and that's whom we meet in the baggy pants, blowing a bubble. When Pauline Kael reminds us that "the whole picture must have been shot during an eclipse," that eclipse is Johnny.

Some of the film is hokey, I admit. Lucifer's burning eyes take us outside Mickey Rourke's mental state and into some kindergarten class of the occult. But Rourke dancing with

Epiphany Proudfoot (Lisa Bonet), while he carries her in his arms, above the wings of his shoes, has a kind of loving menace. He's the angel of death, after all. And Epiphany is Johnny's own daughter. He murders her during one of his violent dream states, in a shabby room in New Orleans, where he'd come looking for Johnny, his own miserable self.

And if we get beyond the movie's skin and the "metaphysics" that Pauline Kael dislikes, and *into* Mickey Rourke, *Angel Heart* becomes much more frightening than its own muddled plot. Rourke's charm on the screen, since his first success in *Diner* (1982), is a gruff, elusive shyness that locates him as a perpetual delinquent lost in a world of adults. He mutters, he slouches, as if he were half-asleep. He's a perfect candidate for a man whose soul and psyche have been split. He *is* Harold Angel, and as he blunders across Harlem and New Orleans, among the living and the dead, wearing a nose shield in the winter, to protect him from a sun that never shines, he looks like some crazed warrior fleeing from himself.

If *Angel Heart* is heavy-handed at times, it's still braver than Bertolucci's *The Last Emperor* (1987), which took most of the Academy Awards, and was a prettified, static portrait of Henry Pu Yi, the last of the Manchus. The chaos and disruptions of Bertolucci's other films are gone. History becomes a gorgeous scrapbook, with the same melodic emphasis from image to image, as we move from the Forbidden City to a garden plot in the People's Republic. Henry Pu Yi remains Henry Pu Yi, no matter what the tumult is.

But Alan Parker rips away that cloth of identity we all wear, whether we are emperors or not. And Harold Angel is only another fragmented dreamer, like ourselves, caught between heaven and hell with his baggy pants.

6 *To Live and Die in L.A.* is a much starker film. Architecture critic Michael Webb marvels at its design, its feel of "impermanence and danger," but calls it "an otherwise forgettable picture." Most movie critics would agree. William Friedkin, who made *The French Connection* (1971), has neglected to give us Popeye Doyle. Instead we have a pair of federal agents, Chance (William Petersen) and Vuke-

vich (John Pankow) who don't have Doyle's irascible honesty or flair. They almost seem invisible, like the landscape. But we aren't in Popeye Doyle's Manhattan. This is L.A., "a city that pretends not to be one," and Chance and Vukevich are children of that town. When one of his informants, a woman he sleeps with (Darlanne Fluegel), tells Chance that she has expenses to cover, he says, "Uncle Sam doesn't give a shit about your expenses. You want bread, fuck a baker."

Chance is trying to trap Rick Masters (Willem Dafoe), a counterfeiter who killed his former partner. In order to set up a sting operation, he has to raise some capital. So he and Vukevich become stick-up men. But the guy they rob happens to get killed, and it turns out that he's also a federal agent on another sting operation. Now we have agents shooting at agents, running after each other's tail on one long, perpetual highway that leads to other highways and the lights of a city that look like Christmas decorations.

Chance and Vukevich tear up Los Angeles the way the Keystone Kops once did. They are the Keystone Kops, but with all the meanness of modern life. The new Kops can't dance on their feet like Fatty Arbuckle. But they can kill people, cars, and streets. Chance himself gets blown away. We mourn him like a missing ghost. We'd gotten used to his blond and blue-eyed presence, but somehow we can't remember his face.

There is no memory here, only little reminders of how we live and hunt like wounded animals. Petersen isn't another "rough trapper" of movie space, like Gable and Gary Cooper. He's someone who can disappear from our psyche in a blink. He's part of our very own amnesia. He lives and dies in L.A., a city that can invent its own future, because it has no real past other than what the Chamber of Commerce bequeathed to it. Hollywood and L.A. grew up together: they're creations of the twentieth-century mind. In some rude manner, they are where "civilization" stops—our dream country, where shoot-outs occur on the highway almost as a matter of fact.

The L.A. Freeway is its own frontier. And Friedkin has captured that frontier sense in short, rapid beats reminiscent of rock video. The music drums at us every minute. We don't have time to ponder character and place. And there are no good guys in Friedkin's L.A. Rick Masters is the artist as psychopath. We watch him prepare his counterfeit bills and "bathe" them in a washing machine. The rituals of his work are much more interesting than those maneuvers of the Keystone Kops (Chance and Vukevich).

Dean Stockwell plays Masters' lawyer, Grimes, with that unemphatic motion he takes with him from film to film. There's a warp in his almost-wooden face, as if he were from another time zone. This is his third incarnation as an actor. I can't help watching him. He always stirs my memory. We were kids together. I saw him in *The Boy With Green Hair* (1948), when he was twelve . . . and I was eleven. He'd come from a family of entertainers. His dad had a part in *Snow White and the Seven Dwarfs:* he was the voice of the Prince. And Dean Stockwell began his own career in film when he was six. His childhood was all over after that. "I quit when I was 16, changed my name, cut my hair off and disappeared into the countryside." But that wasn't much of an occupation, though it lasted five years. Then he went back into the fields of Hollywood, "because I had nothing else I was trained to do."

Stockwell appeared in *Compulsion* (1959), *Sons and Lovers* (1960), and other films, but he lost his "calling" again, after a couple of years. "When we had the hippies and Haight-Ashbury and the love-ins, I dropped out of my career and just went with that." He was like Harold Angel on some dream search.

He got married, moved to New Mexico, and suddenly his career started all over again. "My way of working is still the same as it was in the beginning—totally intuitive and instinctive." But there's that sense of amnesia in his face, the slow, unhurried look that marks him as a child burrowing through time, as if the actor were asking a constant question: Who is Dean Stockwell?

And nobody knows.

# twelve

# The House on Ninety-fifth Street

**1** In an essay that accompanies an omnibus of Gary Winogrand's work *(Winogrand: Figments from the Real World),* curator John Szarkowski writes that Winogrand loved to photograph women on the street. It was "a major preoccupation" that would recur "like malaria throughout . . . his life," perhaps as "an index of his loneliness," or some "atavistic need, in which women represented neither pleasure nor companionship, but magic power."

John Szarkowski could have been talking about my own life, *or* the imagination that was part of so many Hollywood films: women as magic quotients, seen through the eyes of the moguls and other men in positions of power on all the lots of movieland. Women on the screen were a very curious business. Powerful and weak, cold, warm, crazy with desire. What man (and boy) in the audience could ever interpret their needs? Women have become the "treacherous mermaid" of modern times, that underwater goddess who "lures voyagers to their doom," as Dorothy Dinnerstein tells us in *The Mermaid and The Minotaur: Sexual Arrangements and Human Malaise.*

Ah, but what a wonderful doom it was, whether the mermaid happened to be Esther Williams, who could really swim underwater, or Jane Russell, with the magic bra that Howard Hughes designed to hold her bosoms up in *The Outlaw* (1943, 1946, 1950), or Signe Hasso, who frightened the hell out of me when she put on men's clothes in *The House on 92nd Street* (1945) and attempted to escape from the FBI. There was something sinister about Signe Hasso turning into a man. It wouldn't have bothered me in a fairy tale. But this was *film noir.*

And why is it that I can recall her so vividly on the fire escape, in her fedora? Was it because that flight from her own sex was only one more example of how the mermaid could beguile a man? Or she could smother you with her breasts, like Jane Russell, lying on top of Billy the Kid (Jack Buetel), to keep him warm. Her chest "hung over the picture like a thunderstorm spread out over a landscape," as one judge noted in Baltimore, when *The Outlaw* was released for the second time, in 1946. I remember the subway poster of Jane, with a bit of straw in her mouth, challenging my childhood. Jane was a big star before the movie was ever released. *She* was the outlaw, not Billy the Kid. While the movie was being shot (in 1940), twenty-five photographers swarmed around Jane. "Sometimes the photographers would pose me in a low-necked nightgown and tell me to bend down and pick up a couple of pails."

And then, in 1948, I was wounded by an actress in *The Adventures of Don Juan,* one more epic with Errol Flynn. She wasn't Olivia de Havilland. She didn't have all the sweetness of a virtuous wife. She was as lusty as a man. She couldn't have been created in Hollywood. She didn't have the feel of Paramount or MGM. I couldn't imagine her sitting on Mr. Mayer's lap, asking him who she ought to marry. She had a wildness in her that wasn't studio-bred. And she could play that high comedy of adventure and romance as well as Don Juan. It was the first time I'd seen a woman "duel" with Errol Flynn. She didn't flaunt herself like Mae West. She didn't mock. She wasn't Groucho minus the painted mustache. But she had a kind of "masculine" confidence and a beautifully chiseled face.

She was Viveca Lindfors, an actress from Sweden, with two babies sitting in Stockholm, but I didn't know that. She'd march around in different costumes, looking like the queen of Spain, whom she played in the picture, or wear riding clothes, like some prince of the realm. Maybe Jack Warner, who'd signed her, was dreaming of another Garbo. Garbo had worn men's clothes in *Queen Christina* (1933). But Garbo wasn't in my particular galaxy in 1948. It wouldn't have mattered if she was the world's most gorgeous woman. I'd looked up at Viveca Lindfors on the wall, and loved her, not like a little boy, but like the wicked man I wanted to be.

She fell out of my galaxy soon enough. She wasn't meant for

Hollywood. She had much too powerful a persona. The frame exploded around her. And she didn't have Cagney or Bogart to compete with that power . . . after Errol Flynn. She was given a stable of much weaker men: Bruce Bennett, Gordon MacRae, Dennis Morgan, Wendell Corey, Kent Smith, Ronald Reagan.

2    I'd see her from time to time at the Actors Studio, her hair gone completely gray, but the bones of her face as profound as ever. The wrinkles hadn't neutralized her looks. She was still the queen of Spain. I didn't talk to her. What could I say? "Ah, Viveca, I loved you when I was eleven."

Then I got started on this book. Only I couldn't find her at the Actors Studio. I wrote to her. She didn't write back.

A couple of months later I got a call. Viveca apologized. My letter had been lost among her fan mail. Yes, she'd love to talk about Hollywood, but she was leaving for Berlin that afternoon. And so I had to wait another month. She lived in a row house on Ninety-fifth Street, next to that border where East Harlem begins. I thought of Checkpoint Charlie and Berlin, and that schizoid no-man's-land between East and West, where you purchased some paper money and crossed into a maze of empty streets that were like the parcels of a Hollywood set. . . .

Either I was early, or Viveca was late. I rang her bell and nothing happened. I waited and then started walking up the heel of Ninety-fifth Street. I saw a bag lady approach with a big brown dog. As she got nearer I recognized the magnificent cheeks and wrinkled face of Viveca Lindfors. I introduced myself. The dog's name was Willy. He was a golden retriever.

We all climbed up the stairs of Viveca's house. We sat in the kitchen and drank tea, while Willy went out onto the back porch to have a look at the weather.

I grabbed at my notebook. What drew her to Hollywood, I asked. The wrinkled face started to work, and I felt the intelligence under her skin, something as tactile as *touch* itself. "It's a very complex question," she said. "I was an enormous film star in Sweden. I had enormous power. But I did not believe it . . . in those days one had to go to Hollywood. Garbo was the unfortunate myth we all followed.

"If I had stuck it out another two years in Sweden, things would [have been different]. The war put a parenthesis around your life. We all tried to get back to the glamour [of] before the war. I was only twenty-five [in 1946]. I had thirty films behind me. I left a wonderful position. It was stupid . . . I left for another reason. I left because I wanted to develop myself in a way I couldn't have developed in Sweden.

"If I had stayed, probably I would be dead . . . I was pretty neurotic. I had an unbelievable style to find my own passion and rhythm. I couldn't have done that [in Sweden]. What excited me, made me feel terrific, was the intelligence around me. In Sweden you had the old crap game. Journalists asked who I was sleeping with. . . . I'd come from a cold dark country. California had all this space and light. I was very hungry to learn.

"The studios were enormously disappointing. You wandered from make-up to wardrobe. I had a screen test, a hair test. They told me to put pads in my bra. I was absolutely floored when I had to do that. . . . It was an hysterical time in Hollywood. The studios were losing money. Nobody knew what to do. Everybody wanted to wind back the clock to romantic Gary Cooper films. Women went down the drain. . . . McCarthy took the guts out of Hollywood. Women became whores or little girls. . . . I came at the wrong time."

We talked of Errol Flynn.

"Errol was very brilliant, an actor who never understood how brilliant he was . . . that was his tragedy. He could have been a marvelous, marvelous actor. He destroyed himself. I can see why. He was a sex symbol. Like Marilyn Monroe."

"And Viveca Lindfors."

She laughed. "I had tasted the 'dope' of the stage. Women like Garbo and Bergman had never done that. They were the victims of the movies. . . . If I had been a big star, I would have been seduced by all that money." It was an impossible time to make a real impression. "They were such awful movies," the movies that Viveca was in. "One night I went to a little moviehouse in Santa Monica. I saw the [Ingmar] Bergman film about the knight [*The Seventh Seal*]. I was destroyed. It was a devastating moment." She pointed to some phantom Hollywood in her head. "I left Sweden to come to this?"

Jack Warner had invited her to his house for dinner soon after she arrived. "Warner said, 'Don't be nervous, don't be nervous.' It took me two, three years to understand what he meant. It was difficult to have a sense of reality." Your whole existence was "all like a movie." You had to dress up like a doll "to go to a party." Viveca was always "having lunch with people, sitting in photo studios. It's exciting for a week, and then it gets absolutely devastating."

I wanted to know about John Garfield, whom I'd loved much more than Bogart when I was a boy. Mickey Rourke and De Niro, even Brando himself, had been born in Garfield's sensibility, the rough, slow-eyed look, with all its sexual danger. He was that curious urban creature, the Jewish tough, who shouldn't have had much of a career in Hollywood, but his broken-faced handsomeness had gotten him through the gates at Warner Brothers.

"Garfield lived next to us on the beach [Viveca was married to director Don Siegal at the time]. One really did not know what was going on. I had no idea John was blacklisted." When she asked him why he didn't get a particular part, Garfield would shrug his shoulders and say, "Probably I was too short." He was trying to protect Viveca from that insane spiral of the blacklisting process. "He didn't want to put you in jeopardy. I said to myself, If I was in the same position, could I handle it? I was endlessly afraid. If I was called down, would I behave properly? It's like being tortured, like being arrested [without knowing what you had done]."

The moguls had capitulated to the Committee like gigantic mice. They were prepared to skewer members of their own little tribe. The Committee's hearings were like pathological breakfast parties. Walt Disney had accused the Communists of trying to enlist the services of Mickey Mouse. Lives were broken. Careers were ruined. "I am a man of a thousand faces, all of them blacklisted," said Zero Mostel. Judy Holliday, who'd done her own little dance before the Committee, had promised to distance herself from any sort of politics. "I don't say 'yes' to anything now except cancer, polio and cerebral palsy and things like that."

"I was in the wrong place at the wrong time," Viveca said about her nights and days in the gardens of Hollywood.

"Viveca," I said, as dour as Sir Isaac Newton, "I don't think there ever would have been a good time for you."

"If one could live one's life once more . . . It was crumbling all around me [during her years at Warner Brothers]. But you have to think in terms of magic," she said about that peculiar muscle of acting. "In Hollywood, forget it.

"I'm a Strindberg character. You have to lead a very full, strong life. It was a very romantic period before the war. Everybody was crazy . . . turbulent, passionate. We were all mad."

We went upstairs to her study. It was a wondrous, restful room that looked out upon a strange little forest. There was a portrait of Viveca on the wall, from her early years as an actress in Sweden. She was very very dark, like an exotic night creature, a mermaid without a bit of Swedish gloom. Nearby was the photograph that Philippe Halsman had taken of her for the cover of *Life* (Valentine's Day, 1949). It was graceful, antiseptic, the profile of a movie star, with all the "animation" of an icon.

Viveca lent me her autobiography. "Read it," she said, and we would talk again. I kissed her and climbed down the stairs with her golden retriever against my knee.

**3** It was an actress' tale, full of her own sound and fury. *Viveka . . . Viveca,* it was called, like the twin beats of her life. The Swedish star, *Viveka,* comes to the States and is transformed into *Viveca,* the woman with the padded chest. She was born in Uppsala, Sweden, at Nedra Slottsgatan, "the street below the castle." The house where she had lived as a child was later rehabbed, turned into Uppsala's Office for Undeveloped Children.

"I was in love with the American movies, with American movie stars," she wrote. And she understood the mathematics of that "exchange" between Hollywood and her own country. "Swedish actresses were continually achieving world fame through films while male stars were not."

And it was in Viveca's book that I encountered the name of my old nemesis, the beautiful witch in the man's hat: Signe Hasso, the former wife of Viveca's first husband.

Viveca had gone to Rome to make a movie in the middle of World War II, when Cinecittà was still trying to become "a

European Hollywood" under Il Duce. She returned to Sweden, where she was adored. "I couldn't walk the streets without being mobbed."

And then Jack Warner beckoned her to Hollywood. She'd been dazzled by Joan Crawford, Claudette Colbert, Irene Dunne, those women stars of the Thirties who seemed to inhabit a country all their own. And Viveca wanted to become part of that country. But she couldn't really find it in movieland. Warner Brothers was a "cemented city" that looked "like a concentration camp." She'd left her two children behind. "The nightmare was that I began to forget them."

She was supposed to play opposite the Coop in Fritz Lang's *Cloak and Dagger,* but she lost the part to a German actress, Lilli Palmer, who was married to Rex Harrison, who was having an affair with Carole Landis, who killed herself over Rex. . . . That was Hollywood, circa 1948, when Viveca played the Spanish queen in love with Errol Flynn, who "went fishing, and fucking, and paid no attention to his talent." Viveca was fat and bored by the end of the film. She wore hairdos so complicated she "couldn't lie down." Viveca would waste whole afternoons while stagehands polished the big black floor of the throne room.

But she began to feel more and more like a mermaid testing her powers, free to look around for a man "who could help me in my career, free to use my sexuality."

 I returned to the house on Ninety-fifth Street. I had ammunition in my pocket: Viveca's own words, and now I could play like a spider, moving from web to web.

Signe Hasso, I said.

The mermaid's mouth tightened. Was there an ancient wound she didn't want to reveal, the rivalry of women who'd once been married to the same man? "Swedes don't connect much with each other," she said. "How many parts can you have [in Hollywood for women] having an accent?"

What about Cinecittà? I wanted to know more about Mussolini's little empire at the edge of Rome. What was it like making a movie with the madness of war around her? "I'm sure that, looking back, one ought to have been more intrigued," she said. "The Germans were disliked, but they were all over the place. Rome was gorgeous, because there were never any lights. It was dark at night." But Viveca recalled "the lights over the watermelon stands. . . . I've gone through such incredible times, but my diary is always, How do I feel, what did I dream?"

Then I asked her what it was about those American women stars that she adored. "Their open straightness," she said. "It was very hard for European women. . . . [Ginger Rogers and Bette Davis] had a positive quality about their own existence."

She was also "turned on by Jimmy Cagney in *Yankee Doodle Dandy.* . . . There was something so vital [about him]. And Charles Boyer. God, was I in love with him . . . that didn't get me to America."

Boyer wasn't American, of course. He'd come to movieland during the early days of the talkies, when Hollywood was frightened of losing its European markets. Boyer would act in the foreign-language versions of American films . . . until he became a star.

But American actors "during the prewar period"—Gable, Cagney, Cooper—"were interesting men. An enormous respect for each other came across [in their films]. But the war had an incredible effect on the grace of life . . . graciousness went out. We were trying to be realistic [in our films], and became so gross."

She mentioned the American soldiers in her book, those liberators with Hershey bars who'd brought their own particular style of romance to Europe during and after the war, almost like a Hollywood event. They were the modern cowboys, finding yet another frontier in the haunted wildlands of the Ardennes. And I asked her about those cowboys. "They were passionately loved," she said. "They were the heroes. How could you turn them down and not go to America?"

She'd acted with another cowboy, Ronald Reagan, in *Night Unto Night* (1949). Did she have any impressions of the man?

"Not really," she said. "I had no impressions of him." And then she paused to reconsider. "My greatest impression is, he was exactly like he is today. With him, [it was a matter of] learning lines and doing scenes . . . he was a good boy. And an uninteresting actor. You didn't sense a soul there."

He wasn't like Errol Flynn. Flynn was "playing with life all the time. David Niven had the same quality. I was in awe of that. Only later I understood how brilliant [Errol] was. He was drinking all the time. He had a lot to carry [as the star of all the movies he was in]."

Had they been lovers? I was dying to ask, but I didn't. Yes, the moguls had their little love nests, Gable and Garfield had their women, Errol loved to chase fourteen-year-old girls, Tyrone Power had been a male prostitute once upon a time (he was starving when he arrived in Hollywood), Clara Bow and Marilyn might have made love to the milkman, and Mary Miles Minter, childlike star of silent films, did marry her milkman, but that didn't make Hollywood much of a Babylon. The stars had to sweat bullets six days a week. They had brutal schedules. The nickname for Warners was "San Quentin." And each love affair or elopement, documented by Lolly Parsons or Hedda Hopper and mixed with the fantasy life of the gossip columnists themselves, was one more mark of hysteria in an hysterical town.

I still thought it was bold of the mermaid to declare (in her book) that she wanted the freedom to use her sexuality however she wished.

"I always thought I needed someone to help me," she said. "Sexuality was helpful." Ah, we started talking about that curious dance involving humans or crocodiles and God knows what, the dance that defined Hollywood and all its campaigns to discover the new idol, the new sexual snake, and suddenly the mermaid looked years younger, as if the cry of sex was the most primitive call in the world.

"There's always that pull," I said. "That's what people expect from their idols . . . they want to be seduced."

We talked about the crazy travelers we'd become. "It's the curse of the uprooted," she said, "the enormous turbulence of uprooting, the unconscious need to be accepted in [each] new place. . . . I don't think we have adjusted to this century."

I told her it was part of her profession, that double displacement of assuming another persona in another time and another place.

The whole phenomenon of making a film was "getting close to people and then moving on. . . . As the film actress, the star, you have to carry the burden of the film, have to constantly worry about how you look. . . . I was nursing my kids in Europe. I brought them to the studio. I'd say, I'm sorry, I've got to take a break and nurse my kids."

But she couldn't have done that in movieland: the Hollywood actress must always leave her particular shadow, without the added freight of being someone's mother, daughter, or wife. Ol' Jack Warner wouldn't have allowed Viveca to nurse a baby on any of his lots. . . .

5 There were other mermaids in movieland who never really made it, like Faith Domergue, the dark-eyed temptress promoted by Howard Hughes. She was pretty enough, but no one could pronounce her name. And her smoldering looks were wasted in films like *Duel at Silver Creek* (1952) and *Cult of the Cobra* (1955). She burned much too hard in the silliness around her. But it's been forty years since I first saw her face. And I can still conjure up that deep seriousness she had, as if her life depended on all the pushing and pulling of the plot. Faith Domergue.

And of course there were mermaids who stuck around long enough to become regular love goddesses. Rita. Ava. Marilyn . . . and that other Marilyn, the girl from Chicago whom Harry Cohn called his "fat Polack." He changed her name to Kim, gave her platinum hair, and for a couple of years in the Fifties she was the most popular female star in the world. She'd worked as a salesgirl for a while and had promoted refrigerators around the country as "Miss Deep Freeze." She had the surface coldness and dreamlike sexuality that were irresistible during the Eisenhower era. Columnist and movie critic Ezra Goodman described her as having "the face of a madonna, superimposed on the body of an ox."

*Life* photographer Leonard McCombe said that Kim had "the sort of face that looks as if the rest of the body is making love." And a publicist at Columbia felt that Kim's "eyes attracted. They had an almost tigerlike slant." Whatever gifts she did or didn't have, Kim Novak haunted an entire nation. She seemed suspicious in front of the camera, as if someone had pushed her onto the set, and the camera's eye had caught her without her clothes.

She fell in love with Sammy Davis, Jr., wanted to marry him. But Harry Cohn didn't feel that a black dancer with one good eye was suitable for Kim. "I am the king here," Cohn said about his reign at Columbia. "Whoever eats my bread sings my song." He broke up the romance; some people swear he threatened to have Davis killed. Kim had several nervous breakdowns. She withdrew to Monterey.

Harry Cohn died in 1958, the year *Vertigo* was released, starring Kim Novak and Jimmy Stewart. It was Hitchcock's greatest film, and Novak gave an incredible performance for a girl who couldn't act. Hitchcock was shrewd enough to have her play her own split personalities: Kim and Marilyn Novak. She's a shopgirl *and* an "actress" in *Vertigo*. Judy Barton, from Salina, Kansas, who acts the role of "Madeleine Elster," the wife that Gavin Elster, Judy's lover, intends to kill. But we meet her first as Madeleine, the beautiful platinum blonde who goes into trance states, pretending that she's her own great-grandmother Carlotta Valdes, who killed herself out of unrequited love. She draws Scottie Ferguson into the plot.

He's a retired detective of independent means who'd been a lawyer once upon a time. Scottie suffers from acrophobia—a dreadful fear of heights. He has an attack of vertigo in the middle of a chase, and a cop dies because of him. Scottie seems to have a comfortable sort of friendship with his old fiancée, Midge Wood (Barbara Bel Geddes), a commercial artist. During their first scene together, Midge is preparing the designs for a "revolutionary" bra that's supposed to work on the same principle as the cantilever bridge. For all we know, it could have been the very bra that Jane Russell wore in *The Outlaw*. But whosever bra it is, it suggests a nagging sexuality that will plague Scottie (and us) throughout the film.

Midge is still in love with the man. Scottie is blind to that. She doesn't exist for him in any sexual way. He's the perfect chump for Gavin Elster's schemes. The unattached, restless male who can't bear high places. Gavin, an old college acquaintance of Scottie's, asks him to come out of "retirement" and track his wife, Madeleine, who's been wandering about San Francisco in her own dream world. Before he has her committed, he wants to find out where the hell she goes.

Of course, Scottie tracks that other "Madeleine," the double

of Gavin's wife. He falls in love with her, fishes her out of San
Francisco Bay, and puts Madeleine into his own bed . . . like a
mermaid. She wakes up without her clothes, disappears, shows
up at Scottie's door again, and they go wandering together. She
unhinges Scottie's life like an attack of vertigo. She holds him
on a string. She draws him to an old Spanish mission south of
San Francisco, climbs up the mission tower, and Scottie, who
can't follow her because of his vertigo, hears her scream, and
sees her fall to her death.

It was the real Madeleine, already dead, whom Gavin tossed
from the tower, while the other Madeleine, his own creation,
was hiding with him. Scottie goes through an inquest, turns
catatonic, and sits like a stone man in an institution, while Midge
tries to baby him back to health with a little Mozart. "Mozart's
the boy for you."

And the marvel of the film is that Hitch had the least neurotic
actor in the world, Jimmy Stewart, playing a profoundly disturbed man. *His* vertigo becomes our own. He's a stand-in for
every male in the audience over the age of five. Just as Kim
Novak is the ultimate love doll, that mermaid who'd come out
of the sea.

Scottie recovers. It takes a year. He's a total wanderer now,
the man of independent means. He drifts through San Francisco
with all the luck of a sleepwalker, pulled along by his own
dreams. He discovers a ghost on the street, a coarser version of
the dead Madeleine, a shopgirl with brown hair. Judy Barton.
He follows her back to her hotel room, starts to take over her
life. Tells her to quit her job so that he can be with her all the
time.

He's obsessed with Madeleine, his phantom love, and this
shopgirl he's found, this double of Madeleine, would never do.
She doesn't have Madeleine's "aura." But bit by bit, he makes
her into Madeleine. He buys Judy replicas of Madeleine's
clothes, has her recolor her hair. And we begin to feel that
Scottie himself is powerless; he's caught in the fabric of his own
dream.

"I was very intrigued by the basic situation of *Vertigo*," Hitch
told author Donald Spoto, "of changing the woman's hair
color—because it contained so much analogy to sex. This man
changed and dressed up his woman, which seems like the reverse

of stripping her naked. But it amounts to the same thing. I really made the film in order to get through to this subtle quality of a man's dreamlike nature."

And all of us, male and female, are caught up in the dance of this dream. Judy Barton could have disappeared from San Francisco once Gavin's wife was thrown off the tower, but she didn't. She's in love with the man who fell in love with "Madeleine," that mermaid she was playing. And her deepest wish is that her own dream prince, Scottie Ferguson, will also love Judy Barton. But he can't. He can only follow that obsessive path of his desire. He can only love a mermaid.

And in some horrible mood of defeat, the mermaid also realizes this. Unconsciously, of course. Judy Barton wears one of Madeleine's necklaces, a piece of jewelry that once belonged to Carlotta Valdes. And Scottie, the dream detective, realizes that he's been duped. He returns his "Madeleine" to the mission tower to relive that moment of the real Madeleine's fall. This time Judy falls off the tower, and Scottie is left with the vertigo of his own maddened desire.

There are no happy endings here. Hitch doesn't gloss over the horror of Scottie's situation: he's condemned to fall and fall until he dies. Hitch has taken us as close as one can get to that merciless borderland between waking and dreaming, that land of disorientation which has become our very own lives.

*Vertigo* appeared at a time when the whole nation was submerged in some deep sexual slumber. McCarthy had scared the pants off us. A third of Hollywood's output in the Fifties was devoted to Westerns: the past, any past, was safer than the present, no matter how narrowed or anesthetized. So we had Moses, Samson and Delilah, Ben Hur, Bat Masterson, and Billy the Kid. And Kim Novak was the perfect icon. Her face "was blank—except for the eyes, which were deep and haunted. One could call her faceless."

Hitch used that faceless face to reveal our own hunger to design love the way a bridge is designed, or a brassiere. Scottie "built" Judy into some Madeleine who was one more figment from the real world. And Kim Novak imposed herself upon our psyche, for a little while, because she was that mysterious mermaid who meant us no harm.

She was as false as Hollywood. An actress. With tigerlike eyes.

# thirteen

# ℳr. Feathers

1 There's been a babel of books on Hollywood, in every language of the world. Louis B. Mayer alone has at least half a dozen. Every year a wounded lover comes out of the woodwork to write about his or her adventures with a star. Each major studio has an epic or two devoted to its films, its stars, its furniture. One biographer believes Errol Flynn was a Nazi agent. Another believes that Lillian Hellman, who haunted Hollywood in the Thirties, might have been a member of the Comintern. If we read long and hard enough, we discover the two thousand dolls that Joan Crawford had in a secret bedroom of her house, we learn about the love affair between Tyrone Power and Errol Flynn, Gable's false teeth, Faulkner's Hollywood mistress.

But in all the memoirs and books of fact and fable there's so little real imagination, so little meat, that the constant mythologizing doesn't bear much of a bounty. It's odd that an obscure actress named Louise Brooks, rescued from oblivion by Henri Langlois and the Cinémathèque Française, who lived out her last twenty years in bed, a little like Colette, who hated Hollywood and despised her own career, should have written one of the strongest remembrances of Hollywood *and* a remarkable book that cozens up to no one. She's as ruthless about herself as the people around her and is also filled with a ghostly compassion for W. C. Fields, Fatty Arbuckle, and others. Louise is like a grown-up Alice with her own particular Looking Glass and a heartbreaking wit.

The title of the book, *Lulu in Hollywood,* comes from her characterization of Lulu, the restless, immoral seducer of men, in G. W. Pabst's silent classic *Pandora's Box* (1929). Lulu is the ultimate mermaid, the siren who "sings" destruction with each twirl of her body. But Louise's acting is so enigmatic, so removed from guile, and so unmannered, that when she's murdered by Jack the Ripper at the end of the film, it feels like one more seduction. Her sexuality is like a cold electrical storm on the screen. Lulu's never there for the other characters: she exists only for us, the audience that sits in the dark like potential Jack the Rippers and cannot have her.

It was Louise, "in silence and out of her own person, who created the fundamental, the only Lulu," as William Shawn, former editor of *The New Yorker*, writes in his introduction to the book. "Louise Brooks is a femme fatale without any record of fatalities." And it's Shawn who understood that the writer was there all the time in the girl who acted and danced since she was a child, collecting material like the webbed fist of a cocoon, forming Louise. None of those terrible years was wasted, when moguls like Harry Cohn wanted to "interview" Louise while he was half-undressed.

She was born in Cherryvale, Kansas, in 1906. She'd come from a line of "poor English farmers" who arrived in America "on a merchant ship at the end of the eighteenth century." Her dad was a lawyer. Her mom wrote book reviews for the local women's club. Louise was a professional dancer from the time she was ten. "My father thought I had been mutilated when Mother, in the interests of improving my stage appearance, had a barber chop off my long black braids and shape what remained of my hair in a straight Dutch bob with bangs." That "black helmet" of hair became her signature, the sign of her independence, the mark of the mermaid.

At fifteen she left Kansas to study dancing in New York. She appeared in "George White's Scandals," and was also a Ziegfeld girl, *and* the inspiration for Dixie Dugan, a popular comic-strip character who dreams of joining "The Zigfold Follies." "All there is to this Follies racket," says Dixie Dugan, "is to *be cool and look hot*." And Dixie's alter ego, Louise Brooks, had a five-year contract with Paramount before she was twenty. She was only twenty-one when she was in Berlin for *Pandora's Box*. With the coming of sound her career was practically over. "Lulu" began to act in B films. In 1943, she went to New York, "where I found that the only well-paying career open to me, as an unsuccessful actress of thirty-six, was that of a call girl."

But she was too proud to perform in bed. And so she was a salesgirl at Saks: Dixie Dugan takes a fall. It lasted two years. Then she became involved with three different millionaires, but Louise wouldn't marry them. She fell into a deep funk. "There was no point in throwing myself into the East River, because I could swim."

She moved to Rochester in 1956, at the invitation of James Card, curator of Eastman House, who admired Louise. Except for a trip to Paris, financed by the Cinémathèque for its "Hommage à Louise Brooks" in 1958, she remained a recluse. "I have lived in virtual isolation, with an audience consisting of the milkman and a cleaning woman." That's when Louise became her own kind of Colette. She would write and "disintegrate happily in bed with my books, gin, cigarettes, coffee, bread, cheese, and apricot jam."

2 Hollywood, for Louise, "was like a terrible dream I have—I am lost in the corridors of a big hotel and I cannot find my room. People walk past me as if they can not see or hear me. So first I ran away from Hollywood and I have been running away ever since."

But that merciless gift of hers clung to Hollywood no matter how far she ran. "My life has been nothing," Louise said, but that was the camouflage of the writer who has to live inside an abyss of her own making. Movieland had become her dream material; and she was eloquent about what she hated. Not even Scott Fitzgerald or Nathanael West took us as close to the bloody heart of Hollywood. Louise had a wisdom that had come from all that desperate dancing she did. Fitzgerald hadn't been a movie idol. He revealed Monroe Stahr to us, but he couldn't go through the Looking Glass, like Louise. Louise didn't believe in romance. "Staring down at my name in lights on the marquee of the Wilshire Theatre was like reading an advertisement of my isolation."

She recognized the essence of Fatty Arbuckle after he was run out of Hollywood because of Virginia Rappe. He was reduced to directing a series of shorts under another name. "He sat in his chair like a dead man. He had been very nice and sweetly dead ever since the scandal that ruined his career."

She also understood the sheer misery behind the myth of W. C. Fields as the meanest man in town. Fame hadn't "distorted Fields. It was sickness and the clutching fear of being discarded to die on the Hollywood rubbish heap."

And she remembered the Bogart who wasn't "a cinematic saint." He was as lethargic and isolated as Louise. A "fundamental inertia had always menaced his career." Bogart's lisp became an acquired thing, since "too much dialogue betrayed the fact that his miserable theatrical training had left him permanently afraid of words." But with *Casablanca,* Bogey was now big business. Enter Lauren Bacall, "his perfect screen partner, as seductive as Eve, as cool as the serpent."

Then there was John Wayne, the cowboy star of Louise's last picture, *Overland Stage Raiders* (1938). Louise was thirty-two at the time and all but finished as a Hollywood actress. She had no reason to be pleasant or kind to another cowboy. Her own great-grandfather John Brooks had suffered at the hands of cowboys, who "ran wild in a mindless fury of boozing, whoring and gun fighting." Only ex–buffalo hunters, hired as professional killers, could stop the cowboys.

And so, when she arrived on the ranch "where Republic shot all its Westerns," she happened to see a cowboy who was a whole head higher than Louise. "Looking up at him I thought, this is no actor but the hero of all mythology miraculously brought to life."

And he was. He got better and better, in spite of *The Green Berets.* He was the Duke of wisdom, the wild man of the West. He could authenticate an entire genre with one of his very long frowns. Watch him in *The Searchers* (1956), where he reveals an anger and a meanness that undercut his very own legend. He's as bitter as prairie dust. Proud, blind, and brilliant, with his own private country of hate. You can't take your eyes off the Duke. . . .

Louise's sense of worthlessness in movieland, the assumption that beautiful women weren't born to think, but could only become the "Big Joke," the mermaid with the mind of cotton, was enforced by the men around her. Louise felt like an idiot in the company of Herman Mankiewicz, who dawdled with her and gave her books to read. Louise would scribble book reports (like her mother), while Mank's friends ogled the "furniture" of her body.

3  Critic Roland Jaccard wrote that other stars were "phantoms dressed in borrowed light and reduced to male and female objects," while Louise was "the only actress in film history who continually rebelled against this kind of conformist idolatry." The star as anti-star. Many people, according to William Shawn, "think she possesses an erotic eloquence unmatched by that of any other woman ever to have appeared on the screen."

Or, as Henri Langlois said: "There is no Garbo. There is no Dietrich. There is only Louise Brooks."

Lulu had a different idea.

She sensed Garbo's worth, the cruel efficient power of that photogenic face. "From the moment *The Torrent* [Garbo's first American film] went into production, no contemporary actress was ever again to be quite happy in herself." And Lulu was able to catch the particulars of Garbo's screen persona and her greatness. "Garbo is all movement. First she gets the emotion, and out of the emotion comes the movement and out of the movement comes the dialogue. She's so perfect that people say she can't act. People would much rather see someone like Peter Sellers performing than see real acting, which is intangible."

Garbo's favorite director, Clarence Brown, also had a feeling for this sense of the intangible. "She [Garbo] had this remarkable ability to register thought and emotion without doing much of anything. You couldn't see it on the floor, but on screen it came across. I can't explain it—it just happened. That's the Garbo mystery."

It doesn't mean that Lulu wrote fan letters to Greta Garbo. "Every actor has a natural animosity toward every other actor, present or absent, living or dead."

Who else but Louise, the outcast, would have dared admit that? She was so much more than a mermaid and a haunting presence. She was a chronicler who liked to paint herself out of the picture. She called herself "a born loser, who was temporarily deflected from the hermit's path by a career in the theatre and films." But while she rocked in her own isolation cell, Louise missed nothing. She caught Hollywood's clockwork, every single one of its laws. "Old pictures were bad pictures. Pictures were better than ever. An actor was only as good as his last picture. These three articles of faith were laid down by the producers, and business was conducted in a manner to prove them."

That didn't prevent Louise from piercing the mask Hollywood loved to wear, and intuiting the magic beyond much of that mask. "The great art of films does not consist in descriptive movement of face and body, but in the movements of thought and soul transmitted in a kind of intense isolation."

Louise had brought us back to Plato's cave. Prisoners looking at shadows on the wall, while their souls catch fire. Ours was the century of isolation, because all the old fabrics—family, kingdom, country, God—had begun to unravel. And the face we saw in the mirror frightened us. It was a cinematic face, both hot and cold, with the murderous look of the dreamer. Lulu? Jack the Ripper? The people we meet in our daily lives look oddly familiar, like distant doubles of people we'd met before in some moviehouse we can no longer recall.

It happened to Louise herself, that curious dance of an image doubling back upon itself. She'd come to the Ambassador Hotel in L.A. to meet the boy king and his queen: Scott and Zelda. It was 1927, long before Fitzgerald became a screenwriter, so his capital was much higher in Hollywood. They were the perfect cinematic couple, Zelda and Scott. "They were sitting close together on a sofa, like a comedy team, and the first thing that struck me was how *small* they were. I had come to see that genius writer, but what dominated the room was the blazing intelligence of Zelda's profile. It shocked me. It was the profile of a witch."

4 Langlois might have resurrected Lulu in France, but she was still an unremembered ghost in the United States, bedridden with arthritis, living on gin and apricot jam, all alone in her Rochester retreat, until drama critic Kenneth Tynan tracked her down like some kind of detective-angel and wrote about Lulu in *The New Yorker* ("The Girl in the Black Helmet," June 11, 1979). It was one of those

glorious occasions when the written word produces its own thunder that starts to echo and doesn't stop. Tynan recapitulated Lulu's whole career, from the dancing tyke to her days as Dixie Dugan, from Paramount to Pabst, from Saks Fifth Avenue to self-exile. It's a tale of enormous courage, devoted to what Louise herself calls the "cruel pursuit of truth and excellence." And Louise would never be unknown again. It took the Cinémathèque Française and several English film historians and critics—Kevin Brownlow, David Thomson, and Kenneth Tynan—to reveal Louise to us, her American audience, who had developed amnesia about *all* silent films.

"So it is," Louise says, "that my playing of the tragic Lulu with no sense of sin remained generally unacceptable for a quarter of a century." And it is this modern Lulu, this Lulu without tears, that we meet in "The Girl in the Black Helmet."

She flirts with Tynan. "Are you a variation of Jack the Ripper, who finally brings me love that I'm prevented from accepting—not by the knife but by old age? You're a perfect scoundrel, turning up like this and wrecking my golden years!"

But Louise had said on several occasions that she'd never loved a soul. "And if I *had* loved a man, could I have been faithful to him? Could he have trusted me beyond a closed door? I doubt it."

She saw herself as the prodigal daughter, the dancing idiot who belonged to nothing and no one. "Remember when the prodigal son returned the father said, 'He was lost, and is found.' It was the father who *found* the lost son. Somehow I have missed being found."

She had a sad adventure when she was nine, a *mis*adventure that would shape her erotic life. There was an old bachelor in Cherryvale, a certain Mr. Feathers, who liked Louise. He would take her to the flickers and buy her candy and toys. She'd blanked him out of her mind for years and years, until a former neighbor from Cherryvale sent her a photo of Mr. Feathers, "a nice-looking gray-haired man of about fifty holding the hand of a little girl—me." And then that forgotten moment came back. "When I was nine years old, Mr. Feathers molested me sexually. . . . I've often wondered what effect Mr. Feathers had on my life. He must have had a great deal to do with forming my attitude toward sexual pleasure. For me, nice, soft, easy men were never enough—there had to be an element of domination—and I'm sure that's all tied up with Mr. Feathers."

Feathers had become Louise's bête noire and desideratum, the dream lover who could destroy Lulu and satisfy her. One more Jack the Ripper. And the primordial dad who missed finding Lulu for so many years.

She scribbled her memoirs, called it "Naked on My Goat," and then destroyed the manuscript, tossed it down her incinerator. Louise could not "unbuckle the Bible Belt" she'd been born into, the land of Mr. Feathers, of Cherryvale farmers and lawyers and women's clubs . . . book reports and "incest in the barn." Instead of "Naked on My Goat" we have the girl in the black helmet and Lulu's little portraits of Hollywood itself and her life as a reader rather than an actress. Her mother died in 1944, but "she never abandoned me. . . . Each time I read, it's as if I were reading over her shoulder, and learning the words, just like when she read out loud from *Alice in Wonderland*."

And so that woman with a boy's chest and a dancer's powerful legs has entered our consciousness in the Eighties with her own sort of vengeance. Lulu died in 1985, as much a hermit as ever, but with her silvery, silent movements of sixty years ago *and* her words on the page she's become our very own Jack the Ripper, "molesting" us and reminding us too how perverse the idea of pleasure is. A whole new generation has fallen in love with Louise, but she taunts us with her absence-presence and the extraordinary arc of her mind.

We've had Hollywood memoirs by David Niven, Mary Astor, Bette Davis, Gloria Swanson, Lauren Bacall, etc., etc.—some of them good, some of them bad—but none has seized the "flesh" of that place and the sad, ghostly aura of movie people. No one but Louise could have said that Margaret Sullavan's voice "was exquisite and far away . . . like a voice singing in the snow." Or that Chaplin was a perpetual-motion machine, "always standing up as he sat down, and going out as he came in." And when William Randolph Hearst's mistress, Marion Davies, moved with her fourteen-room bungalow from MGM to Warners, it was "like leaving a palace for a stable."

Louise was never false, even about those who praised her. If *Cahiers du Cinéma* had "discovered" Louise, that didn't prevent her from saying: "I think the auteur theory of *Cahiers du Cinéma* is crap; I read the first English issue. It took me two hours and three dictionaries . . . to find out what everybody has known since the beginning of films: that some writers and some directors are jealous of the stars' glory and the auteur theory is just another attempt to wipe the stars off the screen with words."

**5** Why is it that poor Jean Seberg reminds me of Louise? They had little in common, except that both of them had come out of the Midwest. And Seberg wore a "blond helmet" in Godard's *Breathless*. She was also an anti-star, in a way. Otto Preminger had found her at seventeen, after an enormous search, plucked her out of college to be his Saint Joan. He was always discovering people. And *Saint Joan* (1957) should have been one more of his megahits. Graham Greene had adapted Bernard Shaw's play about Joan. And Preminger surrounded Seberg with Anton Walbrook, John Gielgud, and Richard Todd. But the film was ponderous and silly and Seberg was out of place in fifteenth-century France. Otto the Terrible was as stubborn as ever. He put Seberg in a second film, *Bonjour Tristesse* (1958). And then Seberg settled in France. But she could never recapture that excitement or the publicity of a seventeen-year-old at the point of stardom before her first film was ever released.

I wish I could say I'd spoken to Otto about Jean Seberg. She'd fallen out of my memory, like some frozen thing. And then, in 1979, there was the obit. Saint Joan had killed herself. And the story behind her suicide grew into something grimmer than any *film noir*. She'd taken an overdose of barbiturates in the back seat of her car. She was forty years old.

She'd supported the Black Panthers in the Sixties, and the FBI wanted to make her pay for it. J. Edgar Hoover had his Los Angeles office plant rumors in 1970 that Seberg, who was seven months pregnant at the time and married to French novelist Romain Gary, had been having an affair with a prominent Panther, and that *he* was the "Papa" of the child. Shortly after the rumors spread, Seberg went into premature labor and "gave birth to a dead baby, a white female."

"Jean became psychotic," her husband said. She tried to take her life every year "on the anniversary of this stillbirth." She succeeded in 1979.

But I wonder if her psychosis had been helped along without the FBI. She'd been a kind of object lesson in failure ever since *Saint Joan:* the star who didn't become a star, like a deadly fairy tale. Galatea gone bad. The Iowa princess who got turned into a duck.

By the time she appeared in *Breathless,* she looked like Saint Joan lost in a dream. She's Patricia, a young *newyorkaise* who's supposed to be studying at the Sorbonne. She's a sometime journalist who sells the *New York Herald Tribune* in the streets of Paris and has taken up with Michel Poiccard (Jean-Paul Belmondo), a car thief. Michel has murdered a motorcycle cop, and the whole of Paris is looking for him. Godard has fashioned his own meandering thriller from the sensibilities of the Hollywood B film. But there's a crucial difference. The Bs never thrived on such ambiguity and disorder. Hollywood's Poverty Row still had some pretentions. Republic and Monogram liked to think of themselves as smaller, frugal versions of Paramount and MGM.

Godard wanted to exploit the actual chaos of filmmaking. His cops float like kites across Paris. His camera sways like a drunken boat. Godard himself appears in the film as an anonymous man who recognizes Michel and tries to sic the police on him. But no one seems able to catch Michel. He has a curious cloak of invisibility.

Belmondo is lean as electrical wire. His crooked nose lends him a handsomeness that a more conventional face could never have. He's like a knife suddenly come alive. But he's oddly passive with Patricia. "It's foolish . . . but I love you."

Nothing seems to register on her face. She's some kind of Lulu without fun. She sleeps with a journalist to get in his good graces, but she dawdles with Michel.

"You look like a Martian," he says.

And it's true. The image that stares back at us from the mirror is blank, like a lovely doll that has no depths to conceal. She betrays Michel. "I don't want to be in love with you. That's why I called the police."

Michel has time to run. But he won't. "I can't stop thinking of her," he says.

Michel dies, and Patricia stands over him, runs her fingernail across her lip, like a clown imitating Michel. She isn't mean. She's simply a girl without much of a persona. "I'm scared and surprised at the same time." Like a wounded animal, or a clockwork child.

How much of Patricia was there in Jean Seberg . . . or Saint Joan? Her performance is much more frightening now than it must have been in 1960. Belmondo is Belmondo, after all. Watching him on French TV in 1987, I could still recognize Michel Poiccard underneath all the jowls, that quality of being rooted in his own physical presence. But Saint Joan didn't have that charm. Seberg was twenty-one when she played Patricia. And there were premonitions of the woman who had already worn one mask too many.

It's foolish to say that Hollywood killed her. But she couldn't quite recover from *Saint Joan:* the ingenue living in a country of glass. The sad thing is that she *was* Saint Joan, but the voices she heard had nothing to do with God or the fate of France. Preminger had picked the right actress. She did have the frozen, dreamy eyes of a saint who could lead an army into battle. But it would have taken Godard or Brecht (he died in 1956) to have sensed that powerful ice in Jean Seberg. She sank under all the historic armor of Preminger's *Joan*. She was famous as a flop. Would she have survived without all that hurlyburly? God knows, she might have had more of a chance.

# fourteen

# Poisonville

1 Lulu and Hollywood, black helmets and blond, bring me to Sigmund Freud. It was that old Austrian witch doctor who had to remind us that the human animal was "the wishing animal," and no matter what trappings we acquired, cardboard houses, bungalows, or vast estates, our very existence was as problematical as an unfinished fairy tale.

That confusion we often felt at the movie palace, deep pleasure and a kind of primordial fear, rose out of dream figures on a darkened wall. We were cave children caught in some design we couldn't always fathom. The love we had for Brando or Joan Blondell didn't follow any rational plan. If we were crazy about one star and not another, it was because that particular star fell into the fabric of our dreams and we couldn't even say why. Sometimes half the country fell into that fabric, and we were all involved in some long, collective sleep called movieland.

Certain faces haunted us, at least for a while. Consider Al Pacino. He played the young Mafia prince Michael Corleone in *The Godfather*. It didn't matter that he slouched a lot and that his face was slightly disfigured for part of the film: there was romance in the notion of a war hero who became the killer of a crooked cop and the head of a clan. His broken cheek gave him an unorthodox handsomeness, like a fairy-tale frog.

It was 1972, and America was in the middle of a nervous breakdown over the war in Vietnam. Pacino was a new kind of prince: he looked like a grunt, and his slow, willful ways marked him as an amnesiac. While Brando jabbered with cotton in his mouth as the old don, Vito Corleone, Pacino moved like a guy suffering from shellshock.

He was even better in *The Godfather, Part II*, where he was

Michael again. He paddled around with a humped back, like Richard III, poisonous, violent, with spittle under his tongue. But not even that performance could help him now. The film belonged to Robert De Niro, who played the young Vito Corleone in a series of flashbacks that overpowered *Godfather II*. De Niro had had a following ever since Martin Scorsese's *Mean Streets* (1973). He was an interesting, nervous character actor, not a star. But in *Godfather II* the nervousness was gone. He had a lean, classic look, like a Sicilian Mack the Knife. He had no mermaids hovering around him, but he was the romantic heart of the film. The story of Michael Corleone's tribulations took us here and there, but we kept wishing for Vito Corleone (De Niro) to return. He's the fierce object of our desire, the same sort of phantom that Brando had been once upon a time. Perhaps beauty has no gender in our dreams and is childlike and utterly perverse. Or else the star is always feminine, even if she happens to be a man. . . .

But there was no other actor after *Godfather II*. Not Hoffman or Hackman, not Redford, not Pacino himself. De Niro swept us into his whirlwind. He was his own DMZ, and the spaces he inhabited, the shy, savage land in his head, were like that schizoid place America had become after the fall of Saigon.

And then there was *Raging Bull* (1979), another one of Scorsese's portraits of urban life that looked and felt like a war zone. In *Mean Streets,* Scorsese plotted a long, ritualized rumble in a pool hall that was both heartbreaking and funny, because the combatants were like cousins who didn't know how to stop a fight. It was as if the Keystone Kops had invaded Little Italy without their cotton clubs and had to bang at each other with poolsticks until the camera ran out of film. But there were no poolsticks in *Raging Bull*. There was only Jake LaMotta's madness *and* his hands.

De Niro looked like a hungry bullethead lost in the seas of the Bronx. He was profoundly and beautifully dumb. It was no impersonation, or a mimer's sense of Jake LaMotta. That shy, withdrawn man, Robert De Niro, kicked time and space in the pants . . . in his portrait of LaMotta. The screen shrank around him, as if nothing could catch that bull of a man. It was one of those curious acts of possession, like Brando in *On the Waterfront,* or Meryl Streep in *Sophie's Choice,* where the performer has created a new skin. A kind of hallucination occurs that has little to do with "acting," and we have to watch De Niro from our own private moon.

He won his second Academy Award (his first had been for the "supporting" role of Vito Corleone). But there was also a paradox. De Niro had to gain fifty pounds in order to become Jake. And he could never recapture that needlelike Renaissance look. He was powerful and sad as the Yiddish gangster "Noodles" in Sergio Leone's *Once Upon a Time in America* (1984), but he no longer had a face that could force us to howl at the moon.

2     There was no mercy in movieland. The camera had its own primitive need. It either loved a face (and a body) or was neutral to all its charms.

Fifty years ago an unbilled actress, Fern Barry, whose own face seldom appeared on screen, began to "double" certain body parts for other actresses. The camera adored Fern Barry's arms and legs, and often, in particular close-ups, she'd become the arms and legs of Ida Lupino, Bette Davis, or Ann Sheridan. Fern Barry's arms and legs appeared in hundreds of films. "Whenever I go to see a picture," she said, "I see my hands and feet on the screen and I get a thrill out of it."

It sounds a little like Gogol's tale "The Nose," or one of Kafka's parables, where body parts substitute for a person's psyche and soul. Kafka wouldn't have been out of place in Hollywood. He'd have understood the terrain. *The Castle,* after all, reads like a *film noir*.

And *noir* itself is one of the few Hollywood forms that hasn't dated at all. It's no accident that De Niro's best performances have come in "gangster" films, from *Bloody Mama* (1970) to *The Untouchables* (1987), where De Niro was another raging bull, Al Capone. America itself has become that mythic land of crime, where the gangster and the tycoon are central characters, often the same man. With the coming of Prohibition in 1919, gangsters like Capone, Dutch Schultz, and Legs Diamond were almost as popular as movie stars.

Capone was crazy about Caruso. But the Italian tenor happened to die a little too soon (1921), or Capone might have bought him an opera house. Whole gangs of reporters would sit with Al Capone at the opera. He was the most celebrated thug in Chicago, much more famous than Carl Sandburg or Frank Lloyd Wright.

And of course movieland took advantage of Al, featuring a Capone-like gangster in *Scarface, Little Caesar,* and a dozen other films of the time. Ben Hecht worked on *Scarface,* and in his memoirs, *A Child of the Century,* he swears that two of Scarface's henchmen visited him at his Hollywood hotel, wanting to know if Hecht's script was really about Al. Hecht gulls the two gangsters, telling them: "If we call the movie *Scarface,* everybody will want to see it, figuring it's about Al. That's part of the racket we call showmanship."

And the henchmen go away, satisfied.

But the story seems "counterfeit" to me, and mean-spirited, like Hecht's own image of Hollywood.

Movies, Hecht believed, had "lamed the American mind and retarded Americans from becoming a cultured people." Ah, it was Hecht who'd worked on *Gunga Din, The Black Swan,* and *Notorious,* films that had given me all the culture I would need.

"Hollywood's like Egypt," David O. Selznick had told Ben Hecht in 1951. "Full of crumbled pyramids." There's some truth to what Selznick said. It was the time of the witch hunts, when moguls withdrew from movieland or vanished within its walls. But there's also some personal pique in Selznick's declaration of doom. By 1951 he'd lost whatever magic he had. And he was like some Bedouin, looking for another *Gone With the Wind.*

3 There'd always been a kind of doom hanging over Hollywood. From the very beginning local prophets had declared that these "movie people" couldn't last. But as stables and orchards were turned into open-air studios, as the Keystone Kops rampaged in "downtown" Hollywood, as Cecil B. De Mille built his empire among the oranges and the avocados, this little camp of gypsies took hold. Each new generation of gypsies looked back upon the "old" Hollywood and mourned that loss of spontaneity and the pioneering spirit of the first filmmakers. Movies had become big

business, and electricians, carpenters, and actresses stopped eating out of a single lunch pail.

But Hollywood remained a village until World War II, when soldiers and sailors filled the town, on their way to the Pacific. And John Garfield, a refugee from the Group Theatre, noticed the success of New York's Stage Door Canteen and had a particular brainstorm: Why couldn't Hollywood have its own canteen where servicemen could come and meet the stars? He approached Bette Davis. She found an old stable on Cahuenga Boulevard, leased it for a hundred dollars a month, marshaled all the studios to help her, and became president of this phantom society: the Hollywood Canteen. Studio craftsmen gutted the stable. "Carpenters tossed the floor and walls into the street and built new ones; screen cartoonists did the murals with electricians climbing over their backs."

The Hollywood Canteen opened on October 3, 1942, with Duke Ellington, Abbott and Costello, and Rudy Vallee's Coast Guard Band. Eddie Cantor was the first master of ceremonies. He was soon followed by Fred MacMurray, Bob Hope, Bing Crosby, Basil Rathbone, Jack Benny, and John Garfield. The canteen had become the focal point for servicemen *and* the stars, who were imprisoned by their own celebrity and "often had nowhere to go in the evening."

It was at the Hollywood Canteen that Betty Grable met bandleader Harry James, whom she married, after splitting up with George Raft. And Hedy Lamarr found her third husband, John Loder, who was washing dishes at the canteen.

But the stars also did a lot of dancing with servicemen. The canteen was open from seven p.m. to midnight (curfew time in movieland). It was a marathon affair, with seven thousand movie stars and extras working in shifts: the canteen required three hundred volunteers a night. Over a million soldiers and sailors visited the canteen during its first year, soldiers and sailors with terrific appetites, consuming "4,000 loaves of bread" each month, "400 pounds of butter . . . and 150,000 pieces of cake."

Almost the entire Hollywood population had some part in the canteen, except for Garbo and Chaplin, who remained aloof from the proceedings at Cahuenga Boulevard. Even Jean Gabin was there, looking as gaunt as Danny Kaye. He'd come to

Hollywood during the Occupation of France, and served in the canteen kitchen, like other actor-refugees.

Monday was a special night at the canteen, when the movie stars' own mothers were in charge. A soldier might get his coffee from Ginger Rogers' mom, or dance with Betty Grable, while her mom ran the kitchen brigade.

Despite the deep sadness of the war itself, this was probably the best time Hollywood ever had.

Roosevelt was in the White House.

The stars had come down from the hills to sit among soldiers, sailors, and themselves. There was a camaraderie, a lending of one's own spirit, that had long been absent in this company town. But it couldn't last.

Roosevelt died.

The canteen closed. And the Cold War began.

Hollywood tried to be "daring," to deal with racial problems in films such as *Gentlemen's Agreement* (1947) and *Lost Boundaries* (1949). But it was one more Cowardly Lion, without the charm of Bert Lahr. It was too involved with business to take us to the edge of things. Movieland expressed the fears and anxieties of the nation in an almost "accidental" way, in those dream portraits that Barbara Deming described in *Running Away From Myself:* the barren psychic wilderness that lay beneath the story line like the very ruin of our lives. Just behind "the warrior who will win for us, there, if one looks twice, is one whose condition closely resembles that of the lonely figure who worried us at the start." The weave of any film can "effect no translation too total—lest, it seems, we wake."

The soldier comes home to discover that he has no home. Something terrible has happened while he was at play in the fields of war. The women on the "home front" have become much stronger than he could imagine . . . at least that is what he feared. And those wonderful comedies of the Thirties, where Claudette Colbert, Carole Lombard, Jean Harlow, Rosalind Russell, and Myrna Loy could play as hard as William Powell, Cary Grant, or Gable, without giving up a hint of their sexuality, were swept away with the war.

Suddenly we had spider women, like Barbara Stanwyck (with blond hair) and Joan Crawford, who entered male sanctuaries and competed with their beaux. Joan's broad shoulders had never seemed masculine at MGM. When she switched to Warners and played Mildred Pierce, she might have been the sacrificing mama, but she wore the shoulders of a man, and neither Zachary Scott nor Bruce Bennett could occupy much space around Joan.

Only Garfield, with his rough beauty, could match up against her. He was a Dead End Kid, after all, a city boy, and in *Humoresque* (1946) he's a poor fiddler who becomes Crawford's protégé. His sexual musk was as powerful as Joan's, and she kills herself (in *Humoresque*) because she cannot really contain the fiddler.

A different sort of suicide hovered around John (né Julius Garfinkle). He'd started the Hollywood Canteen, sold war bonds, sat with servicemen. But his politics got him into trouble after the war. He wouldn't rat on his friends. And he'd started a Kafka-like dance with the Committee that finally killed him.

Garfield is the man I mourn the most. He made three films after the war, *The Postman Always Rings Twice, Body and Soul,* and *Force of Evil,* that should have established him as the most gifted actor of his generation. But he didn't have Bacall. And Bogey is the guy we remember now, with his lisp, his toupee, and his deadpan looks. He's our Philip Marlowe, Sam Spade, and Casablanca Rick. Garfield's clay was a little too coarse to be mythologized. He wasn't classic enough to be Philip Marlowe or Sam Spade.

4 Marlowe and Spade are the twin gods of *film noir.* Their creators, Raymond Chandler and Dashiell Hammett, have probably had a more significant hold on American films of the Forties and thereafter than any single director or star, with the possible exception of Hitchcock and Bogey himself.

In the Eighties festivals began to proliferate around the world devoted to *film noir* and the *roman noir* (black films and black books). *All* of these festivals—in Havana, Grenoble, Mexico City, Yalta, etc.—were inspired by Hammett and Chandler, and those curious Yankee films of the Forties that cast a spell over the planet with their bleak urban landscapes and misogynous signs: sirens and mermaids, like Lana Turner, Martha Vickers,

Mary Astor, Yvonne De Carlo, Ava Gardner, Joan Bennett, or Jane Greer, who try to sing Garfield and Bogart, Mitchum and Lancaster to their doom.

In October 1987 I took the *train noir* out of Paris with a hundred writers and journalists, rocked all the way to Grenoble, where we were met by half the population of the town. I couldn't believe that so many people would have come out for a tribe of scribblers. They hadn't. They were looking for David Soul (né Solberg), actor-singer and former star of the American cop series *Starsky and Hutch,* which was enjoying a new and profoundly lucrative life in France. But if David Soul was on the black train, I hadn't seen him. He materialized all of a sudden, like a blond commissar in a leather coat. People snaked around him, shouting "Hutch, Hutch," and for a while it felt as if we'd never get out of the Gare de Grenoble.

The next afternoon I took part in a debate with Soviet crime writer Julian Semionov, whose books, one heard, had sold a hundred million copies. I felt like a beetle next to him. He was a big bear of a man, my age, with a cropped head and a complicated beard. He looked like a well-fed pirate. He spoke Russian of course, and German, Spanish, English, but not a syllable of French. His interpreter was a woman with thick hands. He traveled around with her and four other burly people. Rumor had it that Semionov was a colonel in the KGB. I'd have been disappointed if he wasn't. It was the age of glasnost, openness to the West, and I soon discovered that I had more in common, at least rhetorically, with Semionov, than with my own Western comrades in Grenoble. He talked like a Democrat. We both believed that crime fiction had moved outside its own little genre. "Black novels" had burrowed into the fabric of society in a way that "white novels" no longer could. And the *roman noir* had become a kind of international language—little black books with tremors all over the world.

Three films were showing that night at the festival's *nuit du cinéma,* which started at ten and finished at five in the morning. *L'Inspecteur Harry* (*Dirty Harry*), *Police Federale* (*To Live and Die in L.A.*), and *Blade Runner.*

*Blade Runner* had already become an aficionado's classic. It bombed on its first release in 1982. Critics despised it and audiences wouldn't go to see Indiana Jones (Harrison Ford) with a sour face and short, short hair. It was a futuristic detective tale with a Forties feel: Philip Marlowe in some vast Tokyo-town called L.A., where buildings belch fire and police cars can fly. Rick Deckard (Ford) is an ex–blade runner, a special kind of cop who "retires" mutinous androids, or replicants, our own genetic twins, designed by engineers at the Tyrell Corporation. The replicants are soldier-slaves on the off-world colonies. They've been outlawed from our dying planet, because they're much too clever for mere human beings. " 'More human than human' is our motto," says old man Tyrell, the king of genetic engineers.

It's November 2019. A little band of replicants has organized a mutiny in deep space and returned to the planet. Only Deckard can find these "skin jobs." But he doesn't want to go back to work. His former captain tells him: "I need the old blade runner. I need your magic."

He visits the Tyrell Corporation and discovers that Tyrell's assistant, the beautiful Rachael (Sean Young), with coiffed hair, a broad-shouldered dress, and the mascaraed eyes of a Forties princess, is a skin job, implanted with memories of Tyrell's own niece. Rachael's entire history is false. All the songs in her head belong to someone else. But Rachael doesn't know it.

When she kisses Deckard, we realize it's the first time she's ever kissed a man. And when she looks at Deckard's old family photographs, it's with the longing of an amnesiac. The performance is so striking and so particular that when I discovered her in another film (*No Way Out*), as Kevin Costner's sexually aggressive girlfriend, I missed Rachael and the terrible sadness in her darkened eyes.

But that's my own affair.

The rest of *Blade Runner* is concerned with Deckard's destruction of the outlaw band. As he kills the snake woman Zhora (Joanna Cassidy), she falls through pillars of glass that seem as fragile and violent and mysterious as memory itself, and we begin to wonder what kind of skin jobs we all are.

*Blade Runner*'s narrative line is not its real glue. Director Ridley Scott has created a visual force field that tugs at us throughout the film. *His* Los Angeles is a town of pyramids and concrete volcanoes and neon lights that talk of Coca-Cola, an Aztec city of deep tunnels and a deeper sky: it has all the clutter of our

unconscious minds. *Blade Runner*'s visual field swallows up all
of Deckard's strategies. He's a bounty hunter in a world that
has lost its bounty. He's living "off-world" in L.A.

**5** It's nine months after Grenoble. I'm now a member
of AIEP, La Asociación Internacional Escritores Poli-
cíacos, which may be a new kind of Cheka for all I
know. Julian Semionov is our president. We're a universal club of crime writers, come to meet in Asturias, at the
Spanish port town of Gijón, on the Bay of Biscay. It's the first
Semana Negra. Black Week.

We descend like an army upon Madrid, sixty-one writers from
all over the world. Canada. Cuba. Great Britain. Czechoslovakia. France. Bulgaria. Mexico. Germany, East and West. Italy.
Argentina. Sweden. Uruguay. The United States and the Soviet
Union. And the current kingdom of Spain. Our vice-president,
Paco Ignacio Taibo II, who was born in Gijón and now lives in
Mexico City, collects us at the airport. Paco is an historian,
crime novelist, and cultural matador, whose energy has kept the
organization alive. We're dirt poor. The American branch can
barely cover its xeroxing costs. But Paco has brought the Semana Negra home to Asturias. The alcalde of Gijón is sponsor-
ing our gang of roughneck writers. Asturias is in the thick of a
recession. It's cheaper to import coal all the way from China
than to mine the coal beds of Gijón. And so the Semana Negra
is meant to revive the province a little. We'll be joined by a
circus, a choir, and rock bands during our Black Week. And the
port of El Musel in Gijón has been dressed over, turned into a
"black city," in honor of Dashiell Hammett.

We leave Madrid in the morning, waltz across the street from
our hotel to the Estación del Norte. Paco, our Pancho Villa,
has borrowed a prize train, the "Al Andalus Expreso," from
the Spanish railroad. It's like a cattle baron's "estate," with
little plush couches instead of chairs, with curtains, carpets,
tulip-shaped lamps, private shower baths, paneling that had once
belonged to a Spanish king. Now I know why Agatha Christie
wrote *Murder on the Orient Express:* it was for the sheer deviltry
of describing a train like this.

We have a magician on board the Andalusian Express, a little man, bearded and ordinary, and while the writers grant interviews and the journalists drink and smoke, the magician performs card tricks that stun all his guests. He can pick red queens out of your pocket, change a card's complexion from black to red. The magician seems much more powerful than the *literarios* around him. He puts his *cartas mágicas* into a little plastic envelope and goes to sleep.

I rock along on this cattleman's car, where magicians sleep and glass flowers bloom on the wall. I watch the landscape out my window. Castles appear in empty fields. Forests turn blue. A monastery sits behind a train station. I think of that one-armed man, Miguel de Cervantes. Don Quixote no longer seems "quixotic" to me. The old caballero was as rational as a railroad line.

We arrive in Gijón and are greeted by clusters of people, a little orchestra, and the local Communists, who carry a banner that reads: MÁS TRABAJO. The Communists would rather have jobs than a Semana Negra. How can I blame them? We are heroes from another planet, *escritores* who've come to town.

We're bussed to our hotel, the Hernán Cortés, in the heart of Gijón. And before I can change my underpants we're summoned downstairs and like good little troops we get on the bus again. We ride out to El Musel and that little city of crime Gijón has built for the Semana Negra in the very teeth of the harbor. It looks like a piece of property stolen from the *Blade Runner* set. El Musel, a futuristic marvel out of the past. There are derricks and cranes and black dunes of coal. The water is brown at El Musel. Our headquarters is a building called Las Sirenas, and it's here, in the sirens' den, that we get our badges and meal tickets and statues of a little plaster man wearing dark glasses and an overcoat: our patron saint, the *hombre negro* of the week.

*6* We have meetings of AIEP and debates at El Musel. Our delegates from Czechoslovakia, East Germany, Bulgaria, and the Soviet Union talk about the police novel and perestroika. Without perestroika, few of the delegates would have been here. But will we ever see a Czech Sam Spade, a Soviet Philip Marlowe, some hombre negro who dances at the edge of doom, with a siren singing in his ear?

I longed for such a creature. I suppose all of us did.

I was disoriented for the first few days. I'd walk a couple of blocks from the Hernán Cortés and couldn't find my way home. It's that special limbo, the disease of all travelers in the twentieth century: jet lag. But it wasn't all bad. The disorientation heightens the dream state we're in, furthers the dream, and we can't fall back on our own rationality that we covet so much.

I solved the riddle of Gijón. The old port girdles the town. You can close your eyes, walk in any direction, and arrive at the sea.

I stand on the old wall above the Playa de San Lorenzo. No one's out on the beach. I watch the blue, blue Atlantic. The clouds gather in knots, and for a moment I could swear I was witnessing another one of John Eberson's "atmospherics." Then the clouds drop into the sea, and I lose that dream picture of the Loew's Paradise.

*Police Academy 5* is playing at the Teatro María Cristina on the Calle Corrida. It's an old movie palace with marble steps, a gold flowerpot, and a metal grille with a circular design that looks like the endless weave of movies themselves.

I return to El Musel.

"La vida es una novela negra" is written on one of the walls.

Outside Las Sirenas, on the moonscape of El Musel, *our* black city, I wanted to fathom why black novels and black films expressed a need that couldn't be found anywhere else. Stanley Kubrick's *The Killing* (1956), *Atraco perfecto,* is playing at El Musel, in an industrial barn that serves as a movie house. It's pure *noir:* the film is about a racetrack robbery that breaks down time into multiple "tracks" and points of view until we, the audience, live with the abstraction inside Kubrick's head. *Noir* always seems to transmogrify its heroes, turn them into the phantoms of a phantom, our own darkest self, which has no integrated personality and is forever split. Perhaps that's what Black Week is about: the schizoid life of the novelista negra.

 The Communists have dubbed our little black city "Poisonville." And we all have to smile because at least they know their Dashiell Hammett. They're aficionados who want our scalps. "Poisonville" is the nickname of the town where the Continental Op creates bedlam and a bloodbath in *Red Harvest,* Hammett's first novel. The Op had no Bogart to remember him by. He's a faceless fat man who exists in our subconscious. He's been hired to clean up the town and he's gone "blood-simple." Because of him, there are sixteen murders "in less than a week," and Poisonville has become his private slaughterhouse.

The Op has no name or individual life. He's simply an operative for the San Francisco branch of the Continental Detective Agency. He works for the Old Man, who sends him out "to be crucified on suicidal jobs." And like the Op, we wait until someone's machine gun has "settled down to business, grinding out metal like the busy little death factory it was."

When he's with gangsters and crooked politicians, tycoons, and cops, he plays them "like you'd play trout."

But when he leaves Poisonville, it's a town that's waiting to be milked all over again. The Op has accomplished nothing, and the Old Man gives him "merry hell."

In his introduction to *The Continental Op,* critic Steven Marcus reminds us that Hammett's work is filled with conundrums, moral ambiguities that the Op only deepens, and never solves. The Op himself is one more element of the crime. And what we love to call reality is "a construction, a fabrication, a fiction" that the Op tries to deconstruct. But he ends up adding his own fiction to the fiction that is already there.

The Op is a much more complicated character than Nick Charles or Sam Spade. He doesn't have Nora to console him. He doesn't have Effie Perine. He isn't colorful. He isn't kind. He's the most radical figure in all of crime fiction, and the most relentlessly *American,* the Natty Bumppo of detectives—the precursor, the natural man.

He was "born" during Prohibition, when the gangster seized hold of our imagination, and American society "committed itself to a vast collective fiction"—that it could outlaw alcohol and still have a drink. All it did was create "a world of universal warfare, the war of each against all, and of all against all."

It is a world we still inhabit, with or without Prohibition. It is our particular "call of the wild," that belief in the rugged individual (the guy who can get rich whenever he wants), in the idea that money is *everything*—virtue, love, God. Wealth defines our national character: it is the only history we have.

And the Op is the guardian of that society, its very own Baal. He murders all the murderers, and becomes his own murderous angel. Beelzebub and Baal.

Sam Spade was at least a *little* romantic, and Nick Charles was no longer a practicing detective. He disappeared with Nora and Asta, and Hammett himself, who stopped writing detective stories and cannibalized his own material for the radio and comic books, while we have Bogart and William Powell, who haunt us every year at film festivals and Semanas Negras.

But it's the Op who's king at the idled port of Poisonville.

I feel his presence as I have my paella at a fish restaurant in Cimadevilla, the oldest part of town. There aren't any turistas here. I'm the lone yanqui in the place. The man next to me has finished his meal. The camarero brings him a cigar, and the man goes through an entire ritual. He dunks the end of the cigar into his coffee cup, lights the cigar, then browns the sides with the flame of his cigarette lighter. After the cigar is thoroughly "broiled," he takes his first puff. It's a procedure the Op would have admired.

In the neighboring town of Avilés, near the Calle de Fruta and a fourteenth-century façade that could have been attached to the Loew's Paradise, I saw a black swan. The swan had a red beak with a single white band. And so accustomed to Hollywood was I, a walking cinémathèque, that I couldn't take my eyes off this marvelous bird. Now I understood the meaning of Tyrone Power's pirate ship, *The Black Swan,* with its sleek body and black sails. It was almost as magnificent as the black swan of Avilés.

Home at the Hernán Cortés, I watch the wicked witch, Joan Collins, on the tube. *Dynasty* has come to Gijón. And Joan Collins was the siren of the West, as artificial and ageless as Hollywood. We had to fashion a dream city. We had nothing else. Hollywood was the home of all histories without a history of its own.

Paul Newman's face was on the wall of a beauty salon near the Plaza de San Miguel. No other medium had such instant currency—the face of a movie idol.

I look at the silent, sad faces on the street, prisoners of their own beauty in this kingdom that superimposes the twentieth century upon its true medieval self. It's a land of gypsies with light skin. On the Calle Corrida I discover a street puppeteer, a slightly ragged woman with her own little girl in a doll's baby carriage. Her long-haired puppet is almost as ragged as she is. The puppet has wooden shoes and he dances along the Calle Corrida like a little man on the run. He seems to announce that he's not here to amuse. He's as primitive and impersonal as the moon.

Ah, I think, there's still one little corner that Hollywood hasn't touched.

# fifteen

# *Pilgrim's Progress*

## 1

In 1940 a young cartoonist and scriptwriter named Federico Fellini got on a trolley car at Rome's Termini Station and went out to Cinecittà for the first time. The trip took half an hour. The City of Film was located on Via Tuscolana "five miles from the gates of Rome." It sat on a hundred and forty-nine acres of land, with sixteen sound stages, including a special stage "for miniatures, make-up, and animation." It looked a little like the Vatican *and* MGM, with nine acres of gardens and flower beds, three restaurants, an electric power station, and a huge water tank that could hold entire islands and a fleet of ships.

But the young cartoonist wasn't concerned about Cinecittà's acreage or the dimensions of a water tank. He was like a pilgrim who'd come to visit a holy shrine. Born in the seaside town of Rimini, the son of a candy salesman, he ran away from school around the age of seven to "join" a traveling circus. But he was captured after several days and sent home. Still, the love of circuses would remain with him for the rest of his life. Circuses and the "sea" of American films.

"When I was a youngster," Fellini said, "this word, Cinecittà . . . evoked a kind of city in which I wanted to live." For an outsider from Rimini "it was seductive, fascinating; it was the city of cinema, therefore the city of actresses, the city of stars. My generation was born with the myth of the American cinema. We were all entranced by Hollywood stars: Clark Gable, Gary Cooper . . ." And the fact that Italy now had a Cinecittà, "something that resembled Hollywood," enthralled Fellini and obsessed him like the clowns of that mythical circus he'd been carrying in his mind.

There was little he could do about it. The war had come to

Italy and the boy was still a struggling cartoonist. For a while Cinecittà had a charmed "fairy tale" existence. It was "inhabited by a strange population of actors, hangers-on and extras in costume living in an environment of plaster and papier-mâché sets." But it didn't last. Rome was bombed in 1943 after the fall of Mussolini and Cinecittà lay in a kind of enchanted ruin. All film production stopped. The Germans occupied Rome and began a systematic looting of Cinecittà. More bombs fell. "In Cinema City only the walls remained."

The Allies arrived and turned Cinecittà into a refugee camp. But Cinecittà reopened while the refugees still occupied some of the sound stages. And then Hollywood discovered Rome. *Prince of Foxes* (1949), starring Tyrone Power and Orson Welles, was the first American film to be shot at Cinecittà. The majors were in the middle of a crisis, marked by the coming of television and Senator Joe McCarthy, the loss of their movie-theater chains and the rebelliousness of the stars, and they learned to shift more and more of their productions to "Hollywood on the Tiber."

Thus a new scenario began:

The stars invade Rome like planetary beings. Ava Gardner, Rita Hayworth, Errol Flynn, Alan Ladd, Rock Hudson, Elizabeth Taylor, Kirk Douglas, Jennifer Jones, Audrey Hepburn, Gable, Bogart, Sinatra, Brando, Peter Sellers, and Gregory Peck move with their mistresses, lovers, husbands, secretaries, wives, business managers, and make-up men into villas on the Appian Way. Half of Rome's unemployed become "Hollywood" extras for *Quo Vadis?* (1951), *A Farewell to Arms* (1957), *Ben Hur* (1959), and *Cleopatra* (1963), a colossal four-hour bomb that nearly bankrupts Twentieth Century–Fox and kills the American "kingdom" of Rome.

But it was already the age of the "spaghetti Western," with Sergio Leone and his *Fistful of Dollars* (1964). Leone took a TV actor, Clint Eastwood, and turned him into an international star as the tight-lipped, bearded and blond cowboy samurai, the "Man With No Name," who murdered people on the plains of Cinecittà with a cool and deadly hand. Other directors steal from Leone and soon there are hundreds of Westerns on the same lots. "Cinecittà built its own saloons and wooden town fronts—all recycled from one horse opera to the next."

And of course there was Fellini, who shot *La Dolce Vita* (1959) in Cinecittà's Studio Fourteen. The film, which narratized the crazy world of movie stars and paparazzi princes that Rome had become, was an enormous success and Fellini retreated within the caverns of Cinecittà, where he would now shoot most of his films. He was Cinecittà's new lord, with his own apartment inside the walls of Via Tuscolana. As one Italian critic wrote: Fellini "secludes himself in Cinecittà like a voluntary prisoner." And the debris of his old movies, "like the gargantuan head poking out of the Venetian lagoon in 'Casanova' . . . become part of the daily life of cinema city."

That pilgrim of 1940 had rediscovered paradise. The markings of his life were abandoned movie sets. He'd conceived his own autobiography with gum and glue, the phantom of his own opera: Federico Fellini.

2   I'm also a pilgrim. But I didn't have such a clear picture in my head. I was a "Hollywood" brat, just like Fellini, in love with those silver faces. But I never even considered looking for the right trolley to movieland. What would I have found at the end of the line? Brando was in Tahiti. Bogey and Cooper were dead. And I didn't know a thing about Marilyn's crypt. Yet all the journeys I'd made, all the towns I'd lived in—Barcelona, London, Palo Alto, Paris, Austin (Texas), San Francisco, Houston, Monticello (in the Catskills)— were longings for Hollywood, the dream city of magical sets that often *looked* like Paris or Casablanca or L.A., but had that added allure of the temporary, a land of furniture that could be pulled at any moment, dressed again or reduced to common rubble.

What I'd wanted was not a city, but the ultimate set. And I'd been chasing my own tail all this time, searching for Hollywood in Gaudí's lyric Baracelona, in the iron twigs of the Eiffel Tower and the marshmallow domes of Sacré-Coeur, the canals of San Antone, the old Storyville section of New Orleans, the Count of Monte Cristo's island in the harbor at Marseilles. My fate as a moviegoer had been formed much sooner than my experience of the "world," which was only a reflection of what I'd picked up from RKO, Paramount, Warners, Fox, Columbia, Uncle Walt Disney, and MGM. Pinocchio, Dumbo, Bambi,

Frankenstein, King Kong, the Wolf Man, and the Seven Dwarfs were blood brothers of mine.

*Wilson,* a 1944 epic with Alexander Knox, had shaped my sense of politics. I worshipped Alexander Knox, that stern, admirable, and humorless patriarch. The country had turned against Wilson after World War I and wouldn't let Alexander Knox join the League of Nations. Wilson had a stroke and nearly died. I remember a phantom president, wrapped in a blanket, with a monocle in his eye, Moses among the gentiles.

Time socked me in the face forty years after *Wilson,* when I discovered an ancient Alexander Knox in *Gorky Park.* I ignored his trappings as a Soviet general and started to shiver. I couldn't stop thinking of him as my very own dad, Woodrow Wilson.

The friends I had wouldn't have known Alexander Knox. They weren't movie addicts. They were more interested in sneaking into the Polo Grounds than the Loew's Paradise. They didn't even notice when Alice Faye disappeared from the screen in 1945. I was filled with bile. She'd been feuding with Darryl Zanuck at Fox. Zanuck was giving all the meaty roles to Betty Grable. And Alice decided to walk away from musicals. She appeared in *Fallen Angel* (1945), her first *film noir.* It flopped, and Alice Faye retired. I was in the fourth grade. I'd been reading all the fan magazines, and I understood the hierarchy of Hollywood. I scribbled a letter to Twentieth Century–Fox.

"Dear Sirs," I wrote. "Couldn't you fire Mr. Zanuck?"

Fox never answered me. I boycotted most of Zanuck's films until Marlon Brando came along. I wasn't going to miss *Viva Zapata!* (1952) because of my own misgivings about a studio boss. It was a dangerous film. I fell in love with Mexico and Zapata's mustache and the sadness of revolutions. I wondered where the hell *our* Zapata was, with his sombrero, his white horse, his Chinese eyes, and his distrust of politicians. He would have preferred Eisenhower's long silences to the silky songs of Adlai Stevenson.

I also made a new friend. Harry Hurwitz, known as Hesh. We were sophomores at a high school in Manhattan. Hesh lived on a diet of candy bars. He'd discovered Charlie Chaplin at a boardwalk nickelodeon when he was five. He could recite all the movies that Eisenstein had never made. He was his own mad collector, like Langlois of the Cinémathèque Française. He was as skinny as Langlois had been once upon a time, but he didn't have to hold up his pants with copper wire. Harry had a belt. And I don't think he kept his film library in the family tub.

We were dating a pair of twins from Central Park West, and we'd ride the subways together after dropping the twins off at their apartment house; it was during those "midnight runs" on the IRT that we plotted an incredible future for ourselves as Machiavellian princes of the movies, more Monroe Stahr than Louis B. Mayer. We were like a commando unit: we'd rush the walls of Hollywood and write, direct, produce, and act in our own extravaganzas. We wouldn't fall into the trap of that baby face, Orson Welles. We'd subvert RKO from within.

We didn't become moguls, and by the time we finished high school and college there was no longer an RKO to subvert. The studio had stopped making films. But that couldn't bother Harry. He borrowed a Bolex and went into production. I was Harry's diva: the guy who gets to kiss the girl in a field of wheat. He ran out of money and all production stopped. But I remember the parameters of my first screen kiss, the way my head bent to arrive at the young woman's mouth, the slow, deliberate movements of a camera-held kiss, as if I were a piece of geometry that happened to have a face.

I toiled in New York City high schools and Harry taught art. He continued making films, and in 1971 he produced, directed, wrote, and acted in *The Projectionist,* an underground classic about the monomania of our movie culture. The lonely projectionist played by Chuck McCann is haunted by the very films he shows from his projection booth. The booth is both his coffin and his dream chamber. When he climbs down from the booth he becomes one more invisible object, a ghost walking around in a Technicolor world.

The film itself disappeared after a week, and Hesh withdrew to Tampa, where he again taught art. But he wasn't idle. He directed funny sex and horror films under the name of Harry Tampa. He moved to the gardens of Hollywood, wrote, directed, sat in the sun, returned to New York, where we picked up our "collaboration" after twenty-five years. We still had that bond of movies between us, like some magnificent code.

*Bambi* was the first film he'd ever seen. He was four years old.

It was 1942. "It's got mothers dying," Harry said. *"Bambi* was one of the most psychologically devastating films ever made. . . . It prepared you to lose your mother. The Hollywood movie is probably the only medium that is so plugged into our emotions, it's the only place other than in real life where you can feel sexual arousal, sorrow to the point of tears, real terror, and convulsive laughter. . . . There's a scene in *Dumbo* where the mother has been taken away from the child [and put in a circus pen]. Her trunk comes out [of the pen] and cradles the child. It's the most devastating scene in movies . . . her trunk comes out and rocks the baby elephant."

But you couldn't have Bambi and Dumbo all the time. "What audiences really craved was a hit of vicarious emotions intensi-fied, to experience things in a safe arena. It was safe to be stalked by the most monstrous murderers and feel real terror, it was safe to fall in love with beautiful strangers, safe to enjoy the pain of clowns and let them slip on a banana peel. We could all become heroes and lovers. It was audiovisual dope."

Hesh moved back to California and I settled in to collect all the old bones of Hollywood, that lost city of film where Bogart and Betty Grable had lived and worked, with its Garden of Al-lah, Romanoff's, and the Hollywood Canteen, the enormous back lots of MGM and the Republic ranch, where whole civili-zations of cowboys sweated and died and won some mythical West. Most of it had vanished like silver nitrate stock, but I had to go into the belly of the beast and discover how much of movieland was left.

3    I arrived in L.A. like old Leatherstocking, Natty Bumppo, removed from his native ground. I was one more amnesiac near the Pacific Ocean, looking for Chingachgook, his guide and faithful companion. Harry found me, of course. All his projects were on "hold" during a writers' strike that was into its twentieth week. He'd arranged my visit as if he were preparing a "shoot," and we were both in the thick of preproduction, searching for sites.

We entered a Latino 'hood. I saw chain fences among the palm trees, young men drifting in some slow-motion world. I'd read about the "drive-by" shootings in L.A., where rival gangs poked at each other with shotguns and assault rifles from the windows of cars that were becoming a new kind of tank. Gang leaders sported Ponce de León beards, tattooed their fingers, had telephones in their cars, adopted a single color, and relied on a complicated code of hand signals to communicate among their "home boys." There were 600 "sets" (gangs) in L.A., with 70,000 "bangers," kids and old young men who had their infantry training in the streets and were into serious business, killing, selling drugs, and "bringing gold to their mothers." It was venture capitalism gone amok, the sort of tribalism that was familiar to me, one more image of the wild, wild West.

But no one shot at us, and I didn't catch any of the "bangers" wearing gold. We must have entered a fire-free zone, a little marketa where shooting wasn't allowed.

We passed an old movie palace in the shape of a swan.

We passed the pillars of MGM, former home of the junkman and the Boy Genius.

We passed the little white mansion that had been the opening insignia of *Duel in the Sun* and other David O. Selznick productions. The mansion unnerved me. I'd always thought it was a miniature or something, a bundle of trick photography. I hadn't expected it to be standing there in 1988, without David O. Selznick.

We watched the sun on the porch of Selznick's house. "Every cowboy who galloped over the hill had that sun," Harry said.

We passed Twentieth Century–Fox, with tenements peering above the palm trees and the studio walls. I marveled at a building that seemed to grow out of the walls like a beanstalk, or a New York castle from 1910. It was a piece of the *Hello, Dolly!* set.

"Behind those trees is fantasy land," Harry said. "Painted faces and painted façades . . . the actors were all Max Factor. . . . Look at this place. They dressed it with palm trees and stucco and built a huge set out here. Hollywood never existed."

"But the studios were great," I said, staring at my castle.

"Nobody lives in a studio," Harry said.

We got out of the car and approached Paramount's old "Ali Baba" wrought-iron gate at Bronson Avenue and Marathon Street, where Norma Desmond had gone through in her Isotta-Fraschini "bus," with Erich von Stroheim at the wheel. I touched the Moorish gate, but I couldn't summon Ali Baba or anybody else.

We went to the old Warner Brothers, now the Burbank Studios. Harry whistled his way onto the lot. We drove right up to the Western street, which was really a little town, angled so that wherever you were you had a miraculous feeling of depth, like the eye of a movie camera. We walked around in the dirt flats of our own Dodge City. "When we sat in the RKO," Harry said, "this was the town we saw."

The town had few interiors; it was frontage mostly, a skeleton of plaster and wood. Harry pecked at one of the façades with a finger until it began to crumble and reveal a body of chicken wire. We found a trailer behind a Pony Express station, a parking lot behind a wall of leaves, and an entire cave and bear den built out of papier-mâché. "It's phony but it films perfectly."

We drove from Dodge City to smalltown America, with a gazebo and a street of front porches and little stores. "*Strawberry Blonde* was shot here," Harry said. "Three generations learned how to get laid from this block."

And to eat with a knife and fork, to wear a napkin like a bib, and chant a little song of grace before every meal, which was unheard of in the Bronx, where we ate with our fingers while we sucked on chocolate milk with a straw and grabbed whatever food was on the table without thanking the Lord. God lived on some other block.

But I wanted something more substantial than plaster and papier-mâché in Jack Warner's old Cinecittà. And I found a slab of marble with blue veins under the fire escape of what could have been a candy store. "That's stone," I insisted.

"No stone here," Harry said. He scratched the "marble" until it bled a blue ink.

We wandered onto the New York street, which had doubled as a futuristic L.A. in *Blade Runner,* a kind of madcap Little Tokyo where it drizzled all the time. "We're in a twilight zone, walking down streets that don't exist . . . yet they do exist." Harry pointed to the front of a bank. "How many guys got machine-gunned on these steps? Its's Gangsterville, U.S.A."

We walked beyond the plains of the New York street and passed an outdoor warehouse of fake Roman columns and a gigantic storage bin, like Orson Welles' warehouse in *Citizen*

*Kane.* But we didn't find any Rosebuds, not a single childhood sled.

We stumbled upon a whole miniature city, with graveyards of wrought-iron fences and speckled wood, rocketships, fireplaces, tombstones that said HAGAR and PENROD. We'd uncovered an inventory of the world. And Hesh reminded me that the first story films had been made by magicians like Méliès, who'd manufactured his own inventory for the moon.

Hesh stared at the tombstones, the rocketships, the fences, and mile after mile of cable. "It's like the inside of Borges' brain."

4 She was one of the reasons I'd come to Hollywood. She was an icon, like Fay Wray. Both had starred in films about beauty and the beast. But the beast had blotted out all their other beaux. Fay Wray had been wooed by Erich von Stroheim in *The Wedding March*. And not even William Powell or Gary Cooper could compare with the amorous attentions of King Kong. She'll be Kong's lady for the rest of our lives. But I prefer the bride of Dr. Frankenstein, Mae Clarke.

She's supposed to marry Colin Clive. We see her in her wedding dress. She sits down with her bridal bouquet. Boris Karloff comes through the window in his size twenty-six shoes. We watch him lean over Mae Clarke, and it's a horrible, haunting moment. There's no musical score to enforce what we or the monster feel. The silence is like some deep, frozen tower of space that hints at our longing not to be alone. And we realize how handsome Karloff is with bolts in his neck. As he looks at "Elizabeth" (Mae Clarke), there's an incredible visual field. Karloff is the beauty *and* the beast. He deserves Mae Clarke but he doesn't get her. Her rescuers arrive with their torches: Frankenstein is afraid of fire. And Elizabeth is restored to Colin Clive, the film's real freak.

And of course there's that other moment we remember Mae by: she gets a grapefruit in the face in *The Public Enemy* (1931), shot on Jack Warner's New York street, dressed up as Chicago. The film succeeds because of Cagney's graceful dancing body and baby face. He lent a boyish enthusiam to Tom Powers that

Little Caesar (Edward G. Robinson) didn't have. He was lovable and mean, a bootlegger in the Poisonville that America had become during Prohibition. And it was startling to watch the boy gangster "christen" Mae Clarke with the grapefruit. It made him a star.

And Mae Clarke? She was Molly Malloy in *The Front Page* (1931) and appeared with Cagney again in *Lady Killer* (1933). This time Cagney gets to pull her by the hair. She floated through the Thirties, less and less of a star, and was the heroine of a Republic serial, *King of the Rocket Men* (1949).

She was never a classic beauty, like Lombard. She didn't have that animal energy of Harlow, or the killer instinct of Joan Crawford. I couldn't imagine Mae in *Johnny Guitar*. But I didn't care. She was perfect in *Frankenstein,* with Boris Karloff behind her and all that blondness beneath her bridal veil.

She was living at the Motion Picture and Television Country House in Woodland Hills. We arrived at the brick hacienda of the Country House. There were two cookie jars near the dining room, filled with figs and dried banana slices. But we couldn't seem to find Mae. "This is going to be a piece of work," Harry said. Was it the selective amnesia of the movie star? I went into the john. There was a poster on the wall of King Kong, clutching Fay Wray.

Hesh and I sat in the Douglas Fairbanks Lounge. And then, through the window, we saw Mae Clarke, riding down from her cottage on a tricycle. She wore a black bow in her hair. The blondness was gone, but she had that same hawklike profile of Frankenstein's bride.

We took her to dinner at the Calabasas Inn. We had something to celebrate. Mae had given up smoking after sixty years. She ate little meatballs and had a Bloody Mary with a celery stalk. "My peers don't like me because I stopped smoking. I get gentlemen from New York to take me out to dinner."

She'd been born Mary Klotz in Philadelphia, the daughter of a musician who'd played in moviehouses. She was a professional dancer by the time she was twelve. She remembered falling once in Atlantic City, while dancing in sequins. "I fell well." She shimmered from the floor as her costume began making "little designs" of light.

"I was getting ready to go to high school . . . to become an adult and maybe meet a fellah."

Harry told her how Atlantic City had gone to the dogs. "You wouldn't want to go there now."

"I only want to go if I can be a policeman," Mae said. "If I can carry a gun, a gat, and a machine gun."

Ah, I thought, all those gangster films of the Thirties weren't a joke. Mae had really been a gun moll. She recalled the American Film Institute's dinner for Cagney a little before he died. It had been almost half a century since the "grapefruit affair." Cagney talked to her from the stage. "And there's little Mae Clarke. Will you ever forgive me?"

"Of course I forgive you," Mae had said. And she remembered thinking at the time: "Here's an old man who resembles Jimmy Cagney . . . but it wasn't Jim."

She mentioned her father, the movie organist. "Every Saturday I got to go with Dad and sit on his bench . . . as much to watch him as to watch the screen." He had his own cheering section. His fans monopolized the first three rows. "Dad was like a little jockey . . . he came to my shoulders. I would watch the whole show on Saturday. It made me a technician. I saw the value of timing."

She'd made seven films in 1931, including *The Front Page, The Good Bad Girl, Frankenstein, The Public Enemy,* and *Waterloo Bridge.*

"It's wonderful," Harry said.

"Wonderful! It killed me. I overshot the field. Two studios owned me at the same time."

Mae was reluctant to bring up Mary Astor, who'd come to the Country House to die. She would sit in a corner of the dining room, very silent. She never talked. Once Mae had come to dinner wearing a tentlike dress and Mary Astor broke her silence. "You look like Whistler's Mother," she said.

But "she had an Oscar in her little room. . . . I said what everybody says [about the Oscar]. It's heavy."

Mae was staring at the dessert tray. "I'm carrying a hundred and fifty pounds around."

"Come on," Harry said. "You can have a whole dessert and we won't put it in the book."

"Get thee behind me, Satan," Mae said, before she chose a little chocolate pie.

What about Boris Karloff?

"He was a gentle man . . . but so masculine."

Her own favorite among all her films was *Waterloo Bridge*.

I started babbling about *Frankenstein*.

"*Frankenstein* was not a woman's story," she said. But she was fond of the film's director, James Whale, who'd also done *The Invisible Man* (1933), *The Bride of Frankenstein* (1935), and *The Man in the Iron Mask* (1939) before he fell into the usual Hollywood limbo. And in 1959 he drowned in his own swimming pool, one more forgotten man.

"They threw us away," she said of herself and Whale. "They threw us away."

But there wasn't much gloom about her. She was a woman with a touch of lipstick on her unadorned face. "I'm still a little kid with sand in my shoes." She didn't like to disparage people. She wasn't trying to get even.

In 1934, when she was under contract to Louis B. Mayer, she arrived on the lot for *Operator 13,* a film starring Marion Davies, Hearst's mistress, who had her own enormous bungalow inside the walls of MGM. Mae was given a phony wedding ring to wear. "I worked a day or two. I didn't get a call for the next day or the next and the next. I called the studio. 'When do I work?' I was told: 'Could you send the ring in? You've been replaced by Dorothy Peterson.' I was so mad I still have that ring . . . I still have it as a mark of protest. I was replaced because Miss Davies had seen the rushes. 'Too young, too blond, too pretty.'

"Quite a time passed. I became very ill. I had to end my contract. I could not work. I had a complete nervous breakdown. When I got well, my mother told me, When you were the sickest, Miss Davies called. 'When Mae is well, would you and she come and spend her convalescence at the Castle' [San Simeon]. Bear in mind, we never met."

"But you must have seen her on the set of *Operator 13,*" I said.

Mae looked at me. "We never met."

# sixteen

# The First Emperor

**1** It was like a gigantic, sprawling village that some sorcerer had concocted in his sleep. L.A. had swallowed up Hollywood, and now the whole village was Hollywoodian, even the barrio and the "bangers" of south central L.A. The "drive-by" shootings had blended into the fantasy life of the town, like one more exotic rodeo. Los Pocos Locos and the Black Mafia Crip Dogs could have been little corporations among the ruins of Hollywood Boulevard. The gangs wanted gold, just like everybody else. And if New York was the first twentieth-century city, cradled by Ellis Island and mongrels from all over the world who manufactured a "Culture of Congestion" and built skyscrapers that produced "a manmade Wild West, *a frontier in the sky*," L.A. was the *second* "World City, just as complex and cosmopolitan as any city of the past." It was, in fact, the city of the future, "a low-density Babylon," where the skyscraper was transmogrified into a million bungalows.

Life was horizontal, screamed L.A., "a city of bungalow-slums and junk-strewn gardens, a Mexican city, negro city, Japanese city [Korean city, Samoan city, etc.], a city of . . . palm trees and Pepsi-Cola, the city of Philip Marlowe and Charlie Chaplin, of Mickey Mouse and Frank Lloyd Wright."

Another kind of immigrant had fueled this bungalow town—the Hollywood mogul, who hadn't been born in L.A. Nobody is. The mogul was a magician, like Houdini or Méliès or Cecil B. De Mille, and that illusory world he created was only one more picture of L.A., the land of huckster-magicians, where Lombard and Crawford and other "beautiful strangers" danced into our lives.

But the town had gone to bed in the twentieth week of the

writers' strike. Hesh and I waltzed into Musso & Frank without a reservation. Musso's had been Faulkner's favorite grill. Nathanael West had eaten there with Dash Hammett, Dorothy Parker, and poor old Scott Fitzgerald. It had no palm trees. It had never been a cousin to the Cocoanut Grove or the Brown Derby. There were no caricatures of Gable on the walls. It had two rooms and a kind of "proletarian" bar and lunch counter where I could imagine unemployed actors drinking their soup in the middle of the Depression. Hesh and I had our pick of tables. Musso's was a haunted house.

We talked about the curious ethos of Hollywood, where the studios discarded people and also looked after them in their own splintered way. The junkman, L. B. Mayer, who'd sabotaged careers and drummed writers and movie stars out of Hollywood, was one of the chief benefactors of that retirement colony in Woodland Hills. It might never have opened without L.B. Yet the same L.B. was among the first movie execs to capitulate to Nazi propaganda minister Goebbels and "kill" the names of Jews and suspected Jews from the credits of MGM films. He was a businessman after all. He had matzohs and chicken soup at the MGM commissary, but he couldn't afford to lose the German market.

He was also a great ham. "He could play the part of any star in the studio, and play it better. . . . Greer Garson didn't want to play Mrs. Miniver, so Mayer called her into his office and played the role himself. He was the best Mrs. Miniver there ever was. He was hypnotic. And Miss Garson took the part," according to Adela Rogers St. Johns.

*The best Mrs. Miniver there ever was.*

2 We're off to the land of Mickey Mouse, the Disney studio at Burbank. It had once been a gentile enclave, like the FBI. Now its biggest stars, Bette Midler and Richard Dreyfuss, are Jewish, along with its chairman, Jeffrey Katzenberg, and the chief of all Disney enterprises, Michael Eisner.

Katzenberg, the boy from Park Avenue, is a thirty-eight-year-old genius who was already a con man at fourteen, when he helped elect John Lindsay mayor of New York. He's been hyped as the "new" Thalberg. But he doesn't have Irving's pale, deathly look.

He's the Dr. Frankenstein of Mickey Avenue and Dopey Drive, with his own team of "Disnoids," faithful to him and Uncle Walt. The Disnoids have stayed out of trouble in all the films they've inspired. "Put pumpernickel into the Disney toaster . . . and out pops white bread."

But we still got onto the lot. "The rodent is everywhere," Harry said. You couldn't take a step without meeting Mickey Mouse. His button nose was on every mailbox. We walked onto Dopey Drive, entered the old animation building, and discovered the original cels from *Pinocchio* and *Fantasia* on the walls. I drank some water from a paper cup devoted to "Mickey and His Merry Men." Mick was Robin Hood, Donald was Friar Tuck, and Minnie was Maid Marian.

The Mouse was usurping all our myths. He was sixty years old. He'd made billions for Uncle Walt. He first started to talk in *Steamboat Willie* (1928), with Uncle Walt himself delivering the Mouse's voice. He sounded like a boy soprano at the loving edge of hysteria, as if he were caught between a laugh and a cry. His most memorable performance was as the Sorcerer's Apprentice in *Fantasia* (1940). The film was one of Disney's few financial failures, but it couldn't hurt the Mouse, who had already replaced Charlie Chaplin as the most recognizable creature on earth.

One of the Disnoids, Phil Nemy, took us around the place. He told us that Walt Disney had designed the studio with wings. "If it doesn't work, I can sell it off as a hospital," said Uncle Walt, with that businessman's heart of his.

The maestro "brought animals into the building," in preparation for *Bambi*. "He brought in deer." And we spotted a photograph of Disney's animators sitting like students with a live fawn, sketching young Bambi.

We went to the Disney archives. Harry savored all the relics like a kid. The storyboard from *Pinocchio,* the multiplane camera with its three tiers that had created the forest in Bambi and its illusion of depth, long before we'd ever heard of 3-D. "This is the candy store," Harry said.

We saw one of the original Ingersoll Mickey Mouse wristwatches that Emperor Hirohito of Japan had loved so much.

We saw a cartoon of Mickey crying after the death of Uncle Walt in 1966. "Mickey has made this company," Phil said. And the Mickey Mouse watch "kept Ingersoll in business" during the Depression.

Phil was a graduate of Disney University, where all new employees learned about the history and folklore of the house that Uncle Walt had built. "The company looks after its people."

It was a closed world, a fiefdom, Mickey's family, and it didn't matter who was at the head of the line. Walt's spirit presided over the place. He was more than a mogul. He'd tapped into the hysteria of our time—those childhood demons that wouldn't go away. We suffer with Bambi and Dumbo and Snow White, because the arc that ought to take us into "adulthood" has a permanent flaw. We never seem to arrive at that mythic country. Snow White gets her prince, but her real address is that home she's made with the Seven Dwarfs. Dumbo learns to fly, but he's lost without his mom. Bambi grows antlers, but he still belongs in that children's forest with all the other animals. His enemy is Man, the hunter who kills animals out of some perverse sense of play.

Uncle Walt devoted six years of studio time to *Bambi*. He started his own little zoo with a couple of fawns from Maine. These were the fawns Phil had talked about. They "grew" into Bambi and Faline. But Uncle Walt hadn't established his own anitvivisection league on the lot. He wanted his artists to *feel* the tremors of the forest, to live around Bambi and Faline, so they wouldn't be ignorant of animals and would get the animation right—the spring and the frozen beauty of a deer. Uncle Walt was paternal about his creatures. "He loved to act the father of his brood," and he insisted there was "a lot of the Mouse in me." But if the Mouse was like an arrested, asexual child in yellow shoes, Bambi and Faline were not. Mickey belonged to no particular forest. And he didn't have to run from Man.

In praising Disney, a Yale professor once said: "He has given animals souls." I'm not so sure of that. He gave them pants and shoes and a high-pitched voice. Mick is the sweet side of our own nature. He doesn't threaten, because he has no sexual life. Minnie will have to wait a long time for her Robin Hood.

It hardly matters. The Mouse isn't burdened with our own mortality. He doesn't have to get on with his life, like Bambi and Faline. And there's the sorrow of that film. It mirrors our own biology. Voices change. Bambi learns to walk on his wobbly legs. But he cannot solve the riddle of Man, or penetrate that world beyond the forest. The forest itself is "tainted" when Man builds his campfires and brings his hunting dogs, who are unlike the animals of the forest, because they attack and maim for Man's pleasure. And so, even with a biological past, present, and future, Bambi and the others are children until they die, children like ourselves, who cannot leave the forest. And Man is the "other," the fabled adult who doesn't quite understand the forest, feels alone in it, and finds excitement in uncovering its creatures and breaking their backs. . . .

"We're an independent city," says Phil. "We have our own power source, our own first aid. If an earthquake hits, Disney will survive." Once a year the Disnoids have a mock drill, "with an 8.2 earthquake [on the Richter scale]. We estimate the casualties" and move about like a perfect little army.

What else could I want from Walt's children? "This place is junior high school," said another Disney exec. "It's a home for squirrels," Harry said. But I didn't care. Bambi grew up on this lot.

**3** I sail across Hollywood with Hesh and visit Dore Freeman at his private Joan Crawford museum. I feel like Little Nemo on his fabulous bed, caught up in some new Slumberland. Joan Crawford is everywhere: in the bookcases, on the mantels, on the walls, in the toilet too. There was an enormous cutout of Joan that had been on display at the Academy of Motion Picture Arts and Sciences after her death; an inscribed birthday greeting from Milton Caniff, "father" of *Terry and the Pirates,* declaring that Joan was the inspiration for the Dragon Lady, that lovely mean mama of my youth; a mask of Joan that MGM had used for make-up purposes "to build her face"; portraits of Dore with Lana Turner, Elvis, Jean Harlow ("To Kentucky," she wrote), Cary Grant,

Twiggy, Jacqueline Bisset, Leo the Lion, Mae West, and the Dragon Lady, Joan Crawford, who smiled at her ultimate fan with an affection she seldom had on screen.

He was born Isadore Freeman on April 12, 1912, in Louisville, and that's why Harlow had called him "Kentucky." He was the son of a tailor, like Cary Grant. But before he went to work in the publicity department at Metro-Goldwyn-Mayer, he was a messenger boy in New York, where he began his life as a movie fan. "The reason I got that job as a messenger boy was that I could get signatures whenever I wanted."

He'd tried for Garbo's signature and failed.

I asked him how he'd met Garbo. He looked at me as if I were a dunce. "Nobody meets Garbo," he said. He'd come to New York at the beginning of the Thirties and recognized Garbo in the street. "Miss Garbo, may I walk with you?" he asked.

"I don't care what you do," she said, without breaking her stride. And Dore followed Garbo for half a mile until she disappeared into a department store.

A huge dog arrives in the museum. "This is John Michael," Dore said. "He fainted twice today." He was an English mastiff with a devoted wet face. Dore had been offered a lot of cash for his house, but he couldn't sell it. "Where would I put John Michael?"

Dore looked like a speckled Indian with his hair tied in a knot. He reminded me of Brando in *Missouri Breaks*.

His first love had been Gloria Swanson. "But when Joan came on the screen in [*Our*] *Dancing Daughters,* I dropped Swanson and took on Crawford."

He had Joan's studio pass, her Social Security card, cigarette butts. "Everything comes to me . . . even her death certificate," which declared that Joan had died of cardiac arrest. Dore didn't agree. "She loved Hollywood. She loved Joan Crawford. And when she could no longer be Joan Crawford, she didn't want to exist."

She'd become an alcoholic and a recluse near the end. The American Film Institute had wanted to give Joan its Life Achievement Award, but not even the Institute could get Joan out of her apartment in New York. "Dore, honey," she said. "I don't want a fucking tribute. I want a job. Get me a job and I'll come out."

She was a creature of the studios, a Frankenstein monster invented by Louis B. Mayer *and* Billie Cassin, the little girl who'd become a laundress at eleven, whose father had deserted her before she was born. But she had "the diligence of a ditch-digger." A salesgirl in Kansas City, a chorus girl in New York, a part-time prostitute (perhaps), she was picked up by MGM, told to lose her baby fat, and turned into Joan Crawford. It didn't really matter what movie she was in—the drive, the determination, was always there. "The worse the film, the more mesmerizing she is, stalking through the jungle of clichés like a tigress." She'd had four husbands, including Douglas Fairbanks Jr. and Franchot Tone, adopted four children, but her real home was MGM, Warners, and wherever else she worked.

"She woke up like a movie star, she went to the john like a movie star," said director Joseph Mankiewicz. Billie Cassin had no personal life. She'd disappeared inside the phantasmagoria of Joan Crawford, whose first adopted child, Christina, wrote *Mommie Dearest,* one of the saddest adventures of a movie star. "From her throne in the eye of the hurricane, brandishing her magic wand of obsession, ruled the queen of chaos herself: Mommie dearest."

"I thought the book was terrible," Dore said. "Christina was jealous of Joan." I'd loved the book, because it revealed all the pathetic machinery and misplaced passion of the star system—Joan had been one of its great successes, and its profoundest dybbuk, the beautiful schizoid lady with the broad shoulders and big, big eyes. "I had . . . shoulders wider than John Wayne's." She got rid of every single bathtub in her Brentwood house, because she didn't think it was ladylike to sit in dirty bathwater. She answered all her fan mail, thousands of letters a week when Joan was in her glory, but Christina had to make an appointment when she wanted to see her mom. And "when Mommie dearest got mad enough she ripped people to shreds and made them disappear."

"You don't fool around with Joan Crawford," Dore said. "Christina had a stroke. Christopher [her second child] fell off a pole."

But the dybbuk wouldn't desert Dore. "She's still here . . . her spirit is here. I can see her every night when I go to bed and every morning when I get up."

4 We were sitting in Annie Hall's restaurant, The Source, on Sunset Boulevard. It was outside, in The Source's parking lot, that Alvie Singer (a.k.a. Woody Allen) keeps bumping into parked cars. L.A. is "Munchkinland" for Alvie Singer. He cannot survive apart from his particular periscope of Manhattan. He meets Annie's moon-stalked brother Dwayne (Christopher Walken) at a family dinner in Wisconsin. Dwayne hooks Alvie into a conversation about his own suicidal dreams. "I have to go, Dwayne," Alvie says. "I'm due back on the planet Earth."

Walken takes up only a minute or two of screen time. But it's one of those performances that squeezes your ribs. He's a sympathetic Frankenstein.

While Hesh and I are having our carrots and tofu at The Source, a man jogs past the restaurant in a sweatshirt and a blue stocking cap, looking for his own winter in July. It's the moon man himself, Christopher Walken. I don't even bother to blink.

We'd been running around like such maniacs, from Jack Warner's old lot to Dopey Drive and the Calabasas Inn, we hadn't had time to talk about Hesh's trip to China (last spring) with the Museum of Modern Art. It was the first American film retrospective China had ever had. MOMA chose twenty films from its archives, including *The Birth of a Nation, The General, Trouble in Paradise* . . . and *The Projectionist*.

The opening banquet was held in Beijing. "I was mobbed by young people who were trying to get tickets," Harry recalled, "trying to tear the programs away from my interpreter, because tickets were so scarce."

At the Beijing studio Harry stumbled upon "a back lot that looks like Shanghai of the Twenties." It was a Chinese version of Warners' New York street. The Beijing studio had "mostly American equipment. . . . It was self-contained. You could lock yourself in. It had its own hotel and sound stages. I could feel Hollywood. I knew where I was. I was not in China at that moment . . . it was a studio. I was within the walled city" of film.

Harry had also visited another movie set: the clay warriors of Emperor Qin Shi Huang, near the city of Xi'an. The warriors had been discovered standing in enormous pits. They'd been buried for over two thousand years, Qin's own army of the night. There was no China before Qin, nothing but feudal states and princes who warred upon each other. He crushed the warring states, centralized them, and started the Qin (Ch'en) Dynasty. He was the first emperor China ever had.

"And the first movie mogul," I said, because Qin had thought like a mogul and behaved like one. His massive "boneyard" was a miniature of the capital he'd built near the modern city of Xi'an. It contained more than six thousand soldiers, horses, and chariots. Like any mogul, Qin had decided to rebuild the world as he knew it. His army stood in battle formation, its figures utterly lifelike. No two figures had the same expression. Some warriors wear coats of mail. Some carry axes and crossbows. Others ride in chariots. Qin had obliged thousands and thousands of his servants and prisoners of war to pose as models for his army. The models received no rewards.

Hesh was overwhelmed when he saw Qin's army. "The warriors were in a giant airplane hangar. I walked up to them. I had the chills. People made this. I was part of the same race that could make this."

I hadn't seen the warriors, I hadn't been to Xi'an, so I could talk like some wise guy with a thinking cap on his head. "Hesh, it's the monomania of someone trying to reproduce his own planet. I swear, he's the first mogul."

Harry wouldn't listen. "Nobody ever bled from these guys. They were the best soldiers in the world . . . this was a good army."

5 Two days after our lunch at the The Source we visited another ruin: MGM. "Ted Turner owns the library. Lorimar owns the lot. MGM owns nothing but the Lion." The company sat in a futuristic high-rise across from the old studio in Culver City, where Louis B. Mayer was once the sheriff-magician-king.

Hesh and I sneaked onto the Lorimar lot. We saw an old barbershop that could have been there from the beginning of time. But Lorimar's commissary and souvenir shop had arrived long after Louis B. Mayer. We found the Gable Building, the

Garbo Building, the Crawford Building, the Garland Building, the Barrymore Building—pieces of confection no one seemed to care about. The sound stages had huge ice-box doors. There were no standing stages, no back lots. "This studio," Harry said, "it's out to lunch."

We traveled to Westwood, where Hesh uncovered a little cemetery cradled within a complex of tomblike office buildings. Westwood had grown up around the cemetery, had walled it in. It felt like the inner courtyard of those tenements I'd come out of in the Bronx. But the tenements had been livelier than long sheets of glass. We saw a man "doing Marilyn." He was placing flowers in the tiny urn attached to the wall of Marilyn's crypt. Graverobbers had tampered with the wall, and we could still see their marks, but they couldn't get in. Marilyn sat behind a little bunker of concrete. There was a note *with* the flowers: "All my Love, Natalia Fitzhugh."

Marilyn had become America's most exportable "item," the sex goddess as solitary being. She'd slept with the prince of princes, JFK. But she died like a little girl.

Hesh and I went to have dinner at Hymie's with Bill Tuttle, former head of make-up at MGM. Hymie's had been a fish market once upon a time. Now it had waiters dressed like Spanish knights. Bill Tuttle appeared. He was seventy-six and he looked younger and handsomer than all the caballeros at Hymie's, including Harry and myself. He had beautiful, delicate hands. He'd been a violinist during the Depression. He came out of Florida and couldn't find work in Hollywood. "I'll do anything," he told one of the managers at Fox, and was hired as a messenger boy. "I wore a uniform with straps under my shoes." He graduated to the mailroom, where he began sketching people, and was apprenticed to the art department. His boss, Jack Dawn, "was like a Russian general. . . . I did everything. I watched him do all the make-up. I watched him like a hawk." Jack Dawn left for MGM, and Bill followed him there in 1934.

"MGM was very clannish." Bill would sit alone at the counter of Mayer's commissary, the land of chicken soup. MGM's make-up department was in a long row of dressing rooms. "It was a much smaller space than at Twentieth Century." Garbo's dressing room was at the very end of the hall. Neither Bill nor Jack got near her. "Garbo determined how she would be made up."

And Bill moved out of his apprenticeship when the make-up artist for Tod Browning's *Mark of the Vampire* (1935) forgot to show on the set. "Jack Dawn said, 'Son, get your kit and go down there.' I did the whole cast," except for Bela Lugosi. Bill smiled. "I can remember all these things, and I can't remember what happened yesterday.

"MGM was making sixty features a year. It was a busy place. Little by little Jack Dawn was pushing things onto me. I made up Freddie Bartholomew for *David Copperfield*. I worked on the flying monkeys and the Winkies in *The Wizard of Oz*."

We talked about *David Copperfield* (1935). Charles Laughton had the part of Micawber. "I built up Laughton, I worked on Micawber's pointed head. On the fourth day of shooting, Laughton says about Cukor [the director of the film]: 'I can't work with him. He's too feminine.' " And Laughton bolted from *David Copperfield*. That's how W. C. Fields inherited the part. "Fields was a real asshole," Bill said, "a nasty drunk."

Ah, but he was a great Micawber.

We mourned the disaster of colorization, of having to watch *The Maltese Falcon* in computerized reds, greens, and blues. Bogart looked like Santa Claus. "It's brutal," Bill said, before he had some of Hymie's "chocolate suicide cake."

We asked him about MGM's "women." Bill had been married to one of them, Donna Reed. Ava Gardner was difficult but "breathtaking." Eleanor Parker "had one of the most beautiful faces." Jeanette MacDonald was also "a great beauty." Her fan club had a dinner every year at the Beverly Hilton. It was the most powerful fan club in the world.

L. B. Mayer had discovered this empire of women. "He found talent, latched on to them [the women *and* the men], gave them a contract. He had writers who could write for Tracy and Gable, writers who could write for women. . . . They were all available when he needed them.

"I saw dailies for thirty years . . . everything that was shot on the lot," Bill said. But the dismantling of the old studio system had destroyed that kind of attention to detail. The junkman had surrounded himself with master technicians. That was the mark of MGM.

6  I was staying at the Hollywood Roosevelt Hotel. It had opened in 1927, when Hollywood Boulevard was still the hub of movieland. Grauman's Chinese was across the street. The Egyptian, Musso & Frank, and the Hollywood Brown Derby (born in 1929) were a few blocks down on the boulevard. Gable "proposed" to Lombard in booth 54 of the Derby, in front of an avalanche of photographers. And Hollywood and Vine had become America's radioland. The stars would rush from their steak tartare at the Derby to one of the studios on Vine, where they would sing or act out some little drama of the day.

Vine meant nothing now, and the *new* Hollywood Derby was one more tourist trap. But how much did it matter? Disney stood. Fox stood. Paramount stood. And even if MGM had been "nuked," its old sound stages also stood. L.A. was still a movie town.

On the wall of a building near Hollywood and Vine I discovered a mural of the stars sitting in their own little moviehouse. The mural had a childlike persuasion. It wasn't there to impress. It hadn't been painted by some Renaissance master seeking the illusion of depth. The wall was naive and flat and wonderful. The artist had all the monomania and drugged devotion of a movie addict.

Shirley Temple sat in the middle of the entourage, still the reigning queen, flanked by Charlie Chaplin and W. C. Fields and the rest of that Murderers' Row of movie stars. King Kong. Frankenstein. Robin Hood. Brando in his motorcycle jacket. Bogey and Bacall, timeless and together, holding hands. The Duke himself, gallant and ferocious, even on a flattened wall. Butch Cassidy and the Sundance Kid, Hollywood's perfect couple. And Marilyn all alone, in life, in death, and in the mural of a Hollywood *primitif*.

That painter did strive for a bit of dimensionality. He'd packed his moviehouse with faces that fell into a gradually grayer area around the little field of stars up front. The faces in the back rows were as anonymous as any fan, caught in the stupor of a film. And in the lobby was E.T., trying to reach for a telephone.

I was indebted to the *primitif.* He was a son of the movie palace, like Harry and me.

7 I ride upstairs to the Roosevelt's twelfth floor, which has its own concierge and breakfast pantry. The concierge takes me to the "Celebrity Suite," the love nest Gable and Lombard used before they got married. It's a penthouse, two and a half storeys high. It doesn't have Gable and Lombard's bed, but you can feel their aromas for fifteen hundred dollars a night.

The master toilet seat and tank are made of burnished wood. The bar has a raised deck, like a battleship. The concierge and I walk out onto the patio. We're at the "pinnacle" of the hotel, just in back of the Roosevelt sign, in a sunbleached city of Tropicana colors.

"Houdini also stayed here," she says.

Ah, my brain starts to tick. It recalls the little calendars I keep in my head. The magician died in 1926, before there was a "Celebrity Suite."

But I don't doubt for a second that Gable and Lombard slept here. The panorama was perfect for them. They had the entire sweep of movieland at their heels. All they had to do was look out the master window and watch Hollywood Boulevard bleed right into the hills. Gable and his goddess. Him with the false teeth in his mouth. It was like Gatsby's "green light, the orgiastic future" that would never come. The stars had everything and nothing at all. That was the sadness of Hollywood. Their own worlds couldn't compete with the movies they were in. They could never be quite so large as their movie selves, and that's why they built this strange city outside the walls of Paramount and MGM.

Sid Grauman and Louis B. Mayer, Marcus Loew, Mary Pickford and her Black Pirate belonged to the holding company that created the Hollywood Roosevelt, this flamboyant Alhambra of a hotel, named after Teddy Roosevelt, the original Rough Rider, who took all of America under his wing. He turned the Caribbean into his private lake, became the godfather of the Panama Canal, and believed in a United States that had no final frontier.

He was brilliant, honest, ruthlessly energetic, and half-insane. Don Quixote as the great Bull Moose. He would have made a marvelous Hollywood producer.

Movieland was spun out of the same flamboyance, hysteria, and hollowness of heart. It was all appetite. Gable and Lombard and their magic suite. All design. That marvelous toy Venice of *Top Hat*. And artifice, like that army Qin Shi Huang built so he wouldn't get lonely in the nether lands. The moguls erected walled cities as monuments to themselves. *Their* clay soldiers were called actors and actresses, who stood in front of cameras for that nighttime world of film.

I think of Hollywood . . . and Primo Levi, the Italian writer-chemist who got through Auschwitz and committed suicide in 1987, throwing himself down the stairwell of the apartment house where he'd been born. Levi believed that there were no survivors. Auschwitz had left its own killing mark. And he belonged to the tribe of the damned. He had a recurrent nightmare. He would find himself in the countryside, or with his family, or alone at work. And then the scene would dissolve, almost like a film. "The family disappeared. There was no more work. No more countryside. I was still in the camp. And there was nothing real outside the camp."

I'm not trying to compare Hollywood and the Holocaust. I don't have the genius to do that. Nor am I trying to rob Levi of the particulars of his life. But there is something so fundamental about his dream, so frightening, that it speaks to all of us. This is the century when our previous "currencies" have betrayed us. The historical baggage we wear counts for very little. Each of us is an immigrant, uprooted from our past, no matter how much mothering or fathering we give or we get. We're left with a kind of screaming void. Our very own Auschwitz, if you will. And it's in this void that movies first appeared, with their little shadows on the wall that comforted us and also brought us closer to that city of the night, which is our home.

Movieland. Louis B. Mayer. The Loew's Paradise. MGM.

# Notes

ABBREVIATIONS

NYT      *The New York Times*
NYTM      *The New York Times Magazine*
NYTBR      *The New York Times Book Review*


PRELUDE: THE LOEW'S PARADISE

page
7    "dragons, drawbridges, and droshkies" Ben M. Hall, *The Best Remaining Seats,* p. 130.
10    "torridly embellished" John Eberson, quoted in David Naylor, *American Picture Palaces,* p. 77.
10    "pleasure domes . . ." Hall, p. 93.
11    "an American drummer's . . . material dreams" Graham Greene, *The Pleasure Dome,* p. 268.
11    "We sell . . ." Marcus Loew, quoted in David Naylor, *Great American Movie Theaters,* p. 18.
11    "one of the richest . . ." Hall, p. 121.
11    "as he piled . . ." Hall, p. 94.
11    "Donatello's David . . ." Naylor, *American Picture Palaces,* p. 69.
11    "actually a bridge . . ." Naylor, *Great American Movie Theaters,* p. 166.
12    "Eberson was archeologist . . ." Hall, p. 96.
12    "I saw . . ." Eberson, quoted in Naylor, *Great American Movie Theaters,* p. 100.
12    "energy, restlessness . . ." John Canemaker, "Dreams in Motion: The Art of Winsor McCay," p. 5.

*One.* FACES ON THE WALL

14  "the whole future depends . . ." Norbert Weiner, *The Human Use of Human Beings,* p. 7.
15  "on the wrong side of the celluloid" Michael Wood, *America in the Movies,* p. 124.
17  "prey to persistent depression" Barbara Leaming, *Orson Welles,* p. 356.
17  "couldn't stand . . . prisoner in her room" Leaming, p. 357.
18  "an exceptional gift . . ." Wood, p. 58.
18  "Here was a sex object . . ." Wood, p. 57.
18  "Every man I've known . . ." Shifra Haran, quoted in Bob Thomas, *King Cohn,* p. 279.
19  "She smelled dank . . ." Norman Mailer, quoted in Jerome Charyn, "La vie secrète de Norman Mailer," *Le Monde,* August 8, 1986.
20  "I had made enough faces" Greta Garbo, quoted in David Niven, *Bring on the Empty Horses,* p. 181.
22  "When I was twelve or thirteen . . ." Federico Fellini, quoted in Wood, p. 11.
22  "For me movies meant . . ." Italo Calvino, "Autobiography of a Spectator," *Antaeus,* Spring/Summer 1982, p. 29.
22  "American movies of that time . . ." Calvino, p. 31.
23  "did not teach us . . . the difficult" Calvino, p. 32.
23  "the film of which . . ." Calvino, p. 41.
24  "seemed a born aristocrat . . . relationship" Eric Pace, "Cary Grant, Movies' Epitome of Elegance, Dies of a Stroke," *NYT,* December 1, 1986.
24  "struck helpless . . ." Barbara Deming, *Running Away From Myself,* p. 112.


*Two.* PORTRAIT OF THE ARTIST AS BUFFALO BILL

27  "It was like . . ." Marlon Brando, quoted in Truman Capote, "The Duke in His Domain," *The New Yorker,* November 9, 1957, p. 79.
27  "The expression . . ." Edgar Morin, *The Stars,* p. 44.
27  "blueeyed boy" e. e. cummings, "Portrait VIII" ("Buffalo Bill's"), *Complete Poems,* Vol. 1, p. 60.
31  "I wonder if . . ." Paul Newman, quoted in Joe Morella and Edward Z. Epstein, *Rebels,* p. 115.
31  "rough trappers . . ." Morin, p. 46.
31  "break . . ." cummings, p. 60.
31  "a gift certificate . . ." Emanuel Levy, *And the Winner Is . . . ,* p. 224.
32  "The star . . . *garycooperizes* them" Morin, p. 38.
32  "into his own personality" Morin, p. 38.

32 "feels as if . . ." Luigi Pirandello, quoted in Walter Benjamin, "The Work of Art in the Age of Mechanical Reproduction," *Illuminations,* p. 229.

33 "introduces us to . . ." Benjamin, p. 237.

33 "shock effect" Benjamin, p. 240.

33 "Once the film . . ." Morin, p . 39.

34 "heavy . . . high priesthood" Mailer, in Charyn, "La vie secrète."

34 "effect he produces . . . suffering" Harold Clurman, quoted in Mel Gussow, "Lee Strasberg of Actors Studio Dead," *NYT,* February 18, 1982.

34 "father of Method acting . . ." Gussow, "Lee Strasberg."

37 "I know what . . . written for you" Paul Newman to J.C., February 11, 1988.

39 "watersmooth" cummings, p. 60.


*Three. GILDA'S GLOVE*

44 "also be the monster . . ." Hector Arce, *The Secret Life of Tyrone Power,* p. 227.

45 "the biggest electric-train set . . ." "Orson Welles Is Dead at Seventy; Innovator of Film and Stage," *NYT,* October 11, 1985.

45 "He has the manner of a giant . . ." Jean Cocteau, quoted in *NYT,* October 11, 1985.

45 "little odd eyes . . ." Pauline Kael, "Raising Kane," *The Citizen Kane Book,* p. 105.

45 "Overnight . . . phrase book for illiterates" Kenneth Tynan, *NYT,* October 11, 1985.

46 "the dark, Gothic horror style . . ." Kael, p. 115.

47 "film is so vivid . . ." Kael, p. 74.

47 "nigger lips" Louise Brooks, *Lulu in Hollywood,* p. 60.

47 "standard for babies . . ." Nunnally Johnson, quoted in Ezra Goodman, *The Fifty-Year Decline and Fall of Hollywood,* p. 264.

47 "partly paralyzed lip" Ephraim Katz, *The Film Encyclopedia,* p. 135.

48 "He was the loneliest . . ." Jules Levy to J.C., July 28, 1988.

48 "Raft wouldn't die . . . did not resent it" Raoul Walsh, quoted in Goodman, p. 264.

50 "We've got an hour . . . properly sanctified" F. Scott Fitzgerald, *The Last Tycoon,* p. 41.

51 "Few things are sadder . . ." Nathanael West, *The Day of the Locust,* p. 4.

52 "Cary Grant and Betty Grable . . . and sex goddesses" Otto Friedrich, *City of Nets,* p. xiii.

52 "she who . . . aerial maps" Jeanine Basinger, "Betty Grable 1916–1973," *NYT,* July 15, 1973.

56 "fight to the death . . . audience" Arthur Mayer, *Merely Colossal,* p. 23.


*Four.* *ANGEL ON MY SHOULDER*

57 "were the world . . . lacking in form" Calvino, p. 25.

57 "transfiguration . . . essence" Calvino, p. 31.

58 "for all Italian . . . anonymous" Calvino, pp. 32–33.

58 "no relation . . . the world" Calvino, p. 28.

58 "This was . . . reappear" Calvino, p. 35.

58 "counted for so little . . . weren't" Calvino, p. 33.

59 "or the birth of Mickey Mouse" Frank S. Nugent, quoted in John Culhane, " 'Snow White' at 50: Undimmed Magic," *NYT,* July 12, 1987.

60 "declare that our lives . . ." Stanley Cavell, *Pursuits of Happiness,* p. 24.

64 "Private homes . . ." Bruce T. Torrence, *Hollywood: The First Hundred Years,* p. 76.

64 "Hollywood's population . . ." Torrence, p. 87.

65 "was like floating . . ." Louise Brooks, quoted in Kevin Brownlow, *The Parade's Gone By . . . ,* p. 363.

65 "I left the screen . . . was law" Mary Pickford, quoted in Alden Whitman, "Mary Pickford Is Dead at 86; 'America's Sweetheart' of Films," *NYT,* May 30, 1979.

66 "the screen's most adored . . . in the harbor" "Douglas Fairbanks Dies in His Sleep," *NYT,* December 13, 1939.

66 "ate from a solid-gold dinner service . . . on light food" Whitman, "Mary Pickford."

68 "they were children . . . before them" Plato, *The Republic,* pp. 317–18.

69 "would say that . . ." Plato, p. 320.

70 "grown-up children . . ." David Denby, "Russian Revels," *New York,* October 5, 1987, p. 116.

71 "I didn't know Marilyn . . ." Louise Brooks, quoted in Kenneth Tynan, "The Girl in the Black Helmet," *The New Yorker,* June 11, 1979, p. 63.

72 "At Columbia they had . . ." Joan Crawford, quoted in Roy Newquist, *Conversations with Joan Crawford,* p. 46.

72 "Louis B. would have had . . ." Crawford, in Newquist, p. 172.

72 "Men didn't . . . Clark [Gable]" Crawford, in Newquist, p. 63.

*Five.* MOGUL

73  "This frail half-sick . . ." Fitzgerald, *The Last Tycoon,* p. 127.
73  "he would sit . . ." Brownlow, p. 427.
74  "He needed . . . wailing wall" Louis B. Mayer, quoted in Bosley Crowther, *Hollywood Rajah,* p. 188.
74  "history has shown . . ." Brownlow, p. 422.
74  "made more stars . . ." Clarence Brown, quoted in Brownlow, p. 422.
74  "because our people . . ." Samuel Marx, *Mayer and Thalberg,* p. 170.
74  "terrifying" Gary Carey, *All the Stars in Heaven,* p. 174.
75  "He could help you . . ." Danny Kaye, quoted in Crowther, p. 6.
75  "a mental adolescent in perpetuity" Jean Howard, quoted in Marx, p. 228.
75  "We'll have sex . . ." Louis B. Mayer, quoted in Crowther, p. 127.
76  "Irving was a sweet guy . . ." Edgar J. Mannix, quoted in Marx, p. 126.
76  "moonlit ocean" Marx, p. 82.
76  "We can't cater . . . that's how it is" Irving G. Thalberg, quoted in Marx, p. 83.
78  "Trying to control Universal . . ." Brownlow, p. 424.
78  "Since when . . ." Erich von Stroheim, quoted in Marx, p. 33.
79  "I am an artist . . ." Stroheim, quoted in Marx, p. 39.
80  "Of this slim . . ." Norman Zierold, *The Moguls,* pp. 311–12.
80  "rainbows in the dark." Marx, p. 5.
81  "had more laughs . . ." Zierold, p. 314.
81  "administered enemas . . ." Marx, p. 110.
82  "Everybody has . . ." Marx, p. 78.
82  "had the proportions of bombers" Niven, p. 19.
82  "I am like a fireman . . ." Whitey Hendry, quoted in Goodman, p. 325.
83  "They've become Frankensteins . . ." Hendry, quoted in Goodman, p. 326.
83  "It takes ten years . . ." Unnamed Loew's executive, quoted in Carey, p. 155.
83  "his rule of illusion . . ." Zierold, p. 310.
83  "became expert . . ." Marx, pp. 165–66.
    "Phone calls . . ." Marx, p. 166.
84  "As long as Irving lives . . ." Bernard Hyman, quoted in Marx, p. 163.
84  "peerage of producers" Crowther, p. 182.
84  "I don't look Shakespeare . . ." Marx, p. 248.
84  "Isn't God good to me?" Mayer, quoted in Marx, p. 252.

85  "He was like . . . love affairs" Anita Loos, quoted in David Gordon, "Mayer, Thalberg, and MGM," *Sight and Sound,* Summer 1976, p. 187.

85  "I have a woman's body . . ." Elizabeth Taylor, quoted in Friedrich, p. 428.

85  "The more McCarthy yells . . ." Mayer, quoted in Crowther, p. 300.

85  "Nothing matters . . ." Mayer, quoted in Friedrich, p. 437.

86  "Million-Dollar Couch" Zierold, p. 314.

86  "Thalberg has always . . ." F. Scott Fitzgerald, quoted in Bob Thomas, *Thalberg,* pp. 25–26.

87  "Rudolph Valentino . . . haunted house" Fitzgerald, *The Last Tycoon,* p. 3.

87  "He was born sleepless . . ." Fitzgerald, p. 15.

87  "the great upset . . ." Fitzgerald, p. 27.

88  "Of course, he talked that double talk . . ." Fitzgerald, p. 28.

88  "Stahr had ordered something . . ." Fitzgerald, pp. 22–23.

88  "take people's . . ." Fitzgerald, p. 105.

88  "Under the moon . . ." Fitzgerald, p. 25.

88  "The old loyalties . . ." Fitzgerald, p. 28.

88  "He was pale . . ." Fitzgerald, p. 126.

88  "Everywhere floodlights . . ." Fitzgerald, p. 62.

89  "just a shitty little studio then" Henry Blanke, quoted in James R. Silke, *Here's Looking at You, Kid,* p. 27.

89  "We do not want . . ." D. W. Griffith, quoted in Michael Walsh, "Sounds of Silents," *Film Comment,* August 1987, p. 66.

90  "picking up nails . . ." Silke, p. 38.

90  "schmucks with Underwoods" Jack Warner, quoted in Tom Dardis, *Some Time in the Sun,* p. 7.

90  "Jack Warner used to steal . . . their job" Jules Levy to J.C., July 28, 1988.

91  "They kept saying . . . acquiring legitimacy" Arthur Penn to J.C., January 13, 1988.

92  "You're nothing . . ." Jack Warner, quoted in Friedrich, p. 438.

*Six.* *"YOUNG FELLAH"*

94  "Hollywood is afflicted . . ." Goodman, p. 336.

96  "had no rooms inside" David O. Selznick, quoted in Zierold, p. 13.

97  "Conneckticut" Cavell, p. 49.

97  "like seeing history . . ." Kevin Brownlow and David Gill, *Hollywood,* Part 1, "Pioneers."

98  "We had one language . . ." Adela Rogers St. Johns, quoted in *Hollywood,* Part 2, "In the Beginning."

98 "the most imitated woman" *Hollywood,* Part 6, "Swanson and Valentino."

99 "cracked their whips . . ." Brownlow, p. 186.

99 "for being a brave boy" Brownlow, p. 187.

99 "the personality who . . ." Gloria Swanson, quoted in *Hollywood,* Part 6.

99 "I had a fit . . ." Swanson, quoted in *Hollywood,* Part 6.

100 "When sound started . . ." King Vidor, quoted in *Hollywood,* Part 1.

100 "every picture broke boundaries" Agnes de Mille, quoted in *Hollywood,* Part 2.

100 "I think he gave God . . ." Rogers St. Johns, quoted in *Hollywood,* Part 7, "Autocrats."

102 "In Italy I . . ." Rudolph Valentino, quoted in *Hollywood,* Part 6.

102 "preferred making spaghetti . . ." Alvin Krebs, "Pola Negri, a Vamp of the Silent Screen, Dies at 88," *NYT,* August 3, 1987.

102 "tired of cinematic éclairs" Stroheim, quoted in *Hollywood,* Part 7.

102 "Why did he do it?" Karl Brown, quoted in *Hollywood,* Part 7.

102 "This is not the worst . . ." Stroheim, quoted in *Hollywood,* Part 7.

103 "Clara didn't exist . . ." Louise Brooks, quoted in *Hollywood,* Part 12, "Star Treatment."

104 "She was man . . . being Swede" Eleanor Boardman, quoted in *Hollywood,* Part 12.

105 "Jack Gilbert was . . ." Leatrice Joy, quoted in *Hollywood,* Part 12.

105 "would have suffered . . . becomes funny" Vidor, quoted in *Hollywood,* Part 12.

105 "in a beautiful, beautiful place . . ." Samuel Marx, quoted in *Hollywood,* Part 12.

105 "Laurence, the romance . . ." Douglas Fairbanks, quoted in *Hollywood,* Part 13, "End of an Era."

*Seven.* COWARDLY LIONS AND FORGOTTEN MEN

108 "ladies from cold-water flats" Hall, p. 17.

109 "floated in a luminous mist" Hall, p 10.

109 "blinding blondness" Hall, p. 250.

109 "Being a Roxy usher . . ." Hall, p. 132.

109 "glistened like . . ." Hall, p. 170.

109 "hark back . . ." Hall, p. 172.

109 "Roxy West of the Rockies . . . all my shows" Hall, pp. 211–12.

110 "candy salesmen . . . in paradise" Hall, p. 253.

110 "According to Hollywood . . ." Howard Mandelbaum and Eric Myers, *Screen Deco,* p. 102.

110 "dream clubs" Mandelbaum and Myers, p. 100.

110 "people who . . ." Mandelbaum and Myers, p. 112.

111 "The fact that . . ." David Shipman, *The Great Movie Stars,* p. 485.

111 " 'Fred and Ginger' . . ." Arlene Croce, *The Fred Astaire and Ginger Rogers Book,* p. 6.

111 "the working-class princess" Croce, p. 142.

112 "a world of sun . . . be alone" Croce, p. 6.

113 "There's Paramount's Paris . . ." Ernst Lubitsch, quoted in Michael Webb, "The City in Film," *Design Quarterly,* Vol. 136, 1987, p. 17.

113 "artificially lit . . ." René Clair, quoted in Webb, p. 18.

113 "saw a street . . . sensations" Mandelbaum and Myers, p. 166.

115 "committed . . ." Robert Warshow, *The Immediate Experience,* p. 83.

116 "became more . . ." Niven, p. 154.

117 "The gangster . . . modern world" Warshow, p. 86.

117 "without culture . . . of the city" Warshow, p. 89–90.

120 "one of the screen's . . ." Bing Crosby, quoted in Shipman, p. 355.

121 "Hollywood destroyed . . ." Kael, p. 26.

121 "may for a brief period . . ." Kael, p. 23.

121 "brought movies . . . American comedy" Kael, p. 26.

121 "They had gone . . ." Kael, p. 34.

123 certain as the sun: See Shipman, p. 227.

124 "The products . . ." Don Whittemore and Philip Alan Cecchettini, *Passport to Hollywood,* p. vii.

*Eight.* DANCING IN THE DARK (WITH DICK POWELL)

127 "Who cared if . . ." Roger Dooley, *From Scarface to Scarlett,* p. 611.

127 "turn[ed] producer . . ." Zierold, p. 56.

127 "We all have . . ." Clark Gable, in Niven, p. 37.

130 "The only thing . . ." Gable, in Shipman, p. 221.

130 "She went shopping . . ." William Holden, in Goodman, p. 253.

130 "and to many moviegoers . . ." Shipman, p. 225.

133 "Miranda's superbly vulgar personality . . . other star" Charles Higham and Joel Greenberg, *Hollywood in the Forties,* p. 10.

134 "handle the largest . . . all over the place" "Sabu the Elephant Boy Is Dead; Star of Jungle Movies Was 39," *NYT,* December 3, 1963.

135 "sex zombie" Veronica Lake, quoted in Edward Hudson, "Veronica Lake, 53, Movie Star with the Peekaboo Hair, Dead," *NYT,* July 3, 1973.

135 "occupied . . . remote control" Foster Hirsch, *The Dark Side of the Screen,* p. 147.

135 "Kiss me . . . FOR HIRE"!" Veronica Lake, quoted in Hirsch, p. 146.

136 "I will have . . ." Lake, in Hudson, *NYT,* July 3, 1973.

137 "the kind of style . . ." Hirsch, p. 152.

139 "huge, glowing-eyed . . . crash diet" Higham and Greenberg, p. 11.

139 "hacked his way . . . jewel box" "Carole Landis, 29, Is Found Dead With a Suicide Note in Next Room," *NYT,* July 6, 1948.

140 "You can't stop a war . . ." Carole Landis, quoted in "Carole Landis."

*Nine. CHILDREN OF PARADISE*

145 "both unassuming . . ." François Truffaut, in Richard Roud, *A Passion for Films,* p. vii.

145 "one of the greatest . . ." Jean-Luc Godard, quoted in Roud, p. xxvii.

146 "the best school . . ." Bernardo Bertolucci, quoted in Roud, p. xxv.

146 "I have not helped . . ." Henri Langlois, quoted in Roud, p. xxvi.

146 "You couldn't get the women . . ." Ernest Hemingway, "On the Quai at Smyrna," *The Short Stories of Ernest Hemingway,* p. 87.

146 "so they just broke their forelegs . . ." Hemingway, p. 88.

147 "because, Langlois thought . . ." Roud, p. 4.

147 "As soon as she . . ." Langlois, quoted in Roud, p. 9.

147 "fell into . . . the world's screens" Roud, p. 102.

148 "discovered . . . ice cream" Roud, p. 37.

148 "an early Nazi recruit . . . counterseizure" Georges Franju, quoted in Roud, p. 51.

149 "I have hidden films . . . " Lotte Eisner, quoting Langlois, in Roud, p. 55.

149 "No one knows . . ." Roud, p. 42.

149 "I am Scheherazade" Mary Meerson, quoted in Roud, p. 46.

149 "thin, thin . . ." Meerson, quoted in Roud, p. 44.

149 "After the war . . ." Langlois, quoted in Roud, p. 45.

150 "fragile fiction . . ." Georges Sadoul, quoted in Roud, p. 58.

150 "The Cinémathèque was . . ." Truffaut, quoted in Roud, p. 67.

151 "after stealing metal doorknobs" Eric Pace, "François Truffaut, New Wave Director, Dies," *NYT,* October 22, 1984.

151 "said yes, so . . ." Truffaut, quoted in Roud, p. 67.

152 "playing solitaire . . ." Truffaut, quoted in Roud, p. ix.

152 "that really saved him" Roud, p. 157.

152 "There were no pieces . . ." S. Frederick Gronich, quoted in Roud, p. 48.

153 "he continued to suffer . . ." Roud, p. 186.

153 "His heart was bruised . . ." Truffaut, quoted in Roud, p. xv.

155 "Hollywood . . . royal family" Michel Martens to J.C., October 19 and October 26, 1987.

155 "Instead of publicity shots . . ." Katz, p. 646.
155 "Who created . . . capital of America" Martens to J.C.
156 "transparent tigers . . ." Jorge Luis Borges, "Tlön, Uqbar, Orbis Tertius," *Labyrinths,* p. 8.
156 "that while we sleep . . ." Borges, p. 10.
156 "will disappear . . ." Borges, p. 18.
157 "France is the most . . . save movies" Martens to J.C.
157 "Man, the imperfect librarian" Borges, "The Library of Babel," *Labyrinths,* p. 52.
157 "divine disorder" Borges, p. 56.
157 "People conglomerated . . . he died" Martens to J.C.
160 "not even one . . ." Borges, "A New Refutation of Time," *Labyrinths,* p. 223.
160 "more than twenty-four . . ." Borges, p. 230.

*Ten.* TWO-HEADED MAN

161 "expatriates . . . else's rewrites" Kael, p. 25.
162 "play piano . . ." Silke, p. 88.
162 " 'Doctor Korngold' . . ." Silke, p. 94.
162 *I steal from* . . . See Silke, p. 94.
162 "that hit him . . ." Harry Warren, quoted in Silke, p. 94.
162 "sew the dialogue . . ." Stephen Longstreet, quoted in Silke, p. 72.
163 "I grew up . . ." Fitzgerald, *The Last Tycoon,* p. 99.
163 "Writers aren't people . . ." Fitzgerald, p. 12.
163 "long balconies . . ." Fitzgerald, p. 257.
163 "put them on an idea . . ." Fitzgerald, p. 58.
163 "Through the years . . ." Borges, in Richard Burgin, *Conversations With Jorge Luis Borges,* p. 144.
163 "a small thin figure . . ." Marx, p. 251.
163 "permanent-substitute" Daniel Fuchs, "Days in the Gardens of Hollywood," *NYTBR,* July 18, 1971, p. 2.
164 "looked like long . . ." Daniel Fuchs, *Summer in Williamsburg,* p. 75.
164 "bulky faces . . ." Fuchs, *Summer,* p. 153.
164 "Everything here . . ." Fuchs, *Summer,* p. 377.
164 "it is only a beginning . . ." Fuchs, *Summer,* p. 380.
165 "I'm going to Hollywood . . . murder the producer" Fuchs, "Days," pp. 2–3.
166 "thug, harsh and ruthless . . . chocolates" Fuchs, "Days," p. 25.
166 "Fuchs's work . . ." Daniel Golden, "Daniel Fuchs," *Dictionary of Literary Biography,* Vol. 9, Part 2, p. 38.
166 "The bones in their bodies . . ." Fuchs, "Days," p. 2.

166  "caught up in . . ." Golden, p. 38.

167  "I write . . ." Fuchs, "Days," p. 3.

167  "For the boon . . ." Fuchs, "Days," p. 25.

168  "a lonely man . . ." Raymond Chandler, in Frank MacShane, ed., *Selected Letters of Raymond Chandler,* p. 483.

168  "Hollywood recorded . . ." Edward Thorpe, *Chandlertown,* p. 112.

168  "the department-store . . ." Raymond Chandler, *The Little Sister,* p. 88.

168  "has no more personality . . . somewhere else" Chandler, *The Little Sister,* p. 203.

168  "at the glare . . . emptiness" Raymond Chandler, *The Long Goodbye,* p. 224.

169  "We're a big rough rich . . ." Chandler, *The Long Goodbye,* p. 290.

169  "the worst frontier outpost . . ." Frank MacShane, *The Life of Raymond Chandler,* p. 64.

169  "developed the puffing . . ." Mark Girouard, *Cities and People,* p. 364.

169  "sparkling like . . ." Girouard, p. 364.

169  "a boy whose father . . ." MacShane, *Life,* p. 6.

170  "I have lived . . ." Chandler, quoted in MacShane, p. 1.

170  "I had to learn . . ." Chandler, in MacShane, p. 49.

170  "a man without a country" Chandler, in MacShane, p. 13.

170  "a mystery writer with . . ." Chandler, in MacShane, p. 193.

170  "tried to explain . . ." Chandler, in MacShane, p. 233.

171  "She was the beat . . ." Chandler, in MacShane, p. 227.

171  "felt a little like . . ." Chandler, in MacShane, p. 228.

171  "that made his fingers split" MacShane, p. 159.

171  "Chandler the celebrity . . ." MacShane, p. 235.

171  "the distant flashes . . ." Chandler, in MacShane, p. 86.

172  "Samuel Spade's jaw . . ." Dashiell Hammett, *The Maltese Falcon,* p. 1.

172  "He will drink . . ." McShane, ed., *Selected Letters,* p. 271.

172  "The date of his birth . . ." McShane, ed., p. 270.

172  "but that was quite . . ." McShane, ed., p. 270.

173  "Miss Moronica Lake" Chandler, in MacShane, *Life,* p. 126.

173  "*not* a transplanted . . ." Raymond Chandler, "Oscar Night in Hollywood," *The Atlantic Monthly,* March 1948, p. 25.

173  "destroy[ed] . . ." Chandler, in MacShane, p. 123.

173  "magnificent . . ." Chandler, in MacShane, p. 150.

173  "some male idol . . . chicken-strangler" Raymond Chandler, "Writers in Hollywood," *The Atlantic Monthly,* November 1945, p. 52.

173  "tribal dance . . ." Chandler, "Oscar Night," p. 25.

173  "the golden ones . . . shell" Chandler, "Oscar Night," p. 26.

174 "What Hollywood . . ." Raymond Chandler, "Farewell, My Hollywood," *Antaeus,* Spring/Summer 1976, p. 29.

174 "I don't care . . ." Chandler, "Farewell," p. 28.

174 "a sense of exile . . ." Chandler, "Farewell," p. 33.

174 "consistently idiotic" Vincent Canby, quoted in Theodore Gershuny, *Soon to Be a Major Motion Picture,* p. xii.

174 "a bloodless bore" Judith Crist, quoted in Gershuny, p. xii.

175 "My father was . . ." Otto Preminger, quoted in Gerald Pratley, *The Cinema of Otto Preminger,* p. 29.

175 "warmhearted woman . . ." Preminger, in Pratley, p. 34.

176 "the great museums . . ." Whittemore and Cecchettini, p. 500.

176 "He always walked . . ." Preminger, in Pratley, p. 55.

180 "Films are not made . . ." Werner Herzog, quoted in Tom Dardis, *Keaton,* p. 102.

*Eleven. WILDIES*

181 "those dizzy sexpots" Katz, p. 653.

181 "faster and fizzier . . . express train" James Agee, "Comedy's Greatest Era," *Life,* September 5, 1949, p. 74.

182 "an all but brainless . . . mind" Agee, p. 75.

183 "Neither the great names . . . modern France" Terry Ramsaye, *A Million and One Nights,* p. 516.

184 "a foetal Manhattan" Rem Koolhaas, *Delirious New York,* p. 23.

184 "false daytime" Koolhaas, p. 28.

184 "If life . . . Barrels of Love" Koolhaas, p. 29.

184 "electric phantom cities" Koolhaas, p. 55.

184 "If Paris is . . ." George Tilyou, quoted in Koolhaas, p. 32.

185 "For many years . . . tricks" Koolhaas, p. 63.

185 "The world is . . ." D. H. Lawrence, *Studies in Classic American Literature,* p. 7.

185 "England had more . . . have been" Lawrence, p. 9.

186 "in a black spirit . . ." Lawrence, p. 11.

186 "Somewhere deep . . ." Lawrence, p. 10.

186 "to some wild west" Lawrence, p. 12.

186 "spiritual home . . ." Lawrence, p. 27.

186 "inner diabolism" Lawrence, p. 89.

186 "deliberate consciousness . . ." Lawrence, pp. 89–90.

189 "was steeped . . . 'dead gook' " J. Hoberman, "Believe It or Not," *Artforum,* May 1988, p. 13.

190 "a piece of shit . . . a million each" Arthur Penn to J.C., January 13, 1988.

195 "Warren had . . . have a movie" Penn to J.C.

198 "whole elaborate mythology . . . July" Hoberman, *Artforum,* p. 13.

201 "postage-stamp" Leonard Maltin, ed., *Leonard Maltin's TV Movies and Video Guide,* p. 272.

202 "grope boldly . . ." Deming, p. 154.

202 "Movies preserve . . ." Wood, p. 20.

202 "excess of style . . . of unreality" Wood, p. 8.

202 "interchangeable plots . . ." Wood, p. 9.

202 "It was not that popular films . . ." Wood, p. 195.

202 *"Voici le temps . . ."* Arthur Rimbaud, *Illuminations,* p. 42.

204 "a lavishly sombre . . . eclipse" Pauline Kael, "The Current Cinema," *The New Yorker,* April 6, 1987, p. 85.

205 "impermanence . . . not to be one" Webb, "The City in Film," p. 25.

207 "I quit when . . . instinctive" Dean Stockwell, quoted in Lawrence Van Gelder, "At the Movies," *NYT,* July 10, 1987.


*Twelve.* THE HOUSE ON NINETY-FIFTH STREET

208 "a major . . . magic power" John Szarkowski, in *Winogrand,* p. 20.

208 "treacherous mermaid . . . doom" Dorothy Dinnerstein, *The Mermaid and The Minotaur,* p. 5.

209 "hung over the picture . . ." Baltimore judge, quoted in Murray Schumach, *The Face on the Cutting Room Floor,* p. 59.

209 "Sometimes the photographers . . ." Jane Russell, quoted in Schumach, p. 55.

210 "It's a very complex question . . . being arrested" Viveca Lindfors to J.C., March 9, 1988.

212 "I am a man . . ." Zero Mostel, quoted in Victor Navasky, *Naming Names,* p. 178.

212 "I don't say 'yes' . . ." Judy Holliday, quoted in Stefan Kanfer, *A Journal of the Plague Years,* p. 187.

212 "I was in the wrong place at the wrong time . . . Read it" Lindfors to J.C., March 9, 1988.

213 "the street below . . ." Viveca Lindfors, *Viveka . . . Viveca,* p. 34.

213 "I was in love . . ." Lindfors, p. 49.

213 "Swedish actresses . . ." Lindfors, p. 79.

213 "a European Hollywood" Lindfors, p. 101.

214 "I couldn't walk . . ." Lindfors, p. 107.

214 "cemented city . . . concentration camp" Lindfors, p. 144.

214 "The nightmare was . . ." Lindfors, p. 150.

214 "went fishing . . ." Lindfors, p. 164.

214 "couldn't lie down" Lindfors, p. 165.

214 "who could help . . ." Lindfors, p. 167.

214 "Swedes don't . . . nurse my kids" Lindfors to J.C., March 31, 1988.

217 "fat Polack" Harry Cohn, quoted in Thomas, *King Cohn,* p. 329.

217  "the face of a madonna . . ." Goodman, p. 273.

217  "the sort of face . . ." Leonard McCombe, quoted in Goodman, 280.

217  "eyes attracted . . ." Columbia publicist, quoted in Goodman, p. 283.

218  "I am the king . . ." Harry Cohn, quoted in Thomas, *King Cohn*, p. v.

219  "I was very intrigued . . ." Alfred Hitchcock, quoted in Donald Spoto, *The Dark Side of Genius*, p. 432.

220  "was blank . . ." Goodman, p. 273.


*Thirteen.   MR. FEATHERS*

222  "in silence . . . fatalities" William Shawn, in Louise Brooks, *Lulu in Hollywood*, p. vii.

222  "poor English farmers . . . century" *Lulu in Hollywood*, p. 4.

222  "My father thought . . ." *Lulu in Hollywood*, p. 5.

222  "All there is . . ." Dixie Dugan, in Roland Jaccard, ed., *Louise Brooks*, p. 142.

222  "where I found . . ." *Lulu in Hollywood*, p. 38.

223  "There was no point . . ." Brooks, quoted in Tynan, "The Girl in the Black Helmet," p. 66.

223  "I have lived . . ." Brooks, in Tynan, pp. 66–68.

223  "disintegrate happily . . ." Brooks, in Tynan, p. 68.

223  "was like a terrible dream . . ." Brooks, quoted in a letter to Guido Crepax, in Jaccard, ed., p. 144.

223  "My life has been nothing" Brooks, in Jaccard, ed., p. 144.

223  "Staring down . . ." *Lulu in Hollywood*, p. 21.

223  "He sat in his chair . . ." Brooks, in Brownlow, p. 363.

224  "distorted Fields . . ." *Lulu in Hollywood*, p. 74.

224  "a cinematic saint" *Lulu in Hollywood*, p. 59.

224  "fundamental inertia . . . words" *Lulu in Hollywood*, p. 62.

224  "his perfect screen partner . . ." *Lulu in Hollywood*, p. 68.

224  "ran wild . . . to life" Louise Brooks, "Duke by Divine Right," in Allen Eyles, *John Wayne and the Movies*, p. 9.

225  "phantoms . . . idolatry" Jaccard, ed., p. 15.

225  "think she . . ." Shawn, in *Lulu in Hollywood*, p. vii.

225  "There is no Garbo . . ." Henri Langlois, in Roud, p. 95.

225  "From the moment . . ." *Lulu in Hollywood*, p. 88.

225  "Garbo is all movement . . ." Brooks, in Brownlow, pp. 358–59.

225  "She [Garbo] had this . . ." Clarence Brown, quoted in Carey, p. 103.

225  "Every actor . . ." *Lulu in Hollywood*, p. 97.

225  "a born loser . . ." *Lulu in Hollywood*, p. 58.

226  "Old pictures . . ." *Lulu in Hollywood*, p. 86.

226  "The great art . . ." Brooks, in Tynan, p. 77.

226  "They were sitting . . ." Brooks, in Tynan, p. 71.

227  "cruel pursuit . . ." *Lulu in Hollywood,* p. 6.

227  "So it is . . ." *Lulu in Hollywood,* p. 96.

227  "Are you a variation . . ." Brooks, in Tynan, p. 65.

227  "And if I . . ." Brooks, in Jaccard, ed., p. 18.

227  "Remember when . . ." Brooks, in a letter to Guido Crepax, in Jaccard, ed., p. 144.

227  "a nice-looking . . ." Brooks, in Tynan, p. 65.

227  "When I was nine . . ." Brooks, in Tynan, p. 66.

228  "unbuckle the Bible Belt" Brooks, in Tynan, p. 65.

228  "incest in the barn" Brooks, in Tynan, p. 65.

228  "she never abandoned me . . ." Brooks, in Jaccard, ed., p. 24.

228  "was exquisite . . ." Brooks, in Brownlow, pp. 362–63.

228  "always standing . . ." Brooks, in Tynan, p. 72.

228  "like leaving a palace . . ." *Lulu in Hollywood,* pp. 36–37.

228  "I think . . ." Brooks, in Brownlow, p. 363.

229  "gave birth . . ." "The FBI *vs.* Jean Seberg," *Time,* September 24, 1979, p. 24.

229  "Jean became psychotic . . . stillbirth" Romain Gary, quoted in "The FBI *vs.* Jean Seberg," p. 25.

*Fourteen.  POISONVILLE*

232  "the wishing animal" Peter Gay, *Freud,* p. 78.

234  "Whenever I . . ." Fern Barry, quoted in Goodman, p. 321.

235  "If we call . . ." Ben Hecht, *A Child of the Century,* p. 487.

235  "lamed the American . . ." Hecht, p. 468.

235  "Hollywood's like . . ." David O. Selznick, quoted in Hecht, p. 467.

236  "Carpenters tossed . . ." Frank S. Nugent, "Super-Duper Epic: Hollywood Canteen," *NYTM,* October 17, 1943, p. 16.

236  "often had nowhere . . ." Friedrich, p. 108.

236  "4,000 loaves . . . pieces of cake" Torrence, p. 203.

237  "the warrior . . . we wake" Deming, p. 36.

244  "blood-simple . . . a week" Dashiell Hammett, *Red Harvest,* p. 142.

244  "to be crucified . . ." Hammett, *Red Harvest,* p. 108.

244  "settled down . . ." Hammett, *Red Harvest,* p. 114.

244  "like you'd play trout" Hammett, *Red Harvest,* p. 145.

244  "merry hell" Hammett, *Red Harvest,* p. 199.

244  "a construction . . ." Steven Marcus, ed., *The Continental Op,* p. xix.

244  "committed itself . . ." Marcus, in *The Continental Op,* p. xxii.

244  "a world of universal warfare . . ." Marcus, in *The Continental Op,* p. xxiii.

*Fifteen.   PILGRIM'S PROGRESS*

247   "five miles . . ." Aldo Bernardini, "Cinecittà: The Stuff of Legends," *Variety,* February 25, 1987, p. 314.
247   "for miniatures . . ." Bernardini, p. 314.
247   "When I was . . . resembled Hollywood" Bernardini, p. 335.
248   "inhabited by . . ." Bernardini, p. 314.
248   "In Cinema City . . ." Bernardini, p. 314.
248   "Cinecittà built . . ." Bernardini, p. 335.
249   "secludes himself . . . cinema city" Oreste Del Buono, quoted in Bernardini, p. 335.
252   "It's got mothers dying . . . audiovisual dope" Harry Hurwitz to J.C., March 4, 1988.
253   "bringing gold . . ." Mike Redmond, quoted in Robert Reinhold, "In the Middle of L.A.'s Gang Warfare," *NYTM,* May 22, 1988, p. 74.
253   "Every cowboy . . ." Hurwitz to J.C. (All of the following conversations with Harry Hurwitz occurred between July 26 and August 2, 1988).
256   "My peers don't like . . . never met" Mae Clarke to Hurwitz and J.C., July 28, 1988.


*Sixteen.   THE FIRST EMPEROR*

259   "Culture of Congestion" Koolhaas, p. 105.
259   "a man-made . . ." Koolhaas, p. 72.
259   "World City . . . Wright" Girouard, p. 375.
260   "He could play . . ." Adela Rogers St. Johns, quoted in Brownlow, p. 422.
261   "Put pumpernickel . . ." Joy Horowitz, "Touchstone's Magic Touch," *Premiere,* October 1987, p. 34.
261   "If it doesn't work . . ." Phil Nemy to J.C., July 29, 1988 (quoting Walt Disney).
261   "brought animals . . . people" Nemy to J.C.
262   "He loved to act . . . in me" Bosley Crowther, "The Dream Merchant," *NYT,* December 16, 1966.
262   "He has given animals souls" William Lyon Phelps, quoted in "Walt Disney, 65, Dies on Coast; Founded an Empire on a Mouse," *NYT,* December 16, 1966.
263   "We're an independent . . . casualties" Nemy to J.C.
263   "to build her face . . . come out" Dore Freeman to J.C., July 27, 1988.
265   "the diligence of a ditchdigger" Unnamed author, quoted in Peter B. Flint, "Joan Crawford Dies at Home," *NYT,* May 11, 1977.
265   "The worse the film . . ." Shipman, p. 131.

265  "She woke up . . ." Joseph Mankiewicz, quoted in Bob Thomas, *Joan Crawford,* p. 98.

265  "From her throne . . ." Christina Crawford, *Mommie Dearest,* p. 147.

265  "I thought the book . . ." Freeman to J.C.

265  "I had . . . shoulders . . ." Joan Crawford, in Newquist, p. 44.

265  "when Mommie dearest . . ." Christina Crawford, p. 37.

265  "You don't fool . . . get up" Freeman to J.C.

268  "I'll do anything . . . on the lot" William Tuttle to J.C., August 1, 1988.

271  "green light . . ." F. Scott Fitzgerald, *The Great Gatsby,* p. 182.

272  "The family disappeared . . ." Primo Levi, quoted in Alexander Stille, "Primo Levi: Reconciling the Man and the Writer," *NYTBR,* July 5, 1987, p. 5.

## ACKNOWLEDGMENTS

295  "I cannot go to sleep . . ." Lev Nikolayevich Tolstoy, quoted in Michael Ignatieff, "His Art Was All He Mastered," *NYTBR,* August 28, 1988, p. 1.

# Selected Bibliography

ADAMS, CINDY. *Lee Strasberg.* Garden City, NY: Doubleday, 1980.

ALLEMAN, RICHARD. *The Movie Lover's Guide to Hollywood.* New York: Harper Colophon Books, 1985.

ARCE, HECTOR. *The Secret Life of Tyrone Power.* New York: Bantam Books, 1980.

BACALL, LAUREN, *By Myself.* New York: Alfred A. Knopf, 1979.

BACH, STEPHEN. *Final Cut.* New York: New American Library, 1985.

BAZIN, ANDRÉ. *What Is Cinema?* Vol. 1, trans. Hugh Gray. Berkeley: University of California Press, 1967.

BEGO, MARK. *The Best of "Modern Screen."* New York: St. Martin's Press, 1986.

BENJAMIN, WALTER, *Illuminations,* ed. Hannah Arendt, trans. Harry Zohn. New York: Schocken Books, 1969.

BORGES, JORGE LUIS. *Labyrinths,* eds. Donald A. Yates and James E. Irby. New York: New Directions, 1964.

BROOKS, LOUISE. "Duke by Divine Right." In Allen Eyles, *John Wayne and the Movies.* New York: A. S. Barnes, 1976.

——. *Lulu in Hollywood.* New York: Alfred A. Knopf, 1982.

BROWNLOW, KEVIN. *The Parade's Gone By . . . ,* 1968. Reprint. Berkeley: University of California Press, 1975.

BRYFONKSI, DEDRIA, and PHYLLIS CARMEL MENDELSON, eds. "Daniel Fuchs." *Contemporary Literary Criticism.* Detroit: Gale Research Company, 1978.

BURGIN, RICHARD. *Conversations With Jorge Luis Borges.* New York: Holt, Rinehart & Winston, 1969.

CANEMAKER, JOHN. "Dreams in Motion: The Art of Winsor McCay." Katonah, NY: The Katonah Gallery, 1988.

CAREY, GARY. *All the Stars in Heaven.* New York: E. P. Dutton, 1981.

CAVELL, STANLEY. *Pursuits of Happiness: The Hollywood Comedy of Remarriage.* Cambridge, MA: Harvard University Press, 1981.

CHANDLER, RAYMOND. *The Little Sister,* 1949. Reprint. New York: Ballantine Books, 1971.

——. *The Long Goodbye,* 1953. Reprint. New York: Ballantine Books, 1971.

CRAWFORD, CHRISTINA. *Mommie Dearest*. New York: William Morrow, 1978.

CROCE, ARLENE. *The Fred Astaire and Ginger Rogers Book*. New York: Vintage Books, 1972.

CROWTHER, BOSLEY. *Hollywood Rajah*. New York: Holt, Rinehart & Winston, 1960.

CUMMINGS, E. E. *Complete Poems*. London: MacGibbon & Kee, 1968.

DARDIS, TOM. *Keaton: The Man Who Wouldn't Lie Down*. New York: Penguin Books, 1979.

——. *Some Time in the Sun*. New York: Charles Scribner's Sons, 1976.

DEMING, BARBARA. *Running Away From Myself: A Dream Portrait of America Drawn from the Films of the '40s*. New York: Grossman, 1969.

DINNERSTEIN, DOROTHY. *The Mermaid and The Minotaur: Sexual Arrangements and Human Malaise*. New York: Harper Colophon Books, 1977.

DOOLEY, ROGER. *From Scarface to Scarlett: American Films in the 1930s*. New York: Harcourt Brace Jovanovich, 1981.

DYER, RICHARD. *Heavenly Bodies*. New York: St. Martin's Press, 1976.

EAMES, JOHN DOUGLAS. *The MGM Story*, 1975. Reprint. New York: Crown, 1979.

FARBER, MANNY. *Negative Space*. New York: Praeger, 1971.

FITZGERALD, F. SCOTT. *The Great Gatsby*. New York: Charles Scribner's Sons, 1925.

——. *The Last Tycoon*. New York: Charles Scribner's Sons, 1941.

FRIEDRICH, OTTO. *City of Nets*. New York: Harper & Row, 1986.

FUCHS, DANIEL. *Summer in Williamsburg*, 1934. Reprint. New York: Carroll and Graf, 1983.

GAY, PETER. *Freud: A Life for Our Time*. New York: W. W. Norton, 1988.

GERSHUNY, THEODORE. *Soon to Be a Major Motion Picture*. New York: Holt, Rinehart & Winston, 1980.

GERTNER, RICHARD, ed. *International Motion Picture Almanac*. New York: Quigley, 1987.

GIROUARD, MARK. *Cities and People*. New Haven, CT: Yale University Press, 1985.

GOLDEN, DANIEL. "Daniel Fuchs." *Dictionary of Literary Biography*, Vol. 9, Part 2. Detroit: Gale Research Company, 1981.

GOODMAN, EZRA. *The Fifty-Year Decline and Fall of Hollywood*. New York: Simon and Schuster, 1961.

GREENE, GRAHAM. *The Pleasure Dome*, 1972. Reprint. Oxford: Oxford University Press, 1980.

HALL, BEN M. *The Best Remaining Seats*. New York: Clarkson N. Potter, 1961.

HAMMETT, DASHIELL. *The Continental Op*, ed. Steven Marcus. New York: Vintage Books, 1975.

——. *The Maltese Falcon*, 1929. Reprint. New York: Vintage Books, 1984.

——. *Red Harvest*, 1929. Reprint. New York: Vintage Books, 1972.

Hawking, Stephen W. *A Brief History of Time*. New York: Bantam Books, 1988.

Hecht, Ben. *A Child of the Century*, 1954. Reprint. New York: Primus Books, 1985.

Hemingway, Ernest. *The Short Stories of Ernest Hemingway*. New York: Charles Scribner's Sons, 1938.

Higham, Charles. *Errol Flynn*. New York: Dell, 1981.

———. *Warner Brothers*. New York: Charles Scribner's Sons, 1975.

———, and Joel Greenberg. *Hollywood in the Forties*. New York: A. S. Barnes, 1968.

Hirsch, Foster. *The Dark Side of the Screen: Film Noir*. New York: Da Capo Press, 1981.

Horn, Maurice, "American Comics in France: A Cultural Evaluation." In *The American Influence in the World*, ed. Allen F. Davis. Westport, CT: Greenwood Press, 1981.

Jaccard, Roland, ed. *Louise Brooks: Portrait of an Anti-Star*, trans. Gideon Y. Schein. New York: New York Zoetrope, 1986.

Kael, Pauline. "Raising Kane." In *The Citizen Kane Book*, 1971. Reprint. New York: Bantam Books, 1974.

Kanfer, Stefan. *A Journal of the Plague Years*. New York: Atheneum, 1973.

Katz, Ephraim. *The Film Encyclopedia*. New York: Perigee Books, 1979.

Kelley, Kitty. *His Way*. New York: Bantam Books, 1986.

Kirkpatrick, Sidney D. *A Cast of Killers*. New York: E. P. Dutton, 1986.

Kobal, John. *Rita Hayworth*, 1977. New York: Berkley Books, 1983.

Koolhaas, Rem. *Delirious New York*. New York: Oxford University Press, 1978.

Lawrence, D. H. *Studies in Classic American Literature*, 1923. Reprint. New York: Penguin Books, 1977.

Leaming, Barbara. *Orson Welles*. New York: Viking, 1985.

Levi, Primo. *The Periodic Table*, trans. Raymond Rosenthal. New York: Schocken Books, 1984.

Levy, Emanuel. *And the Winner Is . . . .* New York: Ungar, 1987.

Lindfors, Viveca. *Viveka . . . Viveca*. New York: Everest House, 1981.

Linet, Beverly. *Ladd*. New York: Arbor House, 1979.

Locher, Frances Carol, ed. *Contemporary Authors*, Vols. 81–84. Detroit: Gale Research Company, 1979.

MacShane, Frank. *The Life of Raymond Chandler*. New York: Penguin Books, 1979.

———, ed. *Selected Letters of Raymond Chandler*. New York: Columbia University Press, 1981.

Maltin, Leonard. *The Disney Films*. New York: Crown, 1973.

———, ed. *Leonard Maltin's TV Movies and Video Guide*. New York: New American Library/Signet Books, 1987.

MANDELBAUM, HOWARD, and ERIC MYERS. *Screen Deco*. New York: St. Martin's Press, 1985.

MARX, SAMUEL. *Mayer and Thalberg*. New York: Random House, 1975.

MAST, GERALD. *A Short History of the Movies,* fourth ed. New York: Macmillan, 1986.

MAYER, ARTHUR. *Merely Colossal*. New York: Simon and Schuster, 1953.

MORELLA, JOE, and EDWARD Z. EPSTEIN. *Rebels*. New York: The Citadel Press, 1971.

MORELLA, JOE, EDWARD Z. EPSTEIN, and JOHN GRIGGS. *The Films of World War II*. Secaucus, NJ: The Citadel Press, 1973.

MORIN, EDGAR. *The Stars,* trans. Richard Howard. New York: Grove Press, 1961.

MUSEUM OF QIN TERRA COTTA FIGURES, ed. *Terra Cotta Warriors and Horses of Emperor Qin Shi Huang*. Hong Kong: Hong Kong Mau Hai Language Publication, 1987.

*The National Cyclopaedia of American Biography,* Vol. 40. New York: James T. White, 1955.

NAVASKY, VICTOR S. *Naming Names*. New York: Viking: 1980.

NAYLOR, DAVID. *American Picture Palaces: The Architecture of Fantasy*. New York: Van Nostrand Reinhold, 1981.

———. *Great American Movie Theaters*. Washington, DC: The Preservation Press, 1987.

NEWQUIST, ROY. *Conversations with Joan Crawford*. Secaucus, NJ: The Citadel Press, 1980.

NIVEN, DAVID. *Bring on the Empty Horses*. New York: Dell, 1975.

PETTIGREW, TERENCE. *Raising Hell*. New York: St. Martin's Press, 1986.

PLATO. *The Republic,* trans. Desmond Lee, 1955. Reprint. New York: Viking Penguin, 1987.

POWDERMAKER, HORTENSE. *Hollywood: The Dream Factory*. Boston: Little, Brown, 1951.

PRATLEY, GERALD. *The Cinema of Otto Preminger*. London: A. Zwemmer, 1971.

RAMSAYE, TERRY. *A Million and One Nights,* 1926. Reprint. New York: Simon and Schuster, 1964.

RIMBAUD, ARTHUR. *Illuminations,* trans. Louise Varese, 1946. Reprint. New York: New Directions, 1957.

ROSTEN, LEO C. *Hollywood: The Movie Colony, the Movie Makers*. New York: Harcourt, Brace, 1941.

ROUD, RICHARD. *A Passion for Films: Henri Langlois and the Cinémathèque Française*. New York: The Viking Press, 1986.

SCHUMACH, MURRAY. *The Face on the Cutting Room Floor*. New York: William Morrow, 1964.

SHINDLER, COLIN. *Hollywood Goes to War: Films and American Society 1939–1952*. London: Routledge and Kegan Paul, 1979.

SHIPMAN, DAVID. *The Great Movie Stars*. London: Angus and Robertson, 1970.

SILKE, JAMES R. *Here's Looking at You, Kid*. Boston: Little, Brown, 1976.

SONTAG, SUSAN. *Against Interpretation*. New York: Delta, 1966.

SPOTO, DONALD. *The Dark Side of Genius*. New York: Ballantine Books, 1983.

SWANSON, GLORIA. *Swanson on Swanson*. New York: Random House, 1980.

SZARKOWSKI, JOHN. *Winogrand: Figments from the Real World*. New York: The Museum of Modern Art, 1988.

THOMAS, BOB. *Joan Crawford*. New York: Bantam Books, 1978.

———. *King Cohn*. New York: G. P. Putnam's Sons, 1967.

———. *Thalberg: Life and Legend*. Garden City, NY: Doubleday, 1969.

THOMAS, TONY. *The Films of the Forties*. Secaucus, NJ: The Citadel Press, 1975.

THORPE, EDWARD. *Chandlertown*. New York: St. Martin's Press, 1983.

TORRENCE, BRUCE T. *Hollywood: The First Hundred Years*. New York: New York Zoetrope, 1982.

TURNER, LANA. *Lana*. New York: E. P. Dutton, 1982.

WARSHOW, ROBERT. *The Immediate Experience*. Garden City, NY: Anchor Books, 1962.

WEINER, NORBERT. *The Human Use of Human Beings: Cybernetics and Society,* 1950. Reprint. Garden City, NY: Anchor Books, 1954.

WEST, NATHANAEL. *Miss Lonelyhearts & The Day of the Locust*. Norfolk, CT: New Directions, 1962.

WHITTEMORE, DON, and PHILIP ALAN CECCHETTINI. *Passport to Hollywood*. New York: McGraw-Hill, 1976.

WOOD, MICHAEL. *America in the Movies, or "Santa Maria, It Had Slipped My Mind."* New York: Basic Books, 1975.

WRIGHT, WILLIAM. *Lillian Hellman*. New York: Simon and Schuster, 1986.

ZIEROLD, NORMAN. *The Moguls*. New York: Coward-McCann, 1969.

# *Acknowledgments*

1910. Before Chaplin. Before Eisenstein. Long before the Loew's Paradise. The most celebrated man on earth, Lev Nikolayevich Tolstoy, who wasn't a movie star, but simply a Russian count who happened to write novels when he wasn't attending to his farm or sleeping with society women and wenches from his own estate or burdening his wife with a brood of children, this same Lev Nikolayevich had run away from home with his youngest daughter. He didn't get very far. It was very cold. He caught pneumonia and died at a little railway station (Astapovo), a holy man of eighty-two. He'd denounced Shakespeare and cursed his own novels. But he couldn't even die alone. Pathé's cameras had come to record the death of a saint. The vigil at Astapovo was one of the first cinematic events.

But before he died, the ex-novelist told one of his thirteen children, "I cannot go to sleep. I am always composing. I write and it all links itself together like music."

Or a recurrent film. The more he denounced art, the more the demons would plague him. His own novels fell into movieland. Garbo played Anna Karenina *twice*. What would the old man have thought of that beautiful ghost on the screen? Would Garbo have teased him back to novel-writing if he'd lived to a hundred and five?

I loved Anna Karenina—the woman, the book, and the actress, Greta Garbo. I suffered with Anna and would have been a much more devoted lover than Fredric March.

It doesn't matter now. Anna's dead. And I've caught Tolstoy's disease. *I am always composing. . . .*

I can celebrate films only with the words in my head. I thank Count Tolstoy, Greta Garbo, Paul Newman, Arthur Penn, William Campbell, Harold Brodkey, Joy Hurwitz, Rivka Schoen-

feld, John Simon, Jack Temchin, Mae Clarke, the late Dore
Freeman, Malcah Zeldis, Marcia Franklin, Maurice Horn, Ben
Apfelbaum, Paul Bartel, Norman Mailer, Viveca Lindfors, Jules
Levy, Arthur Gardner, Herbert Gold, Frederic Tuten, Douglas
Century, Matthew Affron, Steve Wasserman, Anna Jardine,
MaryJane DiMassi, William Tuttle, Frank Davis, Phil Nemy,
Michel Martens, Faith Sale, and Harry Hurwitz.

# Index